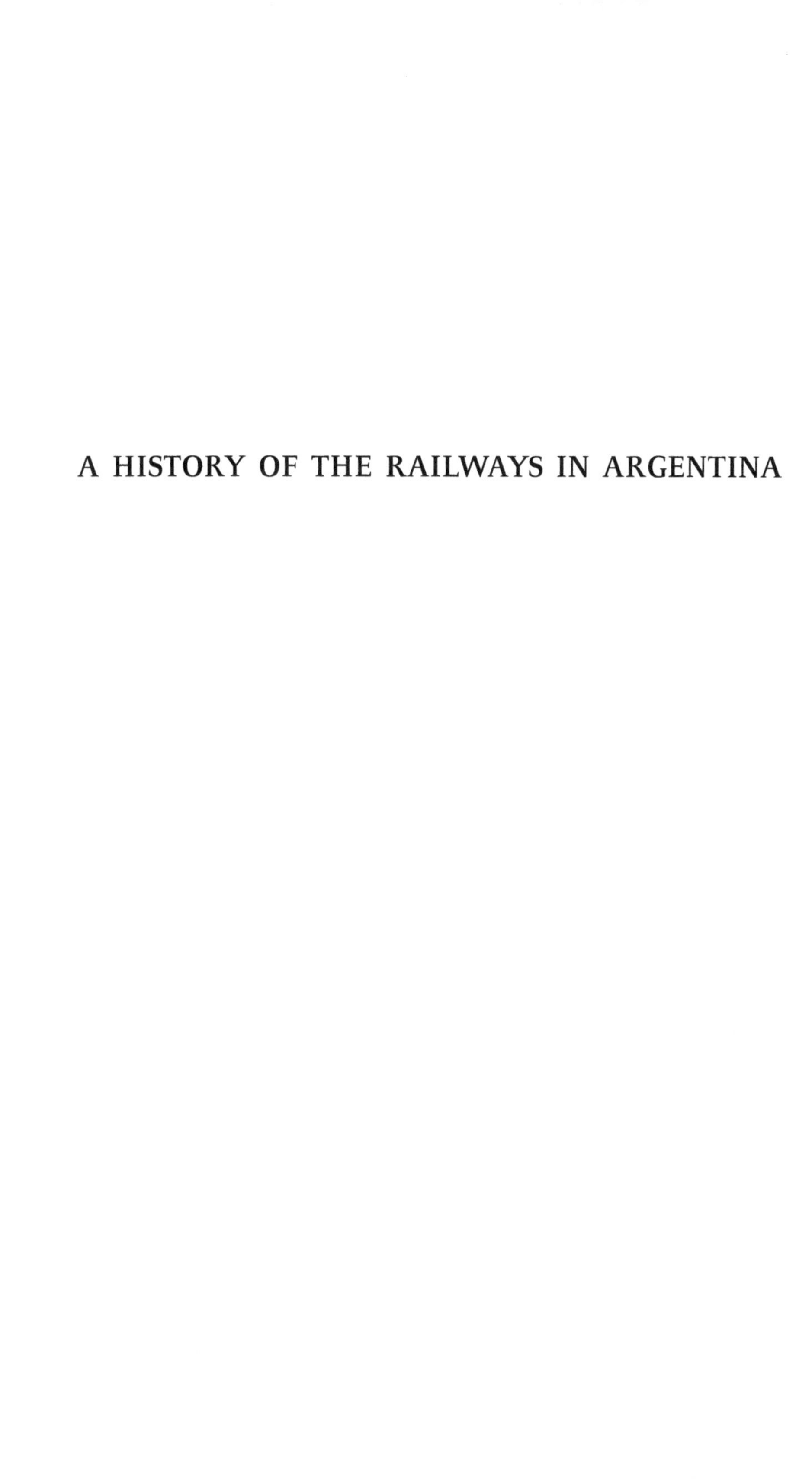

A HISTORY OF THE RAILWAYS IN ARGENTINA

A HISTORY OF THE RAILWAYS IN ARGENTINA

Railway Policies between 1857 and 2015

Mario Justo López, Jorge E. Waddell
and Juan Pablo Martínez

Translated from the Spanish by Paddy Farrell

A History of the Railways in Argentina. Railway Policies between 1857 and 2015

Originally published as *Historia del ferrocarril en Argentina. La política ferroviaria entre 1857 y 2015*

Translated by Paddy Farrell

Lenguaje claro Editora
Portugal 2951, (B1606EFA) Carapachay,
provincia de Buenos Aires, Argentina
www.lenguajeclaro.com
info@lenguajeclaro.com

Typeset by Diana González
Cover design by Miur
Maps by Sergio García, *Todo Trenes* magazine
Cover photograph courtesy of Museo Nacional Ferroviario

López, Mario Justo
A History of the Railways in Argentina: Railway Policies between 1857 and 2015 / Mario Justo López; Jorge E. Waddell; Juan Pablo Martínez. - 1a ed. - Carapachay: Lenguaje Claro Editora, 2023.
350 p.; 23 x 15 cm.

Traducción de: Paddy Farrell.
ISBN 978-987-3764-46-2

1. Ferrocarriles. 2. Políticas Públicas. 3. Infraestructura del Transporte. I. Waddell, Jorge E. II. Martínez, Juan Pablo III. Farrell, Paddy, trad. IV. Título.
CDD 623.63

Hecho el depósito que dispone la ley 11.723.

CONTENTS

Notes on Translation

The Spanish names and abbreviations of railway companies and other important organisations are translated the first time they occur in the text. A list of the private and State-owned railway companies and organisations follows the Contents list.

Currency: £ refers to pounds sterling and $ refers to US dollars; Argentine currency is referred to using the word "pesos". To understand the relationship between these currencies note the following. From 1900 until 1930 their relationships were relatively stable at £1 = $4.85 = pesos 11.45. WW1 caused only transitory changes, which returned to the previous values by 1925. The start of the Great Depresion towards the end of 1929 caused the pound to devalue to £1 = $4.03, and in September 1931 it fell further to £1 = $2.80. The peso suffered much more, and in addition was subject to arbitrary exchange controls. In 1931 it fell to £1 = pesos 13, and in November 1933 it became £1 = pesos 15 to sell and 17 to buy. At the same time a free market arose for £1 = pesos 20. From 1946 a process of acute depreciation began until it completely lost any value. Many approximate methods have been devised in order to relate the present value of a currency to past values, including consumer prices, wholesale prices, prices of certain goods, salaries, etc. With regard to the pound sterling it is not unreasonable to state that the 1900-1930 stable pound is equivalent to rather more than £200 at present.

Weights: all references to weights in tons in the text and tables represent metric tonnes (a metric tonne is equivalent to 1,000 kilograms).

Maps: to give an idea of the scale of the maps, the railway distances from Buenos Aires to Rosario and Mar del Plata are approximately 300 and 400 kilometres, respectively. As the crow flies, the distance from Buenos Aires to the City of Mendoza is approximately 1000 kilometres. 100 kilometres is 62.14 miles.

Prologue

In 2016 "Historia del Ferrocarril en la Argentina" was published by the authors of this English edition. The book, and its antecedent in 2007, filled a gap in the historiography of the Argentine railways by presenting a complete analysis of railway transport in the country, from its beginnings until recent times. For this reason it seems opportune to present an English translation of the work.

Before the first edition in 2007 of this work no other books had been published which offered a comprehensive evolutionary panorama of the railways in Argentina. Numerous works did exist, some of excellent quality, which had been devoted to certain periods in their history. The early years of the country's railways had received much attention, with many investigations dating from their original conception until 1910, 1914 or 1916. However, books on what had happened in the decades of the 20s and 30s were scarce, and studies of the years immediately before the railways were nationalized, and what had then followed, were practically non-existent.

This book aspires to continue the path marked out by those who moved away from politicized history, which had characterized most publications from 1930 until 1970. The works of Paul B. Goodwin (which was translated into Spanish in 1974), of Eduardo A. Zalduendo (1975), of Colin M. Lewis (1983, published in English only) and of Raúl García Heras (thesis presented in 1983, but as yet unpublished) initiated academic Argentine railway historiography. Since then other valuable contributions have been made, such as the study by Andrés Regalsky of French investments in railway lines published in 2002, and the work of Jorge Schvarzer and Teresita Gómez which covers the early years of the "Ferrocarril Oeste" (Buenos Aires Western Railway), published in 2006. In the Bibliography which lies at the end of this book other important works on the history of the railways will be found. The text which follows was nourished on the knowledge there accumulated.

Fundamentally, this book is a work which spreads over many years, so that it has been necessary to select certain events over others during the story. In order to achieve a vision which covers 170 years of history in about 300 pages the book has concentrated on the evolution of what can be called railway policy; that is, the actions of the State towards the provision of a rational public railway policy from a government which determines aims, proposes plans and provides measures towards their achievement.

History, fundamentally, is an intellectual reconstruction of past events based on accepted criteria about the value of documented records and their interpretation. All things considered, the reconstruction will be, as in any proposed description of actual occurrences, sensitive to being qualified as true or false, based on its correlation with those records. But historiography also includes other activities which fall outside that qualification. In the first place, it implies deciding on the subject of study, before starting on the work of reconstruction. The historian chooses to investigate this or that topic and, during reconstruction, discards irrelevant matters and concentrates attention solely on a minimum number of events which form the sphere of study. In the second place, the historian seeks relationships between the events and forms hypotheses which try to explain what has happened. In theory there is a limit to this activity because the selection can not be totally capricious and the hypotheses can not be contradictory or leave out past events. Within these limits, the selection criteria are broad, as also are those used to formulate interpretations and correlations. These activities are not tied to an evaluation of how true they are, but rather only to how useful they are.

Public policy is the question which we have identified as relevant to serve as the criterion for the selection of events and upon which to form relationships. The adoption of a public policy is a complex task, which is carried out in a given environment involving the imposition of overall aims, which in our case and over time can be political unity, social and economic transformation, integration of the national economy, development of the internal market, etc. Starting from there, the adoption of a policy for the railways, or more widely for transport in general, is carried out by selecting from a basic set of available options. The advisability or otherwise of the aims finally chosen, and of the means used to achieve them, make it possible to evaluate the government's decisions. This also forms part of the task which historiography proposes to carry out, but starting always from a reconstruction of events based on identified sources.

The contents of this book is organised on the basis of a succession of six periods, the first five lasting thirty years each, and the sixth for which the period is still unfolding. We postulate that from one period to the next, railway policy has undergone significant change, either in its design or in its application. In general terms, we can say that pragmatism characterised the first period, resorting to public and private capital without distinction or pausing to assess either of these options. Provincial and national State railway policies also coexisted. The adoption of the private company as the protagonist of railway activities was an essential feature of the second period, together with adoption by the State of criteria for their regulation and control. The application of these criteria to private company activities, and the return of the State as a direct agent of railway expansion, distinguished the third period, without the serious financial crisis in 1930 leading to a change in the policy model of the time. Nationalization and the indecisiveness of the enormous new State company which emerged was the most prominent feature of the fourth period. The fifth shows, on the other hand, a panorama of measures, many discontinuous and others contradictory, which led again to a reliance on private company concessions to operate the railways, without failing to note that the relevance of this mode of transport continued the decline which had already started during the previous period. The last period stands out because of the emergency situation which arose from the 2001 financial crisis, which overturned the concession policy and caused a disorderly return of the State as railway impresario.

The translation was undertaken by Paddy Farrell, who not only transformed the Spanish text into English but also consulted closely with the authors with the aim of achieving as much clarity as possible in the new text. From this dialogue there emerged some modifications in the wording, the suppression of certain paragraphs and the addition of others, and the insertion of explanatory footnotes. Apart from these minor alterations, the book has not been significantly changed. The Bibliography has been brought up to date by removing some irrelevant books and adding others which contribute to further understanding of Argentina's railway past. This Bibliography is an important part of the book because everything affirmed in the text is supported by the works listed, which also provide a guide for anyone wishing to continue investigating this subject.

The Authors, Buenos Aires, abril de 2023.

Argentine Railway Companies and Organisations List

Argentine Railway Companies – Before Nationalization in 1948 (Rlwy: Railway FC: Ferrocarril)

AGWR: Argentine Great Western Rlwy	FCGOA: FC Gran Oeste Argentino
ANCR: Argentine Northern Central Rlwy	FCCNA: FC Central Norte Argentino
ANER: Argentine North Eastern Rlwy	FCNEA: FC Nordeste Argentino
ANR: Argentine Northern Rlwy	FCAN: FC Argentino del Norte
ANWR: Argentine North Western Rlwy	FCNOA: FC Noroeste Argentino
AR: Andean Rlwy	FCA: FC Andino
BA&CR: Buenos Aires & Campana Rlwy	FCBAC: FC Buenos Aires a Campana
BACR: Buenos Aires Central Rlwy	FCCBA: FC Central de Buenos Aires
BAEPR: Buenos Aires and Ensenada Port Rlwy	FCBAPE: FC Buenos Aires y Puerto de Ensenada
BAGSR: Buenos Aires Great Southern Rlwy	FCS: FC Sud de Buenos Aires
BAMR: Buenos Aires Midland Rlwy	FCMBA: FC Midland de Buenos Aires
BANR: Buenos Aires Northern Rlwy	FCN: FC Norte de Buenos Aires
BAPGRC: Buenos Aires Province General Railway Company	FCCGPBA: FC Compañia General de la Provincia de Buenos Aires
BAPR: Buenos Aires and Pacific Rlwy	FCBAP: FC Buenos Aires al Pacífico

BARR: Buenos Aires and Rosario Rlwy	FCBAR: FC Buenos Aires a Rosario
BAWR: Buenos Aires Western Rlwy	FCO: FC Oeste until 1890, then FCOBA: FC Oeste de Buenos Aires
BBNWR: Bahía Blanca and North Western Rlwy	FCBBNO: FC Bahía Blanca y Noroeste
CAR: Central Argentine Rlwy	FCCA: FC Central Argentino
CCR: Córdoba Central Rlwy	FCCC: FC Central Córdoba
CLR: Corrientes Light Rlwy	FCEC: FC Económico Correntino
CNWR: Córdoba and North Western Rlwy	FCCNO: FC Córdoba y Noroeste
CRC: Central Rlwy of Chubut	FCCCH: FC Central de Chubut
CRR: Córdoba and Rosario Rlwy	FCCyR: FC de Córdoba a Rosario
EAR: East Argentine Rlwy	FCAE: FC Argentino del Este
EFR: Embarcación to Formosa Rlwy	FCEF: FC de Embarcación a Formosa
ER: Eastern Railway	FCE: FC del Este
ERCR: Entre Ríos Central Rlwy	FCCER: FC Central Entrerriano
ERR: Entre Ríos Rlwys	FCER: Ferrocarriles de Entre Ríos
NCR: Northern Central Rlwy	FCCN. FC Central Norte
PBAR: Province of Buenos Aires Rlwy	FCPBA: FC Provincial de Buenos Aires
PR: Patagonian Rlwys	FCP: Ferrocarriles Patagónicos
RBPR: Rosario and Belgrano Port Rlwy	FCRPB: FC de Rosario a Puerto Belgrano
RST: Rafaela Steam Tramway	FCTR: Tranvía a Vapor de Rafaela
SCTR: San Cristóbal and Tucumán Rlwy	FCSCT: FC de San Cristóbal a Tucumán
SFCGSR: Santa Fe and Córdoba Great Southern Railway	FCGSSFC: FC Gran Sur de Santa Fe y Córdoba
SFPR: Santa Fe Provincial Rlwy	FCPSF: FC Provincial de Santa Fe
TR: Transandine Rlwy	FCT: FC Trasandino
VMRR: Villa María and Rufino Rlwy	FCVMR: FC de Villa María a Rufino
WSFR: Western Santa Fe Rlwy	FCOSF: FC Oeste Santafecino

Argentine Railway Companies – After Nationalization in 1948

FCNGR: Ferrocarril Nacional General Roca	Roca Railway, ex-BAGSR
FCNGSM: Ferrocarril Nacional General San Martín	San Martín Railway, ex-BAPR
FCNGB: Ferrocarril Nacional General Belgrano	Belgrano Railway, ex-French and State lines
FCNGBM: Ferrocarril General Bartolomé Mitre	Mitre Railway, ex-CAR
FCNGU: Ferrocarril Nacional General Urquiza	Urquiza Railway, ex-ERR and ANER
FCNDFS: Ferrocarril Nacional Domingo Faustino Sarmiento	Sarmiento Railway, ex-BAWR
FCNP: Ferrocarril Nacional Patagónico	all the Railways in Patagonia

In 1956 it was decided to create a new State-owned railway company to administrate and develop all the Pailways, called Empresa Ferrocarriles del Estado Argentino (EFEA).

In 1965 EFEA was given a new name: Ferrocarriles Argentinos (FA), which remained until almost all the following privatization concessions were in place. At that point FA and the above State-owned Railways were liquidated, leaving the government as the operator of last resort.

In 1991 Ferrocarriles Metropolitanos S.A. (Femesa. Metropolitan Railways) was created to manage the suburban line sections, separating them from FA.

Privatization Using Concessions (S.A.: Sociedad Anónima)

Cargo Concessions, from 1991

FEPSA: Ferroexpreso Pampea-no S.A.	almost all the Sarmiento, and parts of the Roca and RBPR
NCA: Nuevo Central Argen-tino S.A.	almost all the Mitre, except sections passed to the BAP
FSR: Ferrosur Roca S.A.	almost all the rest of the Roca network
BAP: Buenos Aires al Pacífico	almost all the San Martín, and sections of the Sarmiento and Mitre
FM: Ferrocarriles Mesopotámicos S.A.	the standard-gauge Urquiza network
FGB: Ferrocarril General Bel-grano S.A.	the metre-gauge network, except parts closed or ceded to the State

In 1998 the San Martín and General Urquiza concessions became part of the América Latina Logística (ALL), so the original six cargo service concessions became five, of which four were in the hands of private companies: FEPSA, NCA, Ferrosur Roca and ALL. The fifth was the Ferrocarril Belgrano Cargas, which had been conceded to the Railway Union, but later taken back by the State.

Suburban Passenger Concessions, from 1994 (in the Buenos Aires Metropolitan area)

Metrovías S.A.	the Urquiza and Buenos Aires Subte network
Transportes Metropolitanos San Martín S.A.	the San Martín line, including out to Pilar
Ferrovías S.A.	the northern metre-gauge line, the Belgrano Norte

Transportes Metropolitanos Belgrano Sur S.A.	the southern metre-gauge line, the Belgrano Sur
Transportes Metropolitanos General Roca S.A.	all the Roca suburban network, including out to La Plata
TBA: Trenes de Buenos Aires S.A.	all the Sarmiento suburban network, and the Mitre network out to Capilla del Senór and Zarate

From 1997 the second, fourth and fifth were combined into the Metropolitano (the San Martín, Belgrano Sur and Roca lines), making four concessions in all.

Long-distance Passenger Concessions, from 1992

Initially, by arrangement with the relevant cargo concessions, later between the State and some of the Provinces, particularly with the Province of Buenos Aires, organised by the Unidad Ejecutora del Programa Ferroviario Provincial (UEPFP, Provincial Railway Programme Executive Unit). A fairly successful but short-lived company, Ferrocentral, formed by the suburban company Ferrovías and the cargo company NCA, set up two services: the first from Buenos Aires to Córdoba in 2004, and the second a year later between Buenos Aires and Tucumán.

Government and Other Organizations

Chapter One

Departamento de Ingenieros Civiles	Department of Civil Engineers
La Fraternidad	Brotherhood of Locomotive Drivers and Firemen

Chapter Two

Administración General de los Ferrocarriles del Estado (AGFE)	State Railways Administration
Consejo Nacional de Educación	National Education Council

Dirección de Ferrocarriles	National Railway Board (NRB)
Federación Obrera Ferrocarrilera (FOF)	Railway Workers Federation

Chapter Three

Compañía de Tranvías Anglo Argentina	Anglo-Argentine Tram Company
Compañía Ferrocarrilera de Petróleo	Railway Oil Company
Corporación de Transportes de Buenos Aires	Buenos Aires Transport Corporation
Instituto Argentino para la Promoción del Intercambio (IAPI)	Argentine Institute for the Promotion of Trade
Unión Ferroviaria	Union of Railwaymen

Chapter Four

Banco Internacional de Reconstrucción y Fomento (BIRF)	part of the World Bank
Comisión Económica para America Latina (CEPAL)	United Nations Economic Comission for Latin America
Confederación General Económica	a union business forum affiliated to the governing Party
Consejo Nacional de Desarrollo (CONADE)	National Development Board
Corporación de Empresas Nacionales (CEN)	Corporation of State-owned Companies
Empresa Ferrocarriles del Estado Argentino (EFEA)	Argentine State Railway Company
Empresa Nacional de Transportes (ENT)	National Transport Corporation
Empresas Ferroviarias del Estado (EFE)	State-owned Railway Com-panies
Fábrica Argentina de Locomotoras (FADEL)	Argentine Locomotive Factory
Ferrocarriles Argentinos (FA)	New name for EFEA from 1965
Ferrocarriles del Estado	State Railways

FIAT Materfer	FIAT subsidiary for the construction of passenger coaches (in Córdoba)
Fundación de Investigaciones Económicas Latinoamericanas (FIEL)	Latin-american Economic Reseach Trust
Plan de Mediano Plazo (PMP)	Medium-Term Plan

Chapter Five

Administración de Bienes Ferroviarios (ENABIEF)	Administration of Railway Assets
Administración General de Puertos	Argentine Ports Authority
Autoridad de Transporte del Área Metropolitana (ATAM)	Metropolitan Area Transport Authority
Autoridad de Transporte del Área Metropolitana (ATAM)	Metropolitan Area Transport Authority
Comisión Nacional de Regulación del Transporte (CNRT)	National Comission for Transport Regulation
Comisión Nacional de Transporte Ferroviario (CNTF)	National Railway Transport Comission
Concesión Integral de Explotación (CIE)	Integral Development Concession
Coordinación del Programa de Reestructuración Ferroviaria (UCPRF)	Coordination of the Railway Restructuring Programme
Directorio de Empresas Públicas (DEP)	Corporation of Public Companies
Empresa Nacional de Teléfonos (ENTEL)	Argentine National Telephone Company
Ferrocarriles Metropolitanos S.A. (Femesa)	Metropolitan Railways
Gerencia de Línea Metropolitana (GLM)	Office for the Metropolitan Line
Organismo Administrador de los Bienes del Estado (ONABE)	Organisation for Administration of State Assets
Reglamento Interno Técnico Operativo (RITO)	House Technical Operating Rules
Secretaría de Transporte y Obras Públicas (SETOP)	Secretariat for Transport and Public Works

Sociedad Operadora de Emergencia (SOESA)	Emergency Operating Company
Subsecretaría deTrans-porte Ferroviario	Sub-Secretariat of Railway Transport
Unidad de Gestión Operativa (UGOFE)	Unit for Operational Management
Unidad Ejecutora del Programa Ferroviario Provincial (UEPFP)	Provincial Railway Programme Executive Unit
Unión Ferroviaria (UF)	Union of Railwaymen

Chapter Six

Administración de Infraestructura Ferroviaria Sociedad del Estado (ADIFSE)	State Railway Infrastructure Company
Belgrano Cargas y Logística	Belgrano Cargo and Logistics
Comisión Bicameral de Seguimiento de las Privatizaciones	Bicameral Privatization Comission
Sociedad Operadora Ferroviaria Sociedad del Estado (SOFSE)	State Railway Operating Company
Unidad de Gestión Operativa Mitre Sarmiento(UGOMS)	Unit for the Operational Management of the Mitre and Sarmiento Lines

MARIO JUSTO LÓPEZ

1 | The Combination of Private and Public Capital in the Construction of the Early Railway Lines 1857 – 1886

The construction and exploitation of the early railway lines in Argentina was the result of political events combined with economic factors, both local and international. At the battle of Monte Caseros in 1852 the long-established tyrannical government of Juan Manuel Ortiz de Rosas came to an end. Following this, changes in Argentina's ruling groups took place, as much in the new, re-established national order as in the different provinces. Among the new elite, railway transport mode was seen as the the most efficient tool for consolidation of the fragile national union and a re-affirmation of the authority of national and provincial governments. It also was to be a fundamental instrument for taking forward a social and economic transformation which they considered to be an imperative necessity. This was so much so that the installation of railways was specifically mentioned in the federal constitution of 1853 as one of the means which the new national Congress[1] had at its disposal "to provide that which would lead to the prosperity of the country". This connection with events in its political history explains the delays which the first railway construction projects experienced in Argentina, leaving it trailing in this regard with respect to Mexico, Brazil, Peru and Chile.

The political will of the new ruling groups, however, was only convertible into feasible proposals thanks to being able to rely on

[1] Congress refers to the Argentine Parliament (Congreso) of Deputies (Representatives) and Senators.

favourable external factors, such as the abundant availability of capital looking for new investments, and the existence of newly idle railway construction technology, when in Europe and especially in Great Britain, the rhythm of growth in their own networks began to decrease.

What has been said above is enough to understand why the public authorities had a fundamental role in the task of installing railways, as much in the role of authorising concessions for private initiatives as in acting as promoter, all of which will be seen in more detail in the following pages. Since 1853 the Argentine State had organised itself on the same federal model as the United States of America. Consequently, there existed a national government and several provincial governments. Having accepted a federal form of Constitution, the main question was how to distribute functions and resources between the central government and the local governments. In terms of the arguments which followed, the protagonists were, on the one hand, the Province of Buenos Aires, which defended its provincial autonomy by reason of having reached a higher stage of development; and on the other hand, firstly, the government of the then Argentine Confederation, installed in the city of Parana in the Province of Entre Rios in 1853, and secondly, the government of the Argentine Nation, installed in the city of Buenos Aires in 1862. The constitutional declaration adopting the federal form thus had a real significance, at least until the start of the 1880s decade, when the Province of Buenos Aires, having lost its capital city when it became the federal capital, also lost its predominance and with that the possibility of repelling the range of aspirations of the national authorities. The effect of all this, in terms of public railway policies, was that separate actors emerged, the Province of Buenos Aires and the Nation, which gave rise to different railway systems with their own characteristics. Towards the end of the decade of the 1880s, other provinces followed the example of Buenos Aires and attempted to construct their own systems.

The rivalry between Buenos Aires and the Confederation can be seen at the time as another factor favouring the rapid installation of rails on the soil of Argentina, as both governments began to compete and tried to get ahead in the race for economic change. In addition, however, a contrary effect can be ascribed to that rivalry, as it created for some years a risk of civil war, which did little to facilitate the emergence of the necessary conditions for the raising of the large capital funds which the task required. However, it can be concluded that the confrontation only disadvantaged the Confederation, as it lacked credits in the external market and was not able to organise its public administration and tax collection.

The Railways of the Province of Buenos Aires

It was Buenos Aires which achieved the opening, for the first time in Argentina, of a railway. In August of 1857 the first stretch of line, certainly very short, of what came to be called the Ferrocarril Oeste (FCO), the Buenos Aires Western Railway (BAWR), was promoted by a group of businessmen, traders and politicians in Buenos Aires who obtained a concession from the provincial government and authorisation to constitute a public limited share company, an entity not provided for in the commercial legislation of that time. The take up of shares among local investors was very slow, so the construction work was only able to continue, and the line be inaugurated, thanks to financial support from the authorities. The technology was brought from Great Britain, the construction engineer was from there, and the first rolling stock came from England.

The initial service provided was somewhat precarious, given the scarcity of locomotives and rolling stock, the modest infrastructure and the short journey. However, it was not long before the line captured significant passenger traffic, but not for freight, which remained dominated by the traditional means of transport, the bullock wagon. This was because most of the loads originated beyond the terminus of the line, and the loaders refused to pay the cost of transhipment there. From the beginning, the BAWR was considered an operation of prime importance to the provincial government, which viewed it as an achievement in the task of revolutionising the means of transport and demonstrating the road to progress. This was so much so that in 1860 the government of Bartolomé Mitre, after analysing the circumstances of the line in order to determine a policy to follow with the aim of achieving its growth, devised two bills. The first provided for the acquisition of privately-held shares in the company and contemplated expropriation of the lands through which the line would have to pass, then subdividing and selling them to immigrants or residents. This so as to populate and cultivate them and rapidly increase the still scarce freight traffic. The second bill authorised whatever investment was required in order to extend the BAWR. The bills, written by Minister Sarmiento, were not approved on this occasion, being blocked in the provincial legislature by established interests, but the importance which the government gave to the company indicated that it would take it over in the near future.

Finally, in 1862 a law authorised the provincial Executive to purchase the private shares. The holders received all the funds they had invested plus an annual interest of six percent on them, But at that time a major part of the capital invested belonged to the province.which had also advanced funds via the Provincial Bank to finance works. In this manner the BAWR was organised into a provincial company, with a board appointed by its Governor. This did not mean a management change, since many of the former Directors appointed by the investors continued in their posts.

The company had very slowly extended its line, and this did not change after the province took control. The 10km opened in 1857 had become 39 in 1862 and had reached 160 in 1866, where it remained until 1869. The BAWR reached Chivilcoy and passed through the cities of Lujan and Mercedes. These were relatively populous districts, involved in stockbreeding and developing agriculture. This, together with prudent administration, meant that the company soon achieved a profit and returned outstanding performances thereafter. As the line extended towards the west it was able to increase the freight it carried, permanently displacing bullock carting except for local deliveries to the termini and intermediate stations on the line. Income from freight soon exceeded that derived from passenger traffic.

Towards the end of the 1860s, the BAWR returned to extending its tracks. To the construction of small connections in the city of Buenos Aires was added a branch to Lobos in the southwest, which enabled an increase in the service zone and slowed penetration by competing lines in the future. Also it was proposed to drive forward the construction of the mainline towards the west until it reached the Andes range and the frontier with Chile. Even when this objective, held since the formation of the company, had been abandoned after certain investigations, the company grew. It reached an extension of 240km in 1871, 329 in 1874 and 380 in 1879. Some of the first engineering graduates from the University of Buenos Aires entered its service, and schools for technicians were created in the company organisation. Because of its coverage and traffic activity (in 1879 the BAWR share was 27% of the turnover of all the railway companies in the country) and because of its performance (which had always been above the average over the network), the company became one of the most important as a result.

In addition to the relevant position which it reached, due to its extent and movement of freight and passengers, the BAWR had other characteristics which deserve recording. The railway was conceived as a commercial company almost from the start, at least from the moment when its income showed that making a profit was a possibility. There was a concern to capture more traffic, to reduce costs, and to employ skilled personnel. In general, its directors and staff members defended the interests of the company (to make a profit, grow, and not let itself be bested by rivals) without submitting to other economic or political interests. Awareness of being a company led to its leading personnel being very clear that the railway needed the largest possible service zone. To the original line towards the west were successively added the southwestern branch and a genuinely new trunk line towards the north. Those cases in which defense of the company's interests gave way to exceptional circumstances were few, such as, for example, reducing charges during periods of lost harvests. It can also be said that the Western originated the guidelines which constituted railway policy in the province of Buenos Aires, since on certain occasions its senior staff carried out tasks corresponding to those of public officials, converting themselves into an office for the control of private activity. Likewise, the existence in the state orbit of a railway company with the attributes of the BAWR enabled the provincial government to present a clear and firm front towards private companies, since it could seriously brandish the threat of their expropriation and had the knowledge, through the senior staff of the Western, of the problems and requirements of the companies. In any case, the only obscurity in all of this trajectory of the first years of the oldest railway was its rate of growth. This was slow, and only reached an average of 15km per year between 1860 and 1880. This meant that the company was never able to get close to the interior frontier, as this moved away after fights against the nomadic aboriginal population and subsequent ocupation of the land for raising cattle and the birth of agriculture. The reason for this can be seen in the cronic problem of the financing of public companies. The province financed the new extensions and improvements through the sale of public land and credit from the state bank. But it was clear that both resources had a limit and also that no railway could finance its growth from profits in a dynamic environment like Argentina's at that time, however efficient it was. The impossibility of gaining private capital by issuing shares left only one way to finance a more rapid growth: obtaining that capital by means of loans. This method was tried in the final years of this first stage.

However, the life of the BAWR became very perturbed by the events of 1880. The national government, confronting the province for electoral reasons, intervened in the local government, displaced its authorities and nationalising the city of Buenos Aires, in order to convert it into the national capital. The province, profoundly shaken by the whole event, felt obliged to build a new city 50km south of Buenos Aires, called La Plata, which would serve as its seat of government. The BAWR, as the provincial railway, found its Board moved to La Plata and determined on a new but economically debatable line constructed to re-orient its network towards the new headquarters of the provincial authorities. In any case, the province joined in the euphoria for public works which was characteristic of the country in those years. With external debt as its basis, it began to build the new city of La Plata, with enormous and sumptuous public edifices, the new port of La Plata with a huge and deep central dock, and branches of the BAWR to cover not only the periphery of the new capital but also the zone to the north and south of the province. This excessive indebtedness, which prompted corruption and administrative disorder, could not lead to good results. But the Western continued to be one of the most important railways. Its network grew from 380km in 1879 to 831 in 1886. In that year in generated 19% of the gross product of all the railway companies. But, anticipating what was to occur in 1890, in 1885 for the first time its profit was less than that of the overall average.

The province of Buenos Aires sought to construct its railway system not only based on direct provincial action, which in any case depended on circumstances and not on a clearly defined initial proposal, but also by means of concessions to private companies. The first of these were granted at about the same time as the inauguration of the BAWR, but they only gave rise to lines of short extension and we will refer to these later on. The one which was most successful was the Ferrocarril Sud (FCS), the Buenos Aires Great Southern Railway (BAGSR), commonly known as the Southern Railway. In 1862 the legislature of the province granted to an intermediary promoter, Edward Lumb, a member of the British community resident for many years in the area of the River Plate, the privilege of constructing a railway line 114km long from Buenos Aires to Chascomus. As an incentive for investors, the provincial government would guarantee a minimum annual profit of 7% for forty years, on a maximum investment of 750 thousand pounds sterling (£). The promoter took this proposal to London, where he transferred the concession to a company (BAGSR) which was formed for the purpose and which placed its shares with relative ease. The famous English businessman Samuel M. Peto was contracted to construct the line and provide the rolling stock, in association with Edward L. Betts. The BAGSR did well right from the start. Its traffic was significant. In 1866 its gross product was 29% of the national total for all railways, and this was maintained, at least until 1890, at about 30%. As a consequence, its profits were good and soon became sufficient to do without the state guarantee. Following an offer from the company, it reached an agreement with the government in 1869 which set aside the guaranteed interest rate, replaced it with a subsidy of £500 per mile of any extensions and branches required by the authorities. It was also agreed that the Province would pay what was owed from previous years of the guarantee, with a deduction for the reason that it would desist from demanding a refund if the profits of the BAGSR were high in future years. The length of its line remained unchanged until 1870, in which year there began an uninterrupted expansion which soon converted the Southern Railway into the leading company. The network advanced towards the southwest with its branch to Las Flores and Azul, reached in 1876. It also continued to advance southward, to Dolores in 1874 (the only extension required by the government and which benefitted from the agreed subsidy although never fully paid up) and from there to Maipú and Ayacucho (1880). It had now grown to 563km and was ensuring coverage of an ample exclusive zone.

The importance of the Southern made its Directors fear, in 1881, that it would be expropriated by the provincial government, committed as the latter was to an ambitious policy of public works and rapid expansion of the BAWR. The new Governor, Dardo Rocha, resorted to the threat of expropriation as an alternative to the agreed subsidy by rescinding the guarantee in order to obtain the construction of new branches towards the south. This action of the Provincial government was right in that, as we have said before, its ability to take over the exploitation of a railway was already proven. In addition, the prosperity of the BAGSR and favourable capital market environment meant that the government plans were not considered to be a drawback. Thus the BAGSR committed to continue the construction of branch lines in return for a pledge that they would not be expropriated for twenty years. As a result, lines were opened from Ayacucho to Tandil (1883) and from Azul to Bahía Blanca and its Port (1884). Later, their followed extensions from Tandil to Juárez (1885) and to Tres Arroyos (1886), and from Maipú to Mar del Plata (1886). The total length of BAGSR lines reached 1,249km in 1886. The result of the exploitation left nothing to wish for and was not affected by including new, less developed areas. Every year had shown good performance, frankly exceptional in some years. Consequently, the dividends paid to the holders of ordinary shares were, in practice without interruption, around ten percent and the shares were quoted at multiples of their nominal price.

The success of the Southern was fundamentally due to the business ability of the people managing the company. It is true that it was created in 1862, in political circumstances more favourable than the lines which preceded it, after the battle of Pavón had initiated a process of national unification which raised hopes of more peaceful times (an expectation which was not realized as there was no end to the conflicts, many armed, which afflicted the country). It is worth mentioning some examples which demonstrate this business ability. As in the case of any railway of no great length, the line had difficulty capturing traffic and displacing the bullock cart. But the BAGSR rapidly introduced the possibility of transporting the actual carts, with their cargoes, from its various stations to the terminus at Plaza Constitución, avoiding an additional costly transhipment and obtaining traffic which it would otherwise have lost. Once the branch to Las Flores reached beyond the River Salado and the increase of income permitted charge reductions, the cart was displaced from its zone of influence and reduced to carrying merchandise to nearby stations. In another move, after inauguration of the line to Chascomús, built by a construction company, the Southern itself undertook subsequent extension and improvement works, achieving cost reductions close to 40%. This, together with constant control of everyday costs, led to it being the most efficient of all. From the start, it clearly understood the need to preserve and broaden its exclusive zone of operation. When the BAWR constructed its branch from Merlo to Lobos, with the intention of extending it to Azul, the BAGSR decided to construct its branch to Las Flores and extend it to the same city, which it quickly achieved, avoiding the loss of a large zone towards the southwest. When the Ferrocarril Buenos Aires y Puerto Ensenada (FCBAPE), the Buenos Aires and Ensenada Port Railway (BAEPR), whose very existence had been regarded by the BAGSR as improper interference, wanted to maintain the Riachuelo area as an exclusive zone, the BAGSR applied for and constructed a branch towards there. When its lines reached Bahía Blanca it managed to enclose, between its main line to that new port and the Atlantic coast, a large part of the territory of the province of Buenos Aires, making it difficult for competitors to enter there. Finally, in order to finance the construction of extensions and branches, the company resorted to the capital market by offering novel financial titles. They were called "extension shares", the more common debentures being left aside. These guaranteed the share holders a fixed dividend, higher than that of the more traditional bonds, but less than the developing business had promised to pay to ordinary shareholders. Thus on the one hand, during the early years of the operation of a new section of line, which in general produced smaller returns than those of an established line, it managed to avoid affecting the dividends of the ordinary shares, which in the 80s reached exceptional percentages. On the other hand, it avoided having to contract debts, as was certainly the case with debentures, which could become a heavy burden in difficult times.The extension shares were converted into ordinary shares after a certain period which, given the good times which the company was enjoying, would be another attraction for investors.

The government of the province itself granted other railway concessions, which gave rise to three new companies, none of which achieved the importance of the BAWR and the BAGSR. Towards the end of 1862 service started on the Ferrocarril Norte (FCN), the Buenos Aires Northern Railway (BANR), a minor line first concessioned in 1857. It belonged to a company with British capital which distinguished itself neither by the quality of its service nor by its financial performance. Its track length remained at no more than the 30km of the original concession to link Buenos Aires with the ports of San Fernando and Tigre. It had no serious plans to extend itself. Investments were carried out in an inefficient manner. Successive transfers of the original concession and technical mistakes in the initial works, which forced its immediate reconstruction, led to high over-capitalisation and conspired against satisfactory performance. However, it was able to carry great quantities of passengers by virtue of the areas which it traversed to the north of the city of Buenos Aires. In reality it became no more than a suburban line and only formed part of a major network when purchased by another company in 1889. It enjoyed a 7% guarantee on a capital of 750,000 *pesos fuertes* (pesos backed by gold reserves), about £150 thousand, which became a motive for continuous conflicts with the government. The company's inability to generate profits in relation to its investments led it to claim, year after year, the payment the government had committed to. The authorities questioned the accounts and the quality of service and delayed the payments due. At a certain point, the payments were suspended owing to the bad state of the line, and between the years 1881 and 1883 the disputes were referred by the company to the London Stock Exchange, with the aim of applying pressure on the provincial government, whose credit might be harmed.

In 1865 services began to be offered on the BAEPR. Also concessioned in 1857, this line constructed with British capital linked the capital to a port considered to be a natural harbour for seagoing ships. The concession was transferred twice, without any progress, until in early 1863 William Wheelwright, the well known concessionaire of the Ferrocarril Central Argentino (FCCA), the Central Argentine Railway (CAR), took charge of the project. In spite of this, and of the inauguration of its services to Barracas, the company found it seriously difficult to obtain capital. Only in December 1872 was it able to open the 55km route to Ensenada. In 1874 transfer of the concession to a company formed in London two years before was approved. Its operation was not satisfactory. The line's existence since 1863 had not been well received by the BAGSR, and its short route remained trapped between the BAGSR lines and the River Plate. It did not benefit from a provincial government guarantee. Its profits were very small and consequently the results of investment were very poor. Its status as a secondary line appeared to improve when the nearby city of La Plata and its port were constructed. But the effect of this, which for a while gave it more traffic and improved performance, only emerged in the second half of the 1880s and not before 1886.

The final line with a provincial concession which commenced operations during this period was the so-called Ferrocarril Buenos Aires y Campana, the Buenos Aires & Campana Railway (BA&CR).

Petitioned for by an intermediary local promoter in 1869, the law granting the concession was approved in September 1870, authorising the construction of a railway from Buenos Aires to the port on the River Paraná at Campana. The provincial government did not grant any guarantee of minimum return on investment, but the national government did so by sanctioning a law immediately afterwards, creating the novel situation of a joint railway promotion. The line crossed a zone which would impede a future extension of the BANR, but this small company did not react in any way. The proposal was taken to London by the promoter, who there sold the concession to a company by issuing shares created for the purpose, which in turn contracted the necessary works with another firm at a very high price. The company had bad results given that the line did not produce any returns and the national guarantee was only sufficient to service part of the shares issued. However, in 1883 a new business group, linked to the BAGSR, decided to take over the languishing company, bought a majority of the existing shares, increased its capital and solicited an extension of the concession to the city of Rosario in the province of Santa Fe. The company, now called the Ferrocarril Buenos Aires y Rosario (FCBAR), the Buenos Aires and Rosario Railway (BARR), inaugurated services to its new destination in February 1886, connecting for the first time the systems arising from concessions by the province of Buenos Aires and by the Nation. It also established an efficient administration, became profitable and determined to extend its network even further, in open competition with the lines of the CAR. The company was to grow rapidly and become one of the most important in the country, until reined in by the effects of the the 1890 crisis.

Assessing this period, it can be said that the province of Buenos Aires had in 30 years achieved the construction of an extensive railway system (it had 2,585km in operation by the end of 1886, though the 417km of the BARR had just been put under national jurisdiction), based on its own resources, its internal and external credits and the foreign investors who believed in its policies. It had its own legislation and the private companies were regulated by provincial organisations. Although there were company failures, the actions of the local government had been seen to be efficient. It had given birth to the most important companies. It had imposed unity of gauge for all the lines, obliging successive railways to adopt the broad gauge of the BAWR; and, even though it had never expressly formulated a general railway construction plan, it had distributed the lines assigned to the different companies into exclusive zones as their names suggest: West, North, South.

The National Railways

The government of the Argentine Confederation, based in Parana, attempted to set up a railway company from a time as early as Buenos Aires did, but failed. Only once the new national government was established in Buenos Aires did negotiations with the promoter William Wheelwright conclude successfully, after dealing for five years with President Urquiza and his successor Derqui. In 1862, he was given authorisation to construct a railway from Rosario to Córdoba, the Central Argentine (CAR). The Mitre government proposed granting the same benefits which Buenos Aires had given in the cases of the BANR and the BAGSR; namely, the guarantee of a 7% profit margin and tax exemptions. However, the promoter, based on previous discussions with the Confederation, insisted on and finally obtained a subsidy consisting of land a Spanish league (2.5 km) wide on either side of the full extent of the line, except in urban areas. The granting of this subsidy, exceptional in the history of Argentine railway concessions, followed from a conjunction of distinct factors: the Paraná government's lack of fiscal income, which led it to offer land as its only available resource; the North American origin of the promoter, which led him to follow the example of what was occurring in his place of birth, where for the past ten years this type of subsidy was being given; and the national government's strong desire to achieve a realisation of its project to establish a railway into the interior of the country. The promoter travelled to London where, with help from local businessmen, he was able to set up the CAR. This company placed, not without difficulty, one million pounds worth of shares. Wheelwright himself created more problems than necessary by appearing to compete with the promoters of the BAGSR, which made Barings Bank decline to support the project. This clash would lead to one of the fiercest rivalries between those railways funded by British capital which operated in Argentina, which would only cease at the turn of the century. A significant set of shares in the CAR were acquired by the Argentine government, and, in smaller quantities, by the Buenos Aires provincial government and residents in Argentina.

The new company contracted the construction of this broad-gauge railway to one of the most famous builders of public works at the time, Thomas Brassey, in effect associated with Ogilvie, Wythes and Wheelwright himself. The work was carried out with some delays, occasioned mainly by financial problems. The government delayed in complying with its obligation to hand over the lands of the subsidy and in paying for its subscription shares, which for sure were many. The estimate for the cost of the work which the company had used to calculate the required amount of share capital was too low, and the state of the company and the finance market made any increase impossible. The territory crossed was practically a desert, and in some parts subject to nomadic raids. The line was opened in stages from Rosario, and at last in 1870 trains were able to run over the whole length of the route to Córdoba. The first years in the life of the company were not easy. The lack of traffic worried the Directors, who did not dare to risk additional sums to improve the quantity and quality of the rolling stock, which was becoming insufficient as traffic increased. Until 1878 the company, to remunerate its investment capital, depended on payment of the state guarantee, whose unreliable delivery was a continuing source of conflict. However, the CAR had been conceived as a major company and even though the period of development of its investment took longer to mature than had been envisaged at the start, little by little it increased its income and controlled its costs. Following the colonisation and sale of its lands, for which a new company was formed with shares preferentially offered to investors in the railway, and with the traffic contributed by branches the State constructed, the line progressed and prospered. When the mainline to Córdoba was inaugurated in 1870, the 396km of the CAR represented 54% of the lines in the country. In 1880 this percentage had gone down to 16% because the mainline had not been extended and the branches had not yet been constructed. But its contribution to the gross product of the railway sector was 18.1% and its nett profit had risen to 6.9%.

These improved circumstances led the Directors to solicit the termination of the minimum benefit guarantee in 1881. Negotiations were prolonged because the government, which had not been pleased to find that the CAR would need payment of the guarantee for so many years and would not increase its capital to extend its network, was not disposed to give way on its right to insist on the reimbursement of previous payments. Finally, agreement was reached in 1884 by which the CAR renounced the right to claim from the government the amount necessary to reach 7% annual interest on future capital investment. Likewise, it agreed to repay an amount close to five hundred thousand pounds as a reimbursement for payments made until 1878. The government acquired the right to intervene in the setting of fares and charges if the nett profit exceeded 12% annually, and agreement was reached with regard to capital already invested. All of this, however, did not put an end to the bad relations between the authorities and the company. In the following years, until at least 1887, confrontations occurred as a result of government claims that fares should be reduced because company income had reached the 12%, and the former's unwillingness to recognise new capital increases.

The development of the CAR up to 1886 illustrates some serious problems in early Argentine railway history. It reflects, in the first place, the initial difficulties of the companies which offered a service based on anticipated demands for transport. Consequently, it is a testimony to the need which arose of incentivising the investment of copious sums which could only become profitable after a period, of more or less uncertain duration, during which the development of the area traversed could begin to generate a demand for service. But it also showed, especially to the potential investor, that the possibility of setting up a deal was certain, after initial difficulties were overcome, and that the mechanism of minimum benefit guarantee could be really useful during the stage of investment maturity.

The decade of the 1880s was excellent for the CAR. Although it did not extend its network, traffic continuously increased and reached surprising returns: 14.7% in 1883, 16.8% in 1884, 13% in 1885, 12.4% in 1886. In part, such high profitability can be explained by the company's decision to sacrifice the consolidation of an ample exclusive zone in order to maximise profits. This decision, if it showed good business management for the short and medium term with tight administration, demonstrated a certain lack of understanding of the needs of railway company expansion, which was to have a bad effect in the long term. This paralysis of the CAR facilitated the invasion of its potential zone of operation by dangerous competitors, of which the most aggressive was the BARR. Also, in late 1883 a new railway line had been inaugurated, the broad-gauge Ferrocarril Oeste Santafesino (FCOSF), the Western Santa Fe Railway (WSFR), conceded by the province of Santa Fe, which ran from Rosario to Casilda, south of the CAR line. However, the local character of the company, with little ability to attract capital and its short length (less than 70 km), led to this intrusion not being too damaging.

During 1886 the final stages were opened of the Ferrocarril Buenos Aires al Pacífico (FCBAP), the Buenos Aires and Pacific Railway (BAPR), which linked the Federal Capital with the city of Villa Mercedes in the province of San Luis. This new broad-gauge line was in direct competition with the CAR for traffic from the provinces which form part of the region known as Cuyo (San Luis, Mendoza and San Juan), which could now choose between travelling directly to Buenos Aires on the BAPR or to Rosario via the Andean Railway (see next paragraph) and the CAR. But without doubt the event that led the CAR to change its policy of sacrificing expansion for higher profits was the invasion of the BARR. It did not just open the line between Buenos Aires and Rosario in 1886, but from this port on the River Paraná began an extension northwards diagonally across the province of Santa Fe towards Sunchales, reaching and passing through the area already colonised in the centre of the province. For the CAR there were only two courses to follow: either it reached an agreement with the thrusting new company and eventually merged with it, or it began to extend its network in competition with the former. The Directors, with new members, opted for the second course, which would lead to a rapid expansion of the CAR from 1887.

The national government, towards the end of the 1870s, when the war with Paraguay was drawing to a close and its administration showed signs of becoming organised, ventured with its fiscal resources into railway construction. This was not the result of a doctrinaire approach, in contrast to public services in the hands of private capital, but rather, as in the case of the BAWR, because capital had been reluctant to invest in new ventures and the country's rulers were impatient to see Argentina criss-crossed by rails. On the other hand, what allowed the federal authorities to become railway developers was the fact that, from 1867, the Nation effectively had the benefit of income from the Buenos Aires custom duties, by virtue of what was set out in Article 4 of the National Constitution, as revised in 1860 and 1866. To be precise, the original idea was to finance railway works from additional taxes on exports and imports. All things considered, two lines were constructed by the State, both with junctions to the CAR. In 1873 the first stage of what would be called the Ferrocarril Andino (FCA), the Andean Railway (AR), from Villa Maria, on the Rosario to Córdoba line, to Rio Cuarto. In 1875 its trains reached Villa Mercedes, in the province of San Luis. The standards regulating the construction of the line tried to follow those of the CAR, with the fundamental difference that now the investor was the national State. In collaboration with the Province of Córdoba, it was stipulated that the lands alongside the railway would be expropriated, and later sold in small lots or given to immigrant colonists. Now, of course, given the lack of pressure from private concession holders, the hand-over took place even more slowly than in the case of the CAR example being followed, and colonisation projects remained unfinished. With regard to the capital invested, it was provided by an external loan, guaranteed by the additional customs taxes. Without this loan, the additional tax income would have been insufficient to maintain the flow of the works. The construction was done by contractors of British origin, who also provided a rather meager set of rolling stock.

Once the sections had been handed over for public use, the national government was required to organise its administration, which it did with little conviction and poor efficiency. After a short time it opted to offer the line under lease to a company which had participated in its construction. Only from 1880 did the national State return to actively direct exploitation of the Andean, now able to count on the involvement of a reorganised Departamento de Ingenieros Civiles (Department of Civil Engineers), which had appointed engineers with experience from the BAWR. In addition, the Department took charge of the administrative task of extending the Andean to Cuyo; that is, without contracting a company to do the whole job. The lines from Villa Mercedes (San Luis province) to the cities of San Luis, Mendoza and San Juan formed part of an 1872 concession, the same one which had led to the creation of the BAPR. The original concession holder had in 1878 accepted that the stretch west of Villa Mercedes would be constructed by the State, reserving for itself the construction rights between that city and Buenos Aires, rights which it later transferred to the Pacific Company. The new stages which took the Andean to the capitals of the provinces of Cuyo were opened between 1881 and 1885. With 767km of line in 1886, this railway had a 13.14% share of the national total although its turnover was quite low, constituting only 5.2% of the gross national railway product. Also, its yields were not good. Nevertheless, taking into account the novelty of the enterprise, it was to be expected that in this case the national State, acting as administrator, had initiated a successful venture. The line, though not completely finished, had been constructed in the alloted time and at a reasonable cost.

The other State line began service in 1875 after the opening of the first stage of the route from Córdoba to Tucumán. This was the metre-gauge Ferrocarril Central Norte (FCCN), the Northern Central Railway (NCR). In 1876 the whole trajectory was completed. It had been built by an Italian constructor on behalf of the State. Most of the materials had been imported from Great Britain. Initially the constructor operated the line, but in 1877 the government took charge of the running of the line. For this it appointed an administrator who resided in Córdoba and a supervisory committee based in Tucumán. The results were bad and complaints multiplied because of poor service and reports of illicit arrangements. The Department of Civil Engineers took over the administration in April 1878 and dissolved the committee. The newly appointed administrator acted too independently and clashed with the Department. In any case, the initial construction was deficient in many ways and required repairs, the costs of which enormously exceeded the costs of normal maintenance. From 1880, the line began to be extended northwards towards the cities of Salta and Jujuy, but the mountainous terrain, which the Argentine railway engineers were encountering for the first time, delayed the advance of the rails and several times multiplied the budget approved by the Department of Civil Engineers, which also had undertaken the administrative task, as in the case of the Andean. In addition, branches were constructed to link the main-line with the province of Santiago del Estero, where trains entered the capital city for the first time in 1884, and to the province of Catamarca, where the line reaching Chumbicha was opened in 1886. These works were also carried out under the administration of the Department. Given its length, in 1886 the NCR was a significant enterprise. Its 1,110km amounted to 19% of the total network. But its traffic was rather small. The gross product in that year amounted to 8.8% of the total. Its performance was variable and mostly mediocre.

The experiences of the State as a constructor of railways prompts the following observations. As in the case of the province of Buenos Aires, assigning public funds to the installation of railway lines was the result of a pragmatic, circumstantial approach, given the fact that the timid influx of private capital delayed the growth of the network beyond that acceptable for the social and economic transformation plan. It was not the result of an ideological position in favour of a major involvement of the public sector in the provision of public services. But in a way different to that pursued by the authorities of the leading Argentine province, the State's decision to invest was not followed up with a clear focus on the difficult challenge of the administration of the new enterprises. The federal government was slow to organise the State administration, preferring to lease the lines in service to their constructors. Only after some time did it face up to the task of defining and designating administrative bodies. It committed successive mistakes when doing so, by not appointing the right people. Only from 1880 and until the end of the period did the conduct of the Department of Civil Engineers seem to achieve a minimum level of professionalism. Even so it was not possible to sort out the problem of adequately computing the sums invested, a defect that was to lead, among other consecuences, to not knowing with certainty what the performance was of the AR and the NCR during all the time which they remained in State hands. The new bureaucracy also failed to prepare a budget adjusted to the cost of works in mountainous areas, a defect which gave definite support to those who wanted the works contracted privately. Finally, it is not possible to avoid pointing out that it was the State's incursion into railway enterprises which led to the serious error of committing to the introduction of a range of gauges when, on the advice of its administrators, metre gauge was adopted for the NCR.

At the same time as the construction of the AR and the NCR, as proof of the pragmatism previously mentioned, the national government awarded other concessions, which led to two companies which began to provide services during the period. The Ferrocarril Argentino del Este (FCAE), the East Argentine Railway (EAR), opened its line between 1874 and 1875 from Concordia in the province of Entre Ríos to Monte Caseros in the province of Corrientes, a trajectory of 155km. It was a bad experience as much for the government as for the investors, the result of a poorly conceived and worse executed project. The guarantee offered in the concession was excessive. The concessionaire benefitted by the government lacked influence in the capital market. After many twists and turns, the company was sold to a London finance group of secondary standing, who perceived an opportunity of profitting from the deal by converting themselves into constructors. The result of all this was that the EAR became excessively capitalised and the initial investment was not used effectively. The area traversed did not develop as expected and traffic was always scarce. The company became a hindrance to the government, which had to hand over huge sums in respect of the guarantee, and for the investors, who had made a bad deal apart from a few years before 1885. To all this we could add that the EAR involved the introduction of a third gauge size, the standard-gauge of 1.435 metres, intermediate between the broad-gauge (1.676m) of the already established railways and the narrow (metre-gauge) to which the NCR was constructed.

In 1884 the BAPR, another company with British capital, began to offer services. As we previously mentioned, its origin lay in an act of 1872. Among other lines, the act envisaged a concession for a line between Buenos Aires, Mendoza and the border with Chile. This was solicited by the Chilean Juan E. Clark. The government accepted the request and granted the concession to Clark, but he, as in the previous case, lacked adequate connections in the London financial market. Given that lack, for years he delayed taking forward the company and accepted, as we have said, that the sections between Villa Mercedes (San Luis) and Mendoza and from there to San Juan should be constructed by the national government. In the end the original concessionaire transferred his rights to the sections between Buenos Aires and Villa Mercedes to a share capital company set up for the purpose, called the Buenos Aires and Pacific Railway Company, as previously mentioned. Clark contracted the construction of all the works to it and they in turn hired subcontractors. Though their relationship with the company was not good and led to extended conflict, towards the end of 1886 service was able to open over the whole stretch of 578km between Mercedes (Buenos Aires province) and Villa Mercedes (San Luis province). The final section to the Federal Capital was opened two years later, following another conflict from which the BAPR emerged badly damaged. With the BAPR the zone of Cuyo gained an alternative line to the Atlantic coast, which competed with that of the already existing CAR. In its early years, the company survived thanks to the State's minimum benefit guarantee, although as time passed it grew and became one of the most important railways.

In starting up its railway system, the Nation had more difficulties than the province of Buenos Aires. In addition, the enterprises which it installed, whether by concession to private companies or within the State administration, did not attain the level of efficiency of the BAWR or the BAGSR, except for the CAR in the final years of this period. In the sphere of state enterprises, the BAWR was conceived as a commercial company in its own right; it fought to establish an exclusive zone, it competed with neighbouring companies, and apart from some doubts about its role in promoting other economic activities, its Directors devoted themselves to making it profitable. The AR and NCR national State railways were never administered as commercial companies, exceptions apart, and for that reason their returns were low. Poorly administered and subordinated to political and economic interests alien to them, they did not constitute examples to be followed. It must be recognised that unlike in Buenos Aires, on the one hand the Nation set out to extend its lines over desert territories having no economic activity whatever with the aim of providing a backbone for the country, linking the provincial capitals. On the other hand, at the start it did not have an organised public administration like that of Buenos Aires nor the very effective financial agency of the Bank of the Province of Buenos Aires.

In the Eighties two more provinces launched their own railway schemes: Santa Fe and Entre Ríos. Córdoba also tried, though with limited success. In 1885 Tucumán sanctioned a law granting a railway concession which began to operate services in 1888 (see below). In 1883 Santa Fe opened the first section of the already mentioned WSFR for public service, a concession granted to a local businessman, Carlos Casado, with a lands subsidy. This 58km broad-gauge line ran between Rosario and Casilda, and from 1887 onwards additional sections were constructed. It was a company dominated by the interests of the concessionaire, as a complement to his land deals, and was not subsequently developed. The government of Santa Fe, in addition, after some failed attempts, began to construct another network, this time in metre-gauge, which eventually became the Ferrocarril Provincial de Santa Fe (FCPSF), the Santa Fe Provincial Railway (SFPR). The first section was opened to the public in 1885. A line of credit from a banking house in London was used to finance the works, which were contracted out to a North American constructor. The aim of the new network was to link the agricultural colonies in the centre of the province to the port of its capital, the City of Santa Fe. By 1886 150km of line had been opened, up to the colonies of Lehmann and San Carlos Sud.

With the same funding arrangement as that of the SFPR, the province of Entre Rios was constructing, from 1885, the so-called Ferrocarril Central Enterriano (FCCER), the Entre Ríos Central Railway (ERCR). This central line linked the city of Parana with that of Concepción del Uruguay, over a 288km route which was opened in stages during 1887.

During this period, Córdoba was only able to realise the construction of a short line conceded in 1883 and opened towards the end of 1886. This was the Córdoba to Malagueño Railway, 26km long, constructed with light rails and 75 centimetre (cm) gauge. In the hands of a local businessman, this company was of little importance.

In April 1885 the province of Tucumán conceded a railway line which connected its most important sugar refineries with the provincial capital and the NCR line. This was the Ferrocarril Noroeste Argentino (FCNOA), the Argentine North Western Railway (ANWR). A share company registered in London took charge of this enterprise. The full length of 140km was opened for service between 1888 and 1889.

In 1886 there were 5,826km of railway lines open for public service in Argentina. Of those, 59% corresponded to enterprises under national jurisdiction, 37% were under the Province of Buenos Aires and 4% under the Province of Santa Fe. The gross product of the national railways amounted to 41% and the remaining 59% was that of the Buenos Aires provincial railways. The contribution of the lines in Córdoba and Santa Fe was insignificant. At the start of 1886, following the inauguration of the route from Campana to Rosario of the BARR, the railways in the region of Buenos Aires and those in the rest of the nation became linked, a union reinforced by the opening of the final section of the BAPR to Villa Mercedes. All this, added to the centralising policy of the federal government, led in the years that followed to the disappearance of autonomous provincial railway systems.

General Characteristics of the National and Provincial Railway Policies

The intentions of the different successive Argentine governments in putting forward plans for railway construction faced, as we have already seen, the problem of the lack of disposable capital funding. This circumstance was initially not forseen. On the one hand, in the government there was no clear understanding of the amount of investment required, being based on cost estimates which, in general, failed by being far too small. Also, it was not clear whether enthusiasm for railway construction existed or not among owners of disposable capital in the country. In the end, it finally became clear that the railway adventure demanded huge amounts of capital and that this could not be obtained locally. In the first companies, some initial agreements delayed understanding of this reality. Businessmen in the port city of Buenos Aires indicated that they were prepared to invest in the BAWR, and many of British origin supported the idea of the BAGSR and bought some shares. Likewise others, together with political figures like Urquiza, did the same for the CAR. But the funds which emerged from the pockets of residents in Argentina were definitely scarce, and completely disappeared once the first results from the pioneering companies became known. It follows that at the beginning of the second half of the nineteenth century Argentina did not have a class of people who could contribute to the formation of large companies, including railways, by purchasing shares; that is, the country lacked small and medium investors in sizeable numbers. The scarce amount of available capital belonged to a few people, each of whom was able to undertake their own business deals without needing to depend on financial advisors to determine where they should invest. The habit of looking for a return by means of investments in stocks or shares had yet to develop. And above all, businessmen had alternative investments which, being well understood and profitable, were much more attractive than the purchase of stocks which personally unknown parties promised would pay annual dividends or increase in value. Disposable capital in the country was primarily destined for agricultural and livestock farming or for speculation in land, but not for public works.

Significant numbers of small and medium investors, which jointly could fund large capital sums, were only to be found in the European and US markets. Of all these markets, the main one which had ventured into stock and share negotiations for companies acting outside Britain was London. It was there that investors, banking houses, and stockbrokers existed, willing to enter into negotiations for the purchase of stocks and shares in companies which were going to construct and operate railways in new countries like Argentina. It became the market of choice in the search for capital, above all from Buenos Aires, where there existed a local community of British businessmen and landowners. Also, the possibility of obtaining capital in London for the construction of railways in Argentina was encouraged by the existence of spare capacity in the large railway construction firms which had seen an end of the boom in their activities at the end of the 1840s and 1850s, and being keen to contract for the work, were able to influence some indecisive financial agents. This availability of capital and construction technology correlated with the wish of the governments of Buenos Aires and of the Nation to speed up the delayed modernisation of Argentine society.

Consequently, this early experience demonstrated to the local policy elite that railway policy could only be brought to fruition by attracting this private capital, distant and of unknown ownership. A series of promotional measures were implemented, copied from those made by other governments which found themselves in the same situation and were Argentina's competitors in attracting this capital. The privileges which were conceded to those who invested in railways in newly settled countries included minimum profit guarantees, tax exemptions and subsidies. The various Argentine governments resorted to all of these, although the last instrument was used only in exceptional cases. In general, the Province of Buenos Aires was most unwilling to concede privileges and in all cases strongly challenged the need for guarantees. The Nation, as we have seen, felt obliged to begin by offering lands as a subsidy, although it later limited itself to more general guarantees and to full tax exemptions. From 1880 the influx of foreign capital increased and there was much less need to incentivise it. In general, established companies only obtained tax exemptions for subsequent line extension investments.

The guarantee mechanism was based on a commitment undertaken by the State (national or provincial) to deliver at each year end the necessary sums to ensure that the capital invested achieved a certain profit level, set at 7% in the early years. The commitment was limited to a fixed term of 20 to 40 years. The investing companies undertook to repay to the government any amounts by which the annual profits exceeded the guaranteed minimum percentage. This distinguished guarantees from subsidies. They were, as originally conceived, an advance during the early years, until the line had been finished and development of the transport market ensured a genuine profit. In principle, they were the most powerful instrument available to the authorities for attracting capital. However, their use led to certain problems, which were badly dealt with in many cases. Granting a concession with a guarantee required of the legislature, before approving the relevant law, or of the executive before signing the contract with the concessionaire, that the budget of the proposed works be studied in order to determine an adequate amount up to which the guarantee would apply. It also required the authorities be clear as to how far the guaranteed amount should be raised so as to exceed what alternative investment schemes might offer. Fixing the period during which the privilege would apply was another question which had to be dealt with in a rational manner. Finally, it was important when guaranteeing a railway investment project to reach a judgement as to the future development of the projected line: would its actual future usefulness offset the liabilities incurred by the State, or was the line deemed fully necessary to meet government policy? The lack of a technical bureaucracy made it very difficult to adequately resolve these questions. Only as the railway system began to be installed and some State companies were consolidated, as in the case of the BAWR, did it become more able to evaluate work proposals, determine reasonable returns and fix deadlines for the maturing of investments. But it never faced up to the question of elaborating a plan for railway construction which responded effectively to the final problem. This lack in some cases led to overcapitalisation, guarantees which were excessive or for too long, and the promotion of unsuitable projects. The final challenge for the authorities was the administration of the guarantees. This implied control of expenditures, costs and fares, but suitably qualified government employees were not available to do this. It also implied inclusion in the national or provincial budgets of entries for the payment of owed accounts, which was not normally done. This meant that these administrative arrangements were a permanent source of conflict.

As an alternative to private capital, when this was wary of railway investment in Argentina, there remained the possibility of the governments turning to public capital. An intermediate alternative was to set aside public funds for the purchase of shares in private companies, with the aim of increasing investments when these appeared to be insufficient. This is what happened during the early years of the BAWR and the CAR. But later this alternative was no longer followed. From then on, not only the national government but also those of the provinces of Buenos Aires, Santa Fe and Entre Ríos faced up to the problem by means of direct State investment. Buenos Aires province began to do this with local resources, advances from the provincial bank, and returns derived from the sale of public lands, but the rate of growth of the State lines was very slow. The Nation planned railway construction with funds from customs dues, but immediately dropped the idea as being impracticable. In both cases the governments were forced to take on foreign debts, as did those of Santa Fe and Entre Ríos in the mid-1880s. In the end, the market they turned to was essentially London's, and the capital came from the same type of person who invested in railway companies as recommended by their stockbroker. The difference was, in these cases, that instead of stocks, shares or debentures, loan bonds were being negotiated. This arrangement also led to problems. It required the state to know how far into debt it should place itself, and in what way the servicing of the debt would affect the balance of payments and its fiscal equilibrium. The levels of debt experienced in 1876 and 1885 reached dangerous limits, though in both cases the crisis was overcome without major harm. This was not the case in 1890, when payments ceased at national and provincial levels. The arrangement also required organisation of the public companies, for which their was no previous experience. We have seen that Buenos Aires acquitted itself well in this test, but not so the Nation. Santa Fe and Entre Ríos ended up handing the administration of their railways to the creditors.

Another task which the politicians had to face when they decided to promote railway construction was to put in place certain permanent activities in the public administration, over and above the question of which entity was to be the owner of the capital obtained. Those activities were to do with the planning and control of the new public service, about which we have already said something above. Here it is only necessary to make some general comments. In this first period it can be said that there was no planning by the State, federal or local, which embarked on railway activities, at least not in any explicit way. Never was a general construction plan outlined nor even sketches made of relevant matters to be considered. The railway lines were being installed along routes chosen by their promoters. It was evident that the only traffic which would acquire sufficient volume to justify investment would be that arising from linking the interior to the ports. But over and above this obvious fact, it would have been possible to adopt certain precautions, so as to avoid mistakes like duplication of lines and diversity of gauges. It is true that in this first period the making of decisions on these matters in a country growing its population was almost impossible, and there was a predominant belief that no railway, wherever it was, would be detrimental. As we have seen, the province of Buenos Aires seemed to be moving well towards orienting its lines south, west and north from the capital, assigning to each an exclusive zone. It also decided on a unified broad gauge. All of this perhaps followed from the existence of a technical administration at the BAWR. The nation, on the other hand, seemed to be mainly preoccupied with linking the provincial capitals. With regard to the line gauge we have already seen how it varied according to the circumstances and, in principle, was exclusively concerned with the immediate cost of construction. Regarding control, initially it was linked to the existence of guarantees and not to the fact that it concerned a public service monopoly which involved thousands of people. Only later was it realised that permanent control was required, although quickly the idea emerged that the activities could be self regulated by means of competition. In effect, competent government organisations were not created for these activities, and if the province of Buenos Aires demonstrated greater competence it was owing to the actions of the BAWR staff. Finally, it should be observed, never was the question raised that the State railways, as providers of a public service, should also be controlled by independent entities.

The Impact of the Railway

The emergence of the railway in Argentina produced a radical transformation in society and the economy.

The train displaced the only means for the transport of cargo: the bullock wagon. Of course, as we have seen, in so far as the early railway lines were short, this displacement was gradual. It also depended on the efficiency of the new companies and the skill of their managers. Recall that in the early days of the Southern it captured significant wool traffic, perhaps its most important cargo, by using railway cargo wagons to transport loaded bullock wagons. These would otherwise have avoided transhipment of their cargoes at their local stations and continued their journey to a final destination in Buenos Aires, in competition with the new mode of transport. After a while the wagons disappeared, but a complementary cart traffic survived to provide service for cargo between its point of origin and the nearest station. Transport capacity multiplied many times, journey times shortened, and security increased, and all this contributed to the development of the internal market and permitted the export of agricultural and livestock products.

It followed that as the railway lines were extended, it became possible for lands more distant from ports to be brought into production, thus contributing to their value. Sometimes it has been stated that the construction of railway lines was aimed only at this ultimate objective, and that the places through which the rails passed were determined by the existence of landowners who controlled company decisions and therefore enriched themselves. In the general case, this was not true. Apart from the existence of promoters, required in the early days, and the result of a lack of planned policies later on, the railway companies were, from the beginning, autonomous companies where boards of directors took decisions in line with benefitting their investors. They did not depend on the interests of landowners nor on the wishes of other groups in the country of origin of their capital, such as suppliers of materials and fuel or international commercial companies. Once under way, the preoccupation of those businessmen who understood the rules of railway operation was to develop the transport market, and of course for that it was necessary for lands to produce and international export markets to grow.

Even in those cases where indeed there was a special connection between railway construction and land colonisation, analysis leads to confirmation of the previous assertion. One company which took on the colonisation of lands was the Central Argentine, in accordance with the concession contract and the subsidy it included. Initially, however, the lands were a hindrance, as they needed an allocation of capital, very scarce at the time, and required much troublesome work to attract immigrants. There was uncertainty during the early years. The activity to be developed was not exactly clear and there were doubts as to the agricultural suitability of the soil. Extensive stockbreeding was the only activity in the area. In order to start the colonisation the CAR formed a new company to obtain the necessary capital. But in its inner deliberations the possible destiny of the lands continued to be discussed, and the opinion which emerged was that the best deal would be to sell the land as soon as possible, in large tracts for stockbreeding. The manager who had been appointed to lead the colonisation was let go, because he had used part of the capital of the company to give loans to colonists and many of them had disappeared without making their repayments. But rapid re-selling was not possible because the State held back on its obligation to hand over most of the lands. After some time, the colonies progressed and then sale, rent or actual exploitation of the lands proved to be an excellent deal, beginning in the eighties. However, the land company became completely independent of the CAR and had a separate future history.

Examples of land companies or landowners becoming involved in railway activities are few and of little significance. The Western Santa Fe was promoted by Carlos Casado as a way of boosting his colony at Casilda and to obtain an unjustifiable subsidy from the government of Santa Fe. It was a small company, lacking autonomy and efficiency, which after suffering from the consequences of the 1890 financial crisis was absorbed by the CAR. The province of Santa Fe carried forward, with foreign finance, its railway construction plan to link its ports with the innumerable colonies, in existence or being formed, in the central area of the province. At first this network was called the "Railway to the Colonies", but later became the Santa Fe Provincial Railway (SFPR) when it was transferred to a French company. The provincial policy, which certainly wanted to benefit the colonists, found it possible to achieve this by combining the interests of a railway constructor and a bank, both seeking to benefit from their own part of the deal. Even so, the result was a railway which was operated as an autonomous company.

The construction of railways enabled speculation in land, by means of the purchase of tracts near where the concessioned railway was expected to pass, in the hope of selling it for a better price at a later date. Generally it was the railway promoters and constructors, and not the railway companies, who embarked in this activity. A good example was the Chilean brothers Juan Eduardo and Mateo (Matthew) Clark, promoters and constructors of the

BAPR, completed in 1886; of the Ferrocarril Gran Oeste Argentino (FCGOA), the Argentine Great Western Railway (AGWR); the Ferrocarril Trasandino (FCT), the Transandine Railway (TR); and the Ferrocarril Nordeste Argentino (FCNEA), the Argentine North Eastern Railway (ANER), constructed in the following period. But from the activities of these businessmen, which the 1890 crisis put an end to, it remains clear that their interests did not coincide, and in many cases were in conflict, with the railway companies. In 1886 another promoter, after having acquired enormous tracts of land managed to establish the Ferrocarril Gran Sur de Santa Fe y Córdoba (FCGSSFC), the Santa Fe and Córdoba Great Southern Railway (SFCGSR), which was constructed soon afterwards. However, this railway remained independent of its promoter, its activities were affected by the 1890 crisis, and it ended up being acquired by the BARR.

Another effect of the introduction of the railways was to accelerate the penetration of capitalist methods in Argentina. When in 1854 some traders from the port of Buenos Aires decided to form the company that later became the BAWR, commercial law did not forsee the creation of public limited companies and this concept had to be expressly regulated in the law establishing the company's concession. Little by little, with the sanction of the commercial law code, a regulatory framework began to appear for the creation of public limited companies with large amounts of capital, and later on debentures were legislated for, these being bonds much used by railway companies to attract funds. However, apart from the deficiences of commercial law, it is true that almost all the railway companies were constituted abroad, mainly in London. At the start the government thought that in the future these companies could be re-registered as Argentine companies, or would be able to raise part of their capital in Argentina. The BAGSR, the CAR and the BANR all had a shareholders list in Buenos Aires. But the expectation was frustrated; no foreign company was re-registered in Argentina, or transferred its activities to an Argentine company, and the lists of Argentine shareholders decreased in the cases where they existed. As we have said before, the country lacked the class of persons who provided most of the capital of the railway companies: the small or medium size saver who was accustomed to investing in shares.

The advent of the railway also led to the introduction of new forms of work, of large organisations, of specialist trades which required qualified workers, and the emergence of true industries, such as were the railway workshops. Each company, once in business, raised its own workshop, initially for the maintenance and repair of rolling stock. Some of these also developed into enormous establishments capable of manufacturing carriages and wagons, and all kinds of accessories. However, in no case did they become exponents of heavy industry. The more refined pieces, requiring foundry work, such as wheels, chassis, and actual locomotives, continued to be imported. It has been suggested that the reason for this lay in the promotional policy of the government, which consisted of a total exemption from import duties of railway materials, together with a belief that railway managers would be predisposed to favour industries from their country of origin, even though this might reduce the profitability of their railway. Without discounting these reasons, it seems probable that the lack of development of a heavy railway industry arose from the absence of deposits of iron ore and coal together with a lack of interest from local businessmen to invest in this kind of activity.

The organised work of the railways contributed to the development of two related entities: the trade unions and a welfare system. In 1887, just towards the end of the period reviewed in this chapter, one of the first organised unions in the country had been created, La Fraternidad (Brotherhood) of Locomotive Drivers and Firemen, was officially recognised a short time after, and had started to enroll members from all the companies. A short time before, in 1883, the BAGSR had set up an autonomous retirement fund for its employees, which envisioned making pension payments for those who retired from active service following age 55.

Its network of railway lines changed the geography of Argentina, especially in certain areas. It led to the expansion of Buenos Aires, its principal city, whose suburban expansion followed the rails which extended out from the initial nucleus towards the pampas. It also had a large effect on the location of new towns and cities, or on the growth of small villages which multiplied in size. Only near the path of the railway was it possible for a population to emerge or grow. It is true that the impact the railway had on urbanisation varied according to the area it was in. What has been described until now had happened in the humid pampas, where the new mode of transport started a productive revolution based on agriculture and livestock. Elsewhere, the railway was only an agent of economic transformation, linking certain centres of production, like Cuyo and Tucumán, with the coast without the possibility of developing the areas it passed through.

Finally, it should be noted that the installation of the railways, instigated by the national and provincial governments, contributed to the forging of a special relationship between the country and Great Britain. The great majority of the capital invested in the railways, whether in private or public form, came from there. The majority of foreign investments in Argentina were British, and among these, railway investments were at the forefront. Argentine external debt bonds were purchased mainly by residents in Britain, and until 1886 most of this money was used to construct railways. This relationship developed gradually. In the early stages, the British commercial residents in Argentina played an introductory role. Towards 1886, however, the banking houses in London began to negotiate Argentine stocks and shares without the need for intermediaries. The growing relationship was not an object of criticism, as any idea of economic or political nationalism was nonexistent at that time.

Parque Station, the first terminus in the city of Buenos Aires. The second station building, erected towards the end of the 1860s. *(Photo: Museo Nacional Ferroviario)*

Morón Station on the BAWR. Typical suburban station building, circa 1870. *(Photo: Museo Nacional Ferroviario)*

La Porteña, together with *La Argentina,* were the first two locomotives of the Buenos Aires Western Railway, manufactured by E.B. Wilson in 1856. *(Photo: Museo Nacional Ferroviario)*

Northern Central Railway's Avellaneda. Manufactured in England by Fox Walker in 1874, it was one of the first narrow-gauge locomotives in Argentina. *(Photo: Museo Nacional Ferroviario)*

Olavarría Station on the Southern Railway, built in 1882. A good example of the architectural style developed in the early years of the railways. *(Photo: Museo Nacional Ferroviario)*

MARIO JUSTO LÓPEZ

2 | A Railway System with Private Foreign Companies and Government Control 1887 – 1916

The year 1886 marks the end of a period in the history of Argentina's railways, and the start of a different one. In that year the opening for public use of new sections of the BARR and the BAPR meant that the two railway systems in the country, isolated until then, became linked: that part which had been constructed based on actions of the government of the province of Buenos Aires, and that which had resulted from the efforts of the national government. But in addition, on the 12th of October the presidency passed to Miguel Juárez Celman, who announced a change in policy, consisting of the sale of the state railway companies, as well as a change in the form of the relationship between the government and the private companies acquiring concessions. In addition, the new President decided on a series of measures which resulted in the progressive disappearance of autonomous provincial railway policies.

There has been much discussion as to the motive behind the change of policy. The new President, some of his ministers, and the Governor of the Province of Buenos Aires who took over in May 1887, presented it as a matter of doctrine: the state, naturally a poor administrator, should remove itself from all those activities in which private companies are prepared to invest. In any case, even though these activities provide public services, competition should be promoted, reducing the role of the state to a minimum. At least so affirmed Máximo Paz (previous Governor of the Province of Bs As) although not Juárez Celman. Without negating the sincerity of these statements, no less influential in the change of policy was the conscious realisation on the part of the national and some provincial authorities that excessive fiscal debt had been incurred in the past years and that a crisis in confidence was possible, as the events in 1885 had shown. This was explicitly made public by Juárez Celman, who announced that what the state might receive from the sale of the railway companies would be put towards amortizing the external debt. The policy change was also facilitated by the tendency of the capital markets, in London and other European centres, to become involved in a number of companies without investigating their profitability, relying instead on previous successful examples. The path towards the centralization of railway policy was part of the general policy centralizing process put in place from 1880, during which the provinces began to lose many of the supposed attributes of federalism. Juárez Celman made an important step towards this centralization when he caused a draft bill to be drawn up which would enable Congress to sanction a new law establishing that all railways would come under national government control.

Policy Change and Sale of State Railways

It is certainly the case that already in 1887 the national government had begun to disentangle itself from its railways. The first step was the sale of the most of the AR. Invoking an 1878 law, whose provisions had in practice fallen out of use, all the sections lying between Villa Mercedes (San Luis) and San Juan were offered to Juan E. Clark, the original contractor. At that time he had transferred his rights over the sections from Buenos Aires to Villa Mercedes to the BAPR and had agreed that the sections to Cuyo would be constructed and exploited by the national State. Clark accepted the offer and through his brother Mateo, with the colaboration of a banking house interested in doing business in the country, formed a new company in London, the Argentine Great Western Railway (AGWR), Ferrocarril Gran Oeste Argentino (FCGOA), to which he ceded the rights. The price agreed was approximately £2,450,000.

The concessionaire would benefit from the 7% guarantee provided for in the original law, but over only 80% of the full purchase price. The sale, considered in its own right and in isolation, was a good deal for the state. In a short time, without the need to obtain the agreement of the Congress by virtue of the 1878 law and its antecedents, a buyer was found for a railway over 500km in length, running through economically undeveloped areas, which required major investments to make it function efficiently, and it was handed over for a significant sum, probably more than the state had expended on its construction. However, the action of the government was unable to avoid mistakes. Clark was a controversial businessman. His relationship with the linking company, the BAPR, had deteriorated because of the connecting line near to Buenos Aires, and the existing tensions were carried forward into the new company. The AGWR and the BAPR would be in competition and would clash until the middle of the first decade in the twentieth century. Choosing Clark repeated the Argentine government practice of preferring intermediaries to real investors, which then increased the cost of establishing companies. The result of all this was to divide the railway between Buenos Aires and the frontier with Chile into rival companies instead of a united entity, with the additional aggravation that it allowed Clark to introduce a third entity, the Transandine Railway (TR), Ferrocarril Trasandino (FCT), which started to lay track between Mendoza and the frontier via the Uspallata Pass.

Thus, shortly after taking on the presidency, Juárez Celman was beginning to implement the change of policy he had announced. It is true that modification of the course which had been followed until then had its antecedents. At first the national government had taken on the role of impresario, without much conviction, for lack of private investors agreeing to pay the cost of installing the railways, but then refused to take on the task of administering them. Only in 1876, after the creation of the Civil Engineers Department, did public functionaries emerge with better capacity and willingness to undertake an active role. But in mid-1886, following the resignation of the engineer Guillermo White as head of that Department, still during the presidency of Roca, the actions of the state lost their sense of direction and in the national Congress the tendency to cede activity to private companies took over. Even before Juárez Celman assumed office, a law had established that the rail extensions north of Tucumán be contracted to a private constructor.

The sections of the AR between Villa María and Río Cuarto remained in the public sector. This was the result of not being able to apply the 1878 law to its sale, and recognition of a legal encumbrance in favour of the holders of bonds for the 1881 loan. However, the government petitioned Congress to sanction a law authorising its sale, which was achieved in November 1887. From then on there followed a succession of mistakes. Once again Clark was chosen as the buyer, now associated with another favourite for government concessions (the cunning Charles Henry Sanford). As the sale could not be completed, because of the existence of the encumbrance, a temporary leasing arrangement was agreed, with confusing clauses. The CAR wish to purchase the sections was objected to and, finally, in the face of the continuous failure of the leaseholders to comply, the lease was rescinded, returning this part of the AR to the national state. There it remained until 1909, when it was sold, after blocking attempts in 1891 and 1899, to the linking private companies for an excellent price.

At almost the same time that Congress was approving the bill presented by the Executive to authorise the sale of the rest of the AR, it converted into law a similar bill which authorised the sale of most of the NCR. Thus its main line from Córdoba to Tucumán and the branches to Santiago del Estero and to Chumbicha were offered for sale to interested buyers, who should submit informal offers for a minimum of £3 million (15 million hallmarked gold pesos). A total of four offers were received, and that of the construction company Hume Hermanos was accepted. They were acting as representatives of a group of investors of British origin, rivals of the CAR, which had itself hoped to buy the AR. The price agreed was £3,200,000. Completion of the sale presented certain problems, because the encumbrances in favour of the holders of the 1881 loan bonds still remained in place. In fact, the purchasing company was only a subcontractor of the firm John G. Meiggs

Son and Company, which had operated in the country for many years and wanted to cede the railway to whoever was disposed to make the actual investment. In the end, this investment came from the Córdoba Central Railway (CCR), recently constituted with investors linked to the BAPR in order to construct a line conceded by the province from Córdoba to the frontier with the province of Santa Fe. A mechanism was agreed between all the parties concerned in order to finally complete the contract, by swapping the loan bonds for new debentures issued by the CCR and payment of the remainder in cash from the national government. During those negotiations additional investment was also agreed: to introduce improvements and make repairs to what had been constructed by the state, for a lease during the period which the exchange of titles would require, and an additional lease for the sections to the north of Tucumán which would remain in state ownership. The sums invested by the buyer would benefit from a 5% minimum annual guarantee for a period of 15 years.

Unlike in the case of the AR, the sale of the NCR was not advantageous to the Argentine exchequer. The price received was almost surely at least 20% less than the cost of its construction. Of course in this case, unlike in that of the of the other railway, a major part of the price was destined to paying off the 1881 loan bonds in circulation, which enabled the President to make good on his promise to reduce the foreign debt. On the other hand, a major part of the price for the Andean had been paid in to the National Bank as a capital increase. But over and above that, the operation we are analysing evidenced a series of mistakes, some of them repeating those made in previous cases, which we will now describe. A trunk main line was sold off without having previously planned what to do with the branches and extensions which would remain in state ownership, thus creating a difficult problem to resolve in the future. Alienation of bonds was proceeded with in the face of the existence of creditor guarantees which led, for while, to suspension of the sale and its replacement by a lease, the clauses of which were not properly agreed. The same occurred with the additional lease of the sections to the north of Tucumán. Negotiations were ongoing with those awarded the railway while changing the conditions of the previous public offer, thus violating the principle of equality and depriving all those who had been interested in making an offer. A new business group, whose solvency and efficiency had not been accredited, had been preferred over that of an established company (the CAR) which had been in operation for over twenty years and whose close proximity to the NCR offered the possibility of a more economic exploitation. In the face of all this, the sale of the NCR draws attention to the permanent flaw in the Argentine railway policy of the time: improvisation and lack of a national plan to which decisions about individual lines could be subordinated. Almost at the same time as the law which authorised the sale of the NCR was passed, the Congress approved another two bills granting concessions to lines with the city of Tucumán as their destination. The first of these was the extension from Sunchales to Tucumán passing through Santiago del Estero, applied for by the BARR, which in a frenzy of construction had reached Rosario in barely three years, had crossed the province of Santa Fe from south to north, had constructed branches and was now in a hurry to reach the capital of the northern province, always in competition with the CAR, which was thought to be the most likely candidate to acquire the NCR state line. This concession had been granted without the guarantee of minimum benefit. The second line was approved by Congress at the request of the Governor of the province of Santa Fe in favour of a group of French investors, with whom he had been negotiating the sale of the provincial state railway. This line was to extend from San Cristóbal in north-east Santa Fe towards Tucumán with a trajectory mostly parallel to, and hardly 40km away from, the extension of the BARR. It was to benefit from a 5% guarantee for 55 years. With these two new lines constructed and the network planned for the CCR completed, the country would have three main lines joining Tucumán to the Parana River at Rosario and the coast at Buenos Aires:

1. from Tucumán on the NCR to Córdoba, from there to San Francisco on the Santa Fe border, and then directly to Rosario on the new Cordoba & Rosario Railway (CRR), Ferrocarril de

Córdoba y Rosario (FCCyR)}, which the CCR group was constructing with a provincial concession, all of these tracks being narrow (metre) gauge and having a state guarantee as far as Córdoba;

2. on the BARR, from Tucumán to Santiago del Estero, then on to Rosario, and from there to Buenos Aires, on broad gauge and without guarantee;
3. on the San Cristóbal to Tucumán Railway (SCTR), Ferrocarril de San Cristóbal a Tucuman (FCSCT), where it joined the SFPR, reached the city of Santa Fe and from there to Rosario on an extension which would be opened in early 1892; all of this route on metre gauge track and benefitting from national or provincial guarantees, depending on the particular section.

Did it make sense that as a result of national government policy three railway networks should be constructed between the same or close locations? Accepting the idea, then much in vogue, that all railways are beneficial, did it make sense to grant minimum benefit guarantees to two of them? Ever present improvisation, now linked to imprudent investors and to the progress of railway construction, was beginning to lead to unhappy effects. The passage of time would soon demonstrate that the installation of competing networks would result in no, or very small, returns on investments. This analysis seems to us to be more adequate than the popular revisionist version that so often arises in these cases, without significant supporting evidence, that blames the action of foreign capital exerting pressure, in a surprisingly homogeneous and perspicacious way, in order to take over the former state railways.

The provincial governments which had constructed state railways followed the change in policy of the federal government, though in general with certain delays. The province of Santa Fe, by means of an 1888 law, sought to free itself of what would be from then onward the SFPR. The province of Buenos Aires did the same thing a year later with the BAWR, though already in 1888 it had conveyed a branch from La Plata to the BAGSR. The province of Entre Ríos took the decision in October 1890. The governor of Buenos Aires justified these actions as a matter of doctrine, in which he showed himself to be even more dogmatic than President Juárez Celman. To the administrative incapacity of the state he added the idea that it was the duty of the authorities to promote competition, and during his administration granted whatever concession was requested by supposedly new promoters, while the requests of established companies were obstructed or rejected out of hand. The governments of Santa Fe and Entre Rios, however, justified the sale of their state lines to the fact that the debts contracted to finance their construction had generated charges which were impossible to meet. We will continue with a brief summary of each of the three cases.

The most significant of all the cases, more important even than the national state cases, was that of the BAWR. To understand this, it is necessary to step back a few years, to the Province of Buenos Aires administrations of Governors Dardo Rocha and Carlos D'Amico, in order to then consider the actions of their successor, Máximo Paz. During the mandates of the former two, development of the provincially owned line had been stimulated at an accelerated rate, accumulating for this reason a foreign debt of four million pounds sterling. In addition, the BAWR had extended its services into new areas, such as the city and surroundings of La Plata and its new port, the construction of which had also generated an increase in the debt. Paz, in his first year of office, issued a new loan of a further one million pounds for the BAWR. The excessive external debt thus contracted had become well beyond the capacity of the Province to pay. The money raised had been invested in public works which took a long time to generate significant economic activity and, as a consequence, to increase fiscal income. In the mean time, the interest due on the bonds issued had to be paid. For that reason, in his second year in post, the Governor announced a new railway policy. This was facilitated by the fact that his political supporters were now in a majority in the provincial legislature. Preservation of the provincial railway system was abandoned, and a law was approved enabling the sale of almost all its network. And, finally, it was resolved to accept all bids for railway concessions, so that new companies could compete with already established lines. But all of this required too much time, so much so that the the provincial finances became fragile and the economy of the nation was endangered. The tender for the sale was opened in March of 1890, after investor euphoria had receded. The BAWR was offered at a starting price of 34 million pesos, but it was hoped that more than 70 million would be obtained, based on the supposition that a bidding war would develop between different groups. However, only one group was interested, organised by the British businessman Alexander Henderson. Though he only offered one million pesos more than the starting price, he eventually agreed to pay 41 million pesos. Given that he arranged for £5 million in loans to be issued, the remainder in cash which entered the government accounts amounted to only 16 million pesos. Henderson, as well as having found investors willing to contribute this sum, in order to move the company forward had also negotiated with the neighbouring connected railways, the BAGSR, the BAEPR, and the CAR (which wanted to enter the north of the province of Buenos Aires in pursuit of its rivalry with the BARR) concerning leases for the BAWR branches. In this way, the BAWR only remained in direct control of the original line towards the west, soon to be extended, and was assured of a steady income from the leasing payments agreed with the neighbouring companies, which allowed it to successfully cope with the impending financial crisis. The new BAWR was managed from the start by men closely linked to the BAGSR, with which it maintained cordial relations from then onward, and followed the latter's tradition of efficient performance. The significance for the province of Buenos Aires was the loss of a public company which had been wisely organised and had enabled the rolling out of the most coherent railway policy in the country. The price obtained did not improve the fiscal situation. Even though the refund of five million pounds in bonds against the public debt stayed in the hands of the purchasing company, the cash amount which was placed in the government account in the Bank of the Province of Buenos Aires was insufficient to cover its debt at the Bank, and eventually the Bank failed three years later.

The province of Santa Fe had constructed a metre-gauge railway network with foreign funding, obtained via financial institutions based in London. This was rather vaguely known as the Railway to the Colonies but was eventually called the Santa Fe Provincial Railway (SFPR), as previously mentioned above. It began to grow from 250km opened at the beginning of 1887 to 587km in 1888, 698 in 1889 and 812 in 1890. This also implied an increase in accumulated debt. From February 1888, the annual service charge was £160,000, as well as £170,000 for annual charges servicing loans from the provincial bank. The yield from these investments was negligible, hardly covering the sums involved. Towards the end of that year the provincial exchequer was in difficulties coping with its commitments. The governor José Gálvez believed he had found a solution following the emergence of a group of French investors, comprising a bank and a company providing railway materials. A law authorised the transfer of the provincial railways to a new company formed from these entities, which would take over recovery of the titles of the loans owned by British investors. At the same time, the company would be contracted to continue the expansion of the SFPR network. The Province would grant it a 5% minimum benefit guarantee for 55 years. This transaction had bad consequences. The French company did not recover the titles and stopped servicing the holders from 1890, which led to a three-way conflict between the provincial government, the British investors and the French railway company, which would only be resolved towards the end of the 19th century. As in the case of the Province of Buenos Aires, the transfer of the SFPR to a private company did not prevent the insolvency of the provincial government.

The Province of Entre Rios, as we anticipated in the previous chapter, had taken forward its railway policy by means of a scheme almost identical to that of its neighbour Santa Fe. By June 1887 it had opened the main line of the so-called Ferrocarril Central Entrerriano (FCE), Entre Rios Central Railway (ERCR), between Paraná and Concepción del Uruguay. To do this it had issued a loan, negotiated in London, for £1,530,800 between 1885 and 1886. The following year a new provincial law authorised the construction of four branches for which another loan was issued, for £1,745,000, negotiated in the same way. Servicing the accumulated railway debts rose to £230,000 per year, of which the Nation was responsible for about £50,000. In common with most of the provinces, Entre Rios had then incurred other debts, of which the most significant was to endow a capital sum of £3,200,000 for the new provincial bank. Provincial income was insignificant, and the investments which had occasioned the debts were not profitable. It also followed that in this case the possibility of meeting the loan payments was virtually nil. It was some time before the provincial government became aware of the situation it was in. Only in October 1890 did a law authorise the governor to transfer ownership of the railway lines, of which practically all were open for public service, in exchange for recovery of the titles held by the investors. In this case the operation was carried out more effectively, and the title holders agreed to exchange them for shares in a new company, the Entre Rios Railways (ERRs), Ferrocarriles de Entre Rios (FCER), which took over the main line and branches during 1892. However, just as before, this accion did not prevent the insolvency of the province.

The Advance of Federal Jurisdiction

As well as the sale of the State railway companies, the change in policy implied, of itself, a more favourable attitude to the investment of private capital in the railway transport mode. On the one hand, it accentuated the tendency to accept bids for concessions without serious prior discussions. On the other hand, the minimum profit guarantee remained as an incentive, with some modifications and a new, more attractive, settlement mechanism. The provincial governments, on the whole, also followed the federal government's lead, as much in those provinces which had made incursions into autonomous railway policies as well as in those provinces which had made no moves of that kind.

In reality, the idea of favourably receiving petitions from private entities was based on the belief which Juárez Celman shared with those who had preceded him in the post and which were held by the majority of the individuals who occupied distinguished positions in the politics and economy of Argentina. The railway was the outstanding modern transport mode: efficient, speedy, capable of carrying huge volumes of cargo and large numbers of passengers in the least possible time and with maximum safety. Argentina was an extensive country with vast regions capable of being brought into production. Over the past years governments had begun the task of linking its regions by means of railways, but the existing network was absolutely insufficient and it was imperative to increase its extent as rapidly as possible. As the president declared in 1889: "Today the country needs twenty thousand kilometres of railway lines, if we want to become agriculturists, be an influence in the overseas market and persuade immigrants to penetrate the interior away from the coast". Consequently, this railway policy activity deserved all the support that the State could provide. It was among those activities, like industrial development, which the progressive liberalism of Juárez Celman judged to be deserving of guarantees in order to ensure capital investment. It followed that on the acceptance of any bids for concessions, the new administration would add a modified procedure for the minimum profit guarantee. This happened from 1888, when a presidential decree determined that the entire amount of the guarantee would be paid on each stipulated date, after which the company was required to return to the government any nett profit (that exceeding the amount guaranteed) it might have made. This modified procedure replaced that used until then, which required a determination of the nett profit before the State would pay the difference it owed the company. This was a very important innovation because it avoided the difficulties caused by delays in making payments. On the one hand, investors were assured that the company would on due dates have funds available from which to pay dividends and interest. On the other hand, the government could at the same time expect, in most cases, to be able to enforce the general applicability of certain rules: for example, that a certain percentage of gross income would always be agreed for company development costs and that any deficit over this amount would not be covered by the guarantee. The decree was seen as supportive of any investment in railways. As well as the modified procedure for payments, in the second half of the 1880s the guarantee policy had other built-in characteristics. In the first place, not all concessions received a guarantee. In principle, a prior judgement as to the existence of traffic potential was what justified the granting or not of the guarantee. During the presidency of Juárez Celman 67 concessions were granted. Of these, five were to previously established companies, to which guarantees were never given. Of the rest, 24 received guarantees, and 38 did not. It is true that a case by case analysis will turn up some inconsistances, but in general the stated criterion was applied. In any case, the amount and duration of the guarantee was reduced, mostly to 5% for 20 years, except in the case of the French investments, which were for 5% over 55 years.

The announcements by the president and especially the decree modifying the mechanism for guarantee payments, together with the optimistic climate and euphoria in the capital market led to a faster rhythm of activity, multiplying requests for concessions and an accelerating surge of new companies during the scarcely four years during which the president was in office. This situation became known as the time of fever, mania or madness for railway concessions, and led to certain defects in matters of railway policy, already present in previous administrations, acquiring greater notoriety.

The central error continued to be the lack of planning. At no time did the State pause for study of possible designs for the network, of the lines which seemed to be most necessary, of the most rational way to extend existing lines, of the different requirements which most demanded to be met by the construction of new lines, etc. As in so many other matters, Juárez Celman was aware of the problem. He accepted that railway exploitation was being done, and should be done, in the form of a monopoly, contrary to the belief shared by most of his contemporaries. This moved him to state, in early 1888, that "with the intention of establishing clarity and to avoid the bad effects which could arise from the concession of closely parallel lines in competition with each other, or authorising construction in unsuitable localities, the Executive has just ordered that the National Railway Board and the Department of Engineers proceed to prepare a railway plan and network, taking into account those lines which already exist, those which have been conceded, and those which in their judgement should be established". But, as ever, in spite of this correct diagnosis, nothing was done. The euphoria and concession fever which followed led to the construction of competing lines; the most notorious and absurd case being the long parallel lines from the province of Santa Fe towards Tucumán, which we have already referred to. The diversity of gauges was extended and the idea emerged that two routes should be constructed to any destination, one in broad gauge and another in narrow gauge. Intermediary promoters, now no longer required, continued being successful, and were preferred to established companies, as we have already noted. And, lastly, survival of the guarantee mechanism and lack of foresight raised the commitments of the State in pounds sterling, that is, the external debt, to an obviously imprudent amount. Certainly the railway network began to grow at a rate not seen before. From 1887 to 1890 it rose from almost 6,700km in length to just under 9,500km. The number of companies also grew, from 16 to 23. In 1891 the opening of new lines would reach its highest point since the impetus taken on before the crisis in 1890. The number of kilometres conceded reached an impressive total. Between 1887 and 1889, from the State alone, the 67 concessions given entailed 26,000km. Of those granted, 24 had minimum profit guarantees, as we saw above. These represented 12,200km and 58 million pounds of capital. Most were never taken up, and were declared void from 1891. Many of concessions made were utterly nonsensical. But once agreed they had forced the government to pay annual sums which it did not have nor could raise. However, railway policy during these years did not lead to major difficulties precisely because it was interrupted by the events in 1890. As well as the emergence of some lines which should not have been constructed, and which ended up being absorbed by the State or the larger companies, it was the established companies which were most damaged by the disorderliness of the concessions. Thus the BAGSR had to pay out hundreds of thousands of pounds for third party concessions which if constructed, would have severely damaged its activities.

As we saw in Chapter 1, the national government had not given much attention to controlling the activities of the railway companies which had emerged or had itself created. Control by the public authority was limited to dealing with matters linked to those cases where guarantees existed. Juárez Celman continued that stance, and even sought to reduce the function of the state when he introduced automatic payment of the whole amount of the profit guarantee. However, he rapidly began to modify his position. He had initiated his new policy and procedures in the belief that having railway activities in the hands of private companies, each one efficiently seeking to prosper, would lead to a better overall result. But some of the problems arising in the new companies which had purchased the AR and the CNR, and recurring problems with regard to the EAR, rapidly dissipated that rather naïve belief and, as with all disillutions, led to an exaggerated reaction. The outcome was government measures which fluctuated and lacked coherence. In statements to Congress in May 1888 and 1889 he critisized those companies which had forgotten that "if the government guaranteed interest on their capital, then it was a condition that the company should serve all the necessities and exigences of its traffic, and that its administration and development should be progressive and forward looking." Rules were soon sanctioned which provided for the suspension of the guarantee to any company which did not adequately maintain the condition and quantity of its rolling stock, and which authorised the Executive to retain the guarantee and use it to buy new railway materials. At the same time a reorganisation of the public administration offices was provided for, in order to undertake the necessary control tasks, thus in effect creating a public board, which preceded the National Railway Board, but failed to be staffed with properly qualified senior functionaries. Now close to the end of his government, a decree created posts of auditor for each guaranteed railway, which signified a serious interference in the administration of the companies. Each auditor, as well as having ample powers of inspection, should endorse the accounts and ensure that the nett profit was passed to the government, and where necessary to take charge of the acquisition of locomotives, carriages and wagons. The salary of the auditors would be a charge on the company.

However, up to this point all these measures continued to be linked to the existence of guarantees, leaving the other companies free from state vigilance. Only during the fourth year of Juárez Celman's government did the state become aware that monopolistic public service railway operations required the existence of powers of oversight in the hands of the state itself. This led the Executive to prepare a new General Railways bill, because it understood that the existing legislation did not give the government means to compel the companies to comply with their obligations and improve their services. This bill was not considered by Congress until after the resignation of Juárez Celman in 1890 and it finally became law in November of 1891. While it signified a move forward and aspired, for example, to establish general principles for the setting of fares and charges, its wording was imperfect and without doubt its most immediate effect was to serve as an excuse for a process of centralisation by which all the railways under provincial administration passed into federal jurisdiction. Even from the mid-1880s the national administration had started its drive to eliminate independent provincial policies. Undoubtedly this all followed as a consequence of the federalisation[2] of the city of Buenos Aires. For some time the provincial governments continued to make their own decisions. But the excessive debt which forced the sale of the lines in the provinces of Buenos Aires, Santa Fe and Entre Rios signalled the end of provincial aspirations to maintain railway policies of their own. A while later, one by one, those privately owned railways which remained linked to the provinces also passed into the national sphere. By 1900 the only remaining provincial lines were the ERR and Córdoba North Western railways. A few years later they would also come under national control. In all these cases, the most effective argument was that according to the 1891 law, the lines which crossed

[2] The federal government increased its dominance in 1880 when it declared the City of Buenos Aires to be the Federal Capital of the country.

provincial borders, or could be said to be transporting things or people which would cross those borders, should be under federal jurisdiction. This concentration of all the railway companies under the same authority did not immediately mean that it resolved to exert its control in a clear and direct manner. For some time, the State remained in two minds between the threat of competition and of direct interference.

Crisis, Recovery and Rescinding of the Guarantees

The railway policies of Juárez Celman which we have just described can be viewed as a mixture of irresponsible and overly optimistic behaviour, predominant in economic activities towards the end of the eighties, as much among government figures as in the private sector, both domestic and foreign. However, where this kind of behaviour probably established itself most perniciously was in the domain of monetary and credit policies. The result of this was the crisis, a deep and general crisis which began to unravel towards the end of 1889, became uncontainable in 1890, and led to economic and political effects which lasted until the end of the century. In 1885 there had been a warning when the investment banks threatened to no longer issue loans to Argentina. Suspension of the conversion of paper money into gold, which the government of Roca felt obliged to decree, further agravated the situation. But once the fright was over, the Argentine government did not change course. All public works should have been suspended for a period, new credits should not have been used even when available, everything should have been tightly sealed and all financial issues frozen. But the opposite occurred. No one was capable of resisting the limitless prosperity which appeared to smile on the country.

It can be said that the railway policies of the national government and some provincial governments contributed to the origins of the crisis. The loans taken out for the construction of the State lines, the regime of guarantees which imposed a heavy annual charge on the budget, the existence of foreign-owned companies providing public services which led to currency being sent abroad to pay for materials, fuel and shipping remittances, all of these may have contributed to the cessation of payments by the nation and the provinces. But the real engine behind the crisis was not the balance of payments deficit nor the reluctance of the investment banks to concede new loans, but rather the enormous monetary expansion which two government measures caused from 1887: the guaranteed banking law, and the increase in the capital held by the National Bank, part of which was funded by the sale of the Andean Railway. Railway policies and developments were victims of the crisis rather than its cause. The actions of the State should have been modified on the fly as the operation of the companies crashed head on into depression once the consequences of this and the cessation of payments became evident.

The fall of economic activity and loss of confidence affected all the railway companies, large or small, long established or recent. The bonds and shares of the companies which operated in Argentina began to fall in value, and some fell out of the market over time. The devaluation of paper money, which became particularly serious in 1891, and maintained the price of gold at over 400 until 1894, led to a significant loss of real income for the railways, which collected freight and passenger charges in pesos, whereas the larger part of their outgoings, such as loan interest and payment for materials and fuel, remained constant as they were made in pounds sterling. Thus the crisis produced an abrupt fall in profits and therefore in the dividends received by investors, which soon led to a crash in prices on the stock exchange. The ordinary shares of the Southern Railway, which in 1888 were priced at over 200, fell to 160 in 1890, to about 125 in 1891 and 1892, and about 106 in 1894, but then started a slow recovery. Equivalent Central Argentine shares, which had also stood above 200 in 1888, fell much further to reach 63 in 1893 and recuperate by only a few points in the following years. The aggressive and proud Buenos Aires & Rosario, whose shares almost reached 170 in 1888, saw them fall to 60 in 1893 and fail to rise thereafter. The high dividends of the 1880s were never again repeated, for many years remained in low figures and none were paid by some companies.

The BAGSR and the CAR, which had paid 10% or more in 1887, 1888 and 1889, fell to 5% in the former case and zero, 2 or 3% in the latter case. The BARR fell from 9% to 3%, 2% or zero.

But where the crisis had even graver effects was in those companies in receipt of guarantee payments from the State, mainly the new companies established during the euphoric years of the 1880s. President Pellegrini continued to enforce the decree which designated auditors in each of these companies. In October of 1891 a new law abolished the mechanism for automatic payment of the entire guarantee, and reversed it by demanding that nett incomes should be paid into the state coffers before the guaranteed amounts could be paid out. Even though this rule did not come into effect, since the whole system fell into a moratorium, the same law also allowed the Executive to intervene in the setting of all railway fares and charges, thus creating an important precedent with regard to control of the railways, even though this also had no concrete effect on their actual conduct for some time. Exemption from customs duties and automatic rights to freely import railway materials were also abolished, even though specified in the concessions. Also, as part of the move to reduce tax exemptions, it was determined that the railways should have to pay stamp duties. Regarding payment of the guarantees themselves, the national government complied until December 1890. Thereafter it included these commitments within the clauses of an accord set up in London with a committee of bankers, which provided that for the next three years the payment of guarantees would be replaced by the issuing of bonds in lieu. The accord was only partially complied with as far as the railways were concerned. The situation became even worse when Luis Sáenz Peña assumed the presidency. It was decided not to pay guarantees in the cases of lines only partially in service, and the issuing of bonds was suspended. A new agreement with the financial creditors replaced them with an annual payment by the national government which then would be distributed pro rata between the holders of loan titles according to the interest owed. Although the guaranteed railways were left out of the mechanism, owing to the indifference of financial agents, the government announced that it would also make certain payments to them, within what was possible, in cash. However, few railways received anything before August 1893. From then onwards an annual sum was fixed upon, which as in the case of the banks would be distributed pro rata to all those railways having a guarantee. The sum finally agreed was only about 30% of the annual amount owed, but was paid on time and in full.

The railway companies with guarantees all exhibited approximately the same investment plan. As well as obtaining capital by launching shares, they had issued debentures, which were easier to place than shares, given that the potential profitability was unknown. In most cases, the sums that companies hoped for from debenture or bond issues was higher than that from share issues, and in the case of the French companies formed almost nine tenths of their capital. The debentures obliged the payment of annual interest at a pre-established rate on agreed dates, as well as a percentage for amortization of the capital. This deal had been set up on the presumption that these payments could be made, in the absence of actual profit income, on the basis of the state guarantee. Except for the EAR, as the crisis flared up all the national guaranteed railways had been recently created, and some of them were in the process of obtaining their initial capital. As a consequence, none of them generated any profits, either because they were new enterprises which needed more time to grow, or because their lines had been constructed in areas which were incapable of generating traffic. The failure of the State to carry out its financial obligations from January 1891 was followed by the companies defaulting on their debenture holders, and all faced the risk of liquidation. One after another they fell under financial scrutiny and more or less easily made arrangements with their creditors. The company directors requested that the topic of the unpaid guarantees be included in the discussions about the refinancing of the loans which the Argentine representative was negotiating in London but, as we said above, it was excluded. Towards the end of 1894 the so-called Committee for Guaranteed Railways was formed, which included all the directors of these companies based in Great Britain, but the Argentine government did not acknowledge the Committee, and refused to negotiate with the group. It followed that each company had separately to resolve its situation. At that time there were ten railway concessions in operation with national government guarantees, as well as two provincial railway concessions. Two of them, the BAPR and the EAR, had begun operation before the presidency of Juárez Celman; two emerged from the sale of state railways, the AGWR and the CCR (northern section); the remaining six had begun operation in the years before the crisis. These were the Transandine Railway (TR), the Villa María and Rufino Railway (VMRR), the Bahía Blanca and North Western Railway (BBNWR), the Argentine North Eastern Railway (ANER), the San Cristóbal and Tucumán Railway (SCTR), and the Argentine North Western Railway (ANWR) from Villa Mercedes (San Luis province) to La Rioja. Of all these, seven needed to solicit a legal agreement with their creditors. Only the BBNWR, which had not issued debentures; the EAR, where debentures amounted to half its stock; and the ANWR, which at the start of the crisis had not issued any stock to the public, were free of the need to make an agreement. The creditor agreements always entailed the emission of new bonds to compensate for the delays. Certain projects turned out to be non-viable, such as those of the TR, the SCTR and the ANWR. In some cases, the crisis had prevented completion of the whole project, which resulted in lines which were cut short and could not obtain capital to finish as planned: the BBNWR, the ANER and the ANWR. Two companies, the BAPR and the AGWR, stood out from the group as having been able to move forward and convert themselves into profitable concerns as the effects of the crisis began to diminish. Another two, the VMRR and the BBNWR, were administered by the BAPR.

Once the effects of the crisis weakened and the Treasury began to balance its accounts, facilitated by an increase in exports which created a profitable commercial surplus and limited public spending, the administration of José Evaristo Uriburu, successor of president Sáenz Peña, tried to find solutions to the problems created by the state's unfulfilled payments, whether national or provincial. One of most important matters that needed to be faced up to arose from the debts owed in railway guarantees. The previous president had set up a committee to study the matter and advise the government. But it delayed in its task, and by January 1895 it had barely assessed a third of the cases in conflict. Uriburu, without detriment to making use of the results of that task where possible, set aside the committee and began direct negotiations with each company with the aim of arriving at an agreement to establish an amount to pay by means of new bonds in exchange for the accumulated debt, and rescinding guarantee payments in the future. Initiated in March 1895, negotiations were concluded with seven companies towards the end of that year. The remaining three were settled soon afterwards. Based on this, the Executive presented a bill which approved the agreements reached and authorised an issue of bonds amounting to fifty million gold pesos (approximately ten million pounds) to fulfill them and to cover what was expected to be agreed in pending cases. The difficult negotiations had to resolve a distinct set of questions: (a) to agree an amount for delayed payments; (b) to agree another amount in compensation for the removal of future guarantee payments; (c) to accept or reject company claims which alleged they had been damaged by the State's default, in particular because they had not been able to issue their shares onto the market, or had to place them at low prices, difficulties which arose when the State ceased making payments; (d) to maintain or leave inactive the obligation to return guarantees received previously and arising from the rescinding agreement; (e) to maintain or leave inactive the powers of control, mainly of fares, which featured in the guarantee clauses. Analysis of each one of the agreements enables the drawing of some overall conclusions regarding government actions to do with this theme, without denying that each case had its own characteristics. The State always paid out in bonds the value of which amounted to less than the sum of (a) and (b) above. The claims described in (c) were sometimes compensated for when the reimbursements cited in (d) was set aside, especially as by 1896 there was a shared belief that the guaranteed railways would never achieve profits higher than those guaranteed. While taking that into account, it did not free those companies which received significant sums via their agreements from the obligation of reimbursement. As far as the last question was concerned, the Congress set up a clause which prevented companies from setting new tariffs without the approval of the Executive. Following the exchange of guarantee payments for public bonds, the government reduced its forseeable annual expenditure by a half, though of course the term of its commitments was extended.

The rescinding of the guarantees put an end to disputes arising from them and eliminated this mechanism for incentivising national railway policies. It implied, all things considered, a conversion from what had been thought to be a credit advance into a significantly large subsidy. The real value of this subsidy, however, would not appear so considerable if account is taken of the fact that they were paid at par in public bonds which for many years had a sale value of 60 to 70% of their face value. In two cases, the rescinding agreements not only implied ending the guarantees but also the delivery of the titles as the purchase price from the State for the lines constructed. This was so for the two national concessions constructed by French investments: the SCTR and the ANWR. Among all the construction projects which had been started during the "concession fever" epoch, they were probably those which showed the least likelihood of becoming profitable; the first by being a new metre gauge trunk line installed on a route almost parallel to an existing broad gauge line owned by a first class railway, the BARR; and the second because it consisted of a broad-gauge trunk route extending a few kilometres between Villa Mercedas (San Luis) and La Toma (Córdoba), projected to continue to La Rioja passing through a sparsely populated and infertile region.

Railway Policies in the Last Years of the Nineteenth Century

After the 1887-1896 period, as a consequence of the actions of successive governments and of the financial crisis, railway policies in Argentina acquired new characteristics. These characteristics, with modification only as to details, would continue for a further fifty years as the railway policy of Argentina.

The railways, unlike what had happened previously, remained tied to national jurisdiction. They were owned almost entirely by private companies with the great majority funded by capital raised in Great Britain, and each one operated, or aspired to, in an exclusive zone. The State reduced its empresarial function, though it did not abandon it completely, as appeared to happen during the presidency of Juárez Celman. The State lines ran through areas which were marginal or difficult to develop, away from the humid pampa which provided the major part of railway traffic. The lines which remained in government ownership owing to Juárez Celman's erroneous privatization policies continued to grow, due to the construction of previously planned branches and extensions or to link unfinished sections, but mainly because the State had acquired the two ill-conceived companies mentioned above as a result of the process of rescinding guarantees. Following the crisis, the public sector appeared to be an unwilling impresario of railways, until finally it adopted the subsidiary role of replacing public companies in the places which they did not reach.

The State modified its function as promoter of railway expansion, though precise guidelines were not stated. It continued to ignore its task of network planner, letting the system grow more from private than public initiatives. The incentive of railway guarantees had disappeared, and help from public funds was only available for private companies in a small number of cases where the State saw a subsidy for the lines as being essential, all of them for lines running towards frontier zones. Despite this, it retained the tax exemptions, although within certain limits and having introduced the idea, not specified for many years, that established companies might become subject to certain aspects of taxation.

It began to emerge that it was necessary to provide for the control of railway activity because of its public service nature, independently of any existing guarantees or other pecunary obligations on the State. In spite of this change and rooted in the absence of planning, the State continued for some time to defend the idea that promoting competition could be used as a tool to mold the behaviour of the private companies. This indecision began to collide more and more with the positions adopted by the established private companies, which had started to defend, one by one, a strategy of ensuring zones of operation, of combining with rivals, of uniting by means of takeovers or mergers and of eliminating the risks of clashes. After the turn of the century the British-owned companies, following the example of the Southern and Western railways, undertook a reorganisation to reform their lines into groups of companies within defined zones at the end of the process.

The policy resulting from the change of direction undertaken by Juárez Celman and the actions which followed in order to resolve the consequences of the crisis, set out in broad terms in 1896, required certain more specific approaches which would take ten years to be adopted. The matters pending were, basically, to establish how the State would exercise the control function, and how far should the public interest go towards reducing taxes in the railway sector.

The crisis of 1890 slowed down the rate of growth in the Argentine railway network, though not immediately. During 1891, based on the spurt of concessions given in previous years, for which finance was already assured, significant extensions were still being brought into operation. But from then on, the companies were primarily struggling to survive, in the case of the new lines, and to restore profitability, in the case of the established lines. Regarding the latter, it should be taken into account that profits of about 10% in 1888 had fallen to only 2 or 3% or, exceptionally, 4%. By 1896, the effects of the crisis ameliorated and the problem of the liquidation and termination of the guarantees left behind, railway activities could return to concentrating on growing the system. Consequently, the government began again to pay attention to the requests of the numerous new concessions. During the ten years from 1897 until 1906 this task was done, curiously, with neither the Congress nor the Executive having shown any significant assimilation of previous bad experiences, and without facing up to pending matters arising from the fiscal restucturing and liquidation of the crisis put into practice from 1891 to 1896. Among the consistent features of the new concessions awarded during these ten years we can note that they were not aligned with the development of any general plan for railway construction, that the intention was to extend networks of different gauges, that fantastical submissions were approved with no previous investigation as to the business abilities of the petitioners, that new concessionaires were favoured over established companies, and that the prevailing notion for controlling their activities, as to quality and charges for services, was to be by means of introducing competition.

The previously mentioned matters pending were not resolved, though neither were they ignored. During debates in Congress about new bills for granting concessions, in general it was held that the government should increase its powers to intervene in the setting of fares and charges. The currency revaluation had been damaging for the producers and a benefit for the railways, as they had been able to increase their tariffs, following various discussions once the price of gold had more than doubled, and they were now unwilling to reduce them. The Chamber of Representatives approved a declaration which asked for intervention by the Executive on the matter. The minister of public works, Emilio Civit, during discussions of the matter in relation to a submission for a concession, admitted that fare control deserved attention because "a railway always implies monopoly and privilege, not only in terms of the nature of the concession itself, but also by hindering cooperation and leaving the company almost entirely free to set fares as it would itself wish". For Civit, this justified the presentation of a bill about general intervention in the setting of transport fares, but he did not bother to draw one up. Despite this omission, a rule began to appear in the majority of new concessions: fares would be modified if nett profits exceeded 6% of capital, where the profits would be calculated from gross incomes with an allowance for costs set at about 50%.

With regard to the taxes railway companies should pay, the granting of complete exemptions continued to be questioned. It became a rule that the importation of railway sleepers would not be exempted, which obliged the companies to use the hard wood of the country. In some cases customs duty exemptions were limited to materials for railway construction, but not to those required for service operations. Municipal taxes were excluded from the exemptions.

In those years there were discussions as to the way in which the State should carry out its function as a railway business agent, which it still retained. At the end of 1899 the Executive presented a bill to create the Administración General de los Ferrocarriles del Estado (AGFE, State Railways Administration), organised along the lines of the private companies but released from the hobbles of the Accountancy Law. However, this matter was not carried forward. Soon afterwards, a law was passed sanctioning an ambitious plan to extend the State lines, including towards coastal ports.

It was not surprising, given those circumstances, that when two of the most important companies announced they had reached an agreement to merge, that this news would be badly received by Congress and in public opinion. At the end of 1901 the Buenos Aires & Rosario and Central Argentine railways celebrated an agreement crowning their tentative reciprocal relationship, which had begun in 1899, and putting an end to the most significant clash between two companies in the entire history of railways in Argentina. After long discussions they had resolved to form a single company, unite their networks, exchange their shares with compensation for differing quotation values, set up a new Board of Directors, accept the resignation of some members of the former Boards, and agree which senior staff members of the former companies would occupy senior positions in the new one. Until then, any company reorganisations had involved the absorption of small companies by large ones, or agreements between larger companies to colaborate without merging, as in the case of the Southern and Western companies. The announcement made, petitions from interest groups were presented to the government asking that the merger be rejected, and some congressional representatives were upset. However, the Director General of the National Railways Board, Alberto Schneidewind, produced a report which pointed out it was necessary to adopt a different policy to that demanded by the general opinion about the case and which had been followed until then. It affirmed that the agreement being celebrated, in the form of the purchase of the CAR by the BARR, was a merger which united two companies hitherto in conflict which, by means of previous takeovers, had grouped together six lines of different origin, ruled by 24 concession laws which differed in respect of tax exemptions granted and tariff intervention arrangements, among other matters. The government should take advantage of the merger in order to equalise the regime in all parts of the unified system and gain agreement on matters in dispute deferred until then. The merger of two companies was advantageous for the general interest, in spite of the current opinion. It would lead to more economical administration, permit reduced tariffs, do away with conflicts at junctions, improve train connections, facilitate better control of the services provided, etc. The course followed by the authorities should be to recognise the merger, but to insist in exchange on the acceptance of new norm which would address the problems previously identified, establish rules for tariff interventions, regulate specific new tax exemptions, and in a practical case, take the opportunity to resolve the urban problem caused by level crossings on lines entering the capital city. After considering Schneidewind's ideas, the companies made an offer from which the Executive drew up a bill which can be thought of as the embryonic stage of the railway policy which would finally be adopted in 1907. Having accepted the merger, the government moved away from the idea that introducing competition was the best defence of the public interest against that of the companies, and moved towards the public interest justifying the intervention of the State in the setting of tariffs and in the kind of service offered. The bill established that fares would be as set out in an appendix table, which represented reductions on those currently in use; in addition the Executive would be able to revise them every five years, or at any time lower them if gross income exceeded 17% of officially recognised capital. A comprehensive range of tax exemptions was to remain for 25 years, but a special contribution was imposed, 1% of gross income, destined for the National Education Council.

The bill was not debated, and the Congress continued with its undefined and contradictory policy. However, the economic and political reality was changing, and this change had a significant effect on railway legislation. The established companies were operating more and more efficiently, helped by the continuing progress of the Argentine economy. If by 1896 they could be considered to have overcome the effects of the 1890 crisis, and had again moved into profitability, then by 1901 their improved situation had permitted the stronger ones to absorb some of the smaller ones; and by 1906 the plan was to begin thinking of extending the consolidated networks into new areas, a plan coinciding with the expansion of those areas which were under more intensive agricultural production. Competition between companies, which some legislators counted on to regulate railway activities, was not easily realised. The British-owned railways, one by one, were moving away from the aims they had pursued before the crisis, though they carried them over for a few more years. After the merger between the BARR and the CAR there followed the drawing together of the BAPR and the AGWR, which until the beginning of the twentieth century had competed for the traffic to Cuyo. The only remaining railways in conflict were the two standard gauge lines of minor importance in the Mesopotamian region, the ERR and the ANER, which would only begin to come together towards the end of the period. The only achievement of the competition policy, by the early years of the twentieth century, had been to interest French investors in constructing lines in zones until then exclusively served by British companies. Between 1901 and 1904 a number of concessions of this kind were granted: the branch from San Francisco to Villa Maria of the SFPR; the network from Buenos Aires to Rosario of what became part of the Buenos Aires Province General Railway Company (BAPGRC); and the concession given to Diego de Alvear for a line which later formed part of the Rosario to Belgrano Port Railway (RBPR). With the exception of this last line, the new constructions were justified, as well as by providing competition, in that they were metre gauge lines which extended the metre gauge network into areas not otherwise served. The latter justification applied to the granting of an extension to Buenos Aires of the CCR, a new incursion into the railway ambit of the province of Buenos Aires, although now under a policy which was not to last much longer. But the magnitude, in size of network and volume of traffic, which had been achieved by the established British railway companies, now merged or about to become so, made it doubtful that French competition would achieve the results forseen by its supporters, leaving aside the damage that might occur as result of seriously mistaken investments. In the ten most important British companies, some of them controlled by the larger ones, the capital invested in 1896 reached nearly 100 million pounds, with over 14,000km of lines in service. In 1901, the capital had only risen to 108 million pounds, with almost 17,000km of lines open. But by 1906 the capital was 134 million, with more than 20,000km in service.

To the expansion of the economy in general and to the prosperity of the larger railway companies, which had returned to paying 6 or 7 percent dividends, was added a change in the government cabinet following the 1904 presidential election, which was accentuated when the vice-president José Figueroa Alcorta replaced President Manuel Quintana when he died in March 1906. The new head of state formed his cabinet mainly from members of the "Coalition", and the Public Works ministry fell into the hands of Miguel Tedín, of the Republican party led by Emilio Mitre, who for some time had been pushing for the need for a major state involvement in the provision of public services. Mitre's position coincided with a debate which was taking place at that time in several European countries, which favoured putting the public authorities in charge of railway services. Towards the mid-nineteenth century railway construction had been, basically, in the hands of private companies. As time went on, the governments of some countries had taken over their operation, for political or economic reasons, depending on the circumstances. The most quoted example of this was the railways of Prussia around 1880. It was asserted that in the case of state enterprises the absence of investors, who expected dividends, would enable lower fares and better services. It was also argued that railways managed by the state could be used to implement policies protecting certain economic activities. In other cases, public authorities had provided part of the capital required for construction but operation of the line remained in private hands although under strict state control. French railways were often mentioned as examples of this second option. Lastly, some railway systems remained entirely in the hands of private

determine that the 17% limit together with an additional rule that set the maximum operating ratio (relation between operating costs and gross income) at 60%, resulted in the railway companies having a maximum profit of 6.8% before the government could insist on a reduction of their fares. This was reasonable, as was the tax of 3% on nett profits, since both were similar to those existing in other countries. Even though it was true that such a tax did not compensate for the income the State would not receive, as stipulated by the 40-year general tax exemption, this came about because the railways deserved state support. Over and above these themes, it was clear that the main objection to the bill came from a handful of Representatives who defended the idea of beneficial competition, which the bill would destroy. From their inception, the current policies had created a disorganised situation which treated the companies unequally. Congress continued to grant concessions with tax exemptions for more or less extensive periods, while the periods of established companies with similar privileges were close to expiry. Some Representatives defended this inequality as a way of facilitating competition. However, the bill evened out the concessions, which diluted the benefits of unfair priviliges for new concessionaires. It also eliminated the actions of "intermediary agents", who used their influence to obtain special benefits with the only aim of using them to negotiate with the actual investors.

The equilibrium of Law 5315, which denoted Emilio Mitre's bill once it was sanctioned on 30th September, 1907, is its most outstanding characteristic. The State reaffirmed its powers and began to receive a tax income, and the companies acquired a stable set of regulations within which they could plan their activities. The tax exemptions and the new tax formed a sort of counter-balance. But also, if the companies entered into the regime of the Mitre Law they should accept the permanent control of the National Railway Board with respect to their capital and activities, and limit their profits to not exceed 6.8%, as long as their operating ratio did not reduce it below that figure. The new law, which in reality constituted a framework not only for the companies but also for the future work of Congress, entailed a modification and refining of the policies followed until this point. The questioning of foreign investments, which had arisen with the crisis of 1890 and reappeared on the horizon from time to time, ceased. The government, which before had opposed mergers, came to accept and take advantage of them to reaffirm control by the state. The law created a climate within which facilitated a more rapid growth of the network during those years when investment capital was available. It was understood that there was an agreement between the State and the investors. They were able to obtain the return on their capital to which they aspired, but not beyond a level which would unduly raise the cost of services to users. The companies in general felt that under the law they were being treated more fairly than in the recent past. This leads up to the final question with respect to Law 5315 and the change of direction in railway policy. Not all the companies found themselves in the same situation. There were major companies, in general funded by British capital; and minor companies, some recently set up with French capital. The uniformity of the legislation, the new regime of tax exemptions for 40 years and the new fixed-rate tax of 3% on nett profits could be seen as a game winning result for the former group. This might be true, but at the same time it recognised that in the hands of such companies the railway system operated efficiently, that in the public interest it was more advisable to protect them rather than subject them to competition from new, unproven businesses, and that the State should, within this frame, impose itself as the controlling authority over the providers of public services under equal terms. The railway policy as it emerged after the series of events from 1887 to 1896, having elected the private companies as the protagonists of the system's activities, was thus specified by choosing the public authority to control these activities rather than by leaving them to the freedom of the market.

The Railway Companies in 1916

The growth of the economy in Argentina during the first years of the twentieth century can be observed in a number of indicators, all of which coincide. For example, produce from the area sown with the main crops cultivated in the temperate pampa region (wheat, maize, flax, oats, barley), which constituted one of the principal railway cargoes, went from 4,700,000 hectares (ha) in 1900 to nearly 10,000,000ha in 1907 and about 13,000,000ha in 1913. The larger railway companies, having consolidated exclusive operating areas in the most dinamic region of the national economy, and propelled by the new regulatory framework of the Mitre Law, continued to grow but at a more rapid pace. The Southern grew from operating over more than 4,000km of lines in 1907 to nearly 6,000km in 1913. The Western grew even more, proportionally, from 1,600km to almost 3,000km between the same dates. During this period, the Buenos Aires & Rosario, merged with the Central Argentine, grew from 4,000km to just under 5,000km, and the Pacific from about the same extension to 5,500km. The networks of the new French companies which were conceeded at the start of the century also entered service, involving 2,066km more of track by 1913 (RBPR 798km, BAPGRC 1,268km). As a consequence, the railway network in Argentina experienced remarkable growth during the period, which can be divided into four stages: very rapid growth from 1887 to 1891; slow growth from 1892 to 1896 due only to projects conceived before the financial crisis; slow growth based on new concessions from 1897 to 1906; and a return to rapid growth from 1907 to 1913. In last three years before 1916, in the face of an international recession, the pace of growth fell abruptly. All this is clearly set out in Table 3.

The expansion of the railway network entailed large amounts of capital entering the country, raised by each of the companies in the European market, the major part in London and a smaller amount in Paris. For example, the BAWR issued shares for £18 million between 1902 and 1913; The BAGSR issued a similar amount but between 1907 and 1913; the merged BARR and CAR increased its capital by £15 million during these years, as did the BAPR group. The new investments accentuated the characteristics which were already present in the British companies from the beginning. Their capital was formed from thousands of small and medium sized contributions from investors attracted by the promise of better returns than those available from current local investment possibilities. Although there were big investors, such as commercial banks, investment banks, pension funds, stock exchange agents and various commercial companies, the total they accumulated amounted to not more than 10 or 15% of the capital held by each company. Each continued to manage its affairs independently, guided by a self-renewing board of directors which was not subordinate to the interests of any other company. On the other hand, the railways funded by French capital, from the first one, the SFPR, to the more recent BAPGRC and RBPR, concentrated on investments by banks and industrial companies, apart from relatively very small share issues.

The growth of the network led to an increase in rolling stock. The Western, Southern and Pacific railways between them rose from having 1.300 locomotives, 1.194 coaches and 26.043 goods wagons in 1906 to having 1.703, 1.895 and 36.087 respectively in 1914.

Celebration of the centenary of the May Revolution[3] found the railway companies in a prosperous situation, which was marked by a grand international exhibition in Buenos Aires from May to December, 1910. The railway system as a whole had acquired an outstanding reputation, distinguished as one of the largest in the world. It was an important sector of the Argentine economy, and even though it could be said that it had grown in step with it, it was also true that the economy itself had expanded and would continue to do so thanks to the conditions which the railway system had created. Advances in farming production, access to international markets at competitive prices and the rise in foreign commercial activities could only have occurred as they did when the transport system was able to provide efficient carriage of goods. But, in addition, it had helped to develop regional economies, as in the production of sugar in Tucuman or of wine in Cuyo; and had contributed to the formation of a significant national market demonstrating widespread growth, which was already the largest in Latin America.

[3] On 25th May 1810 an open meeting in Buenos Aires voted to secede from the Spanish Empire. Actual independence was not achieved until 1816.

Amid the expressions of national pride which were common during celebrations of the May Revolution, the railways occupied a prominent position. Only ten nations were ahead of the country in having more extensive railway networks, but among them were the principal European Powers, and states with enormous territories like Russia, the United States, Canada, Australia and India. On the other hand, the Argentine network was seen to be growing rapidly and a widely shared opinion held that it would continue to grow for many years, until it reached 200,000km. Railway policy had established an equilibrium which generated confidence in the principal stakeholders. Ninety percent of the system was in the hands of private companies. The larger ones, having consolidated their zones, had a history of achieving acceptable average profits, and even though the minor companies still had not achieved equally flattering results, it was felt that rising traffic and optimism arising from the growth of the economy would take them to parity with the major lines. The State had taken on a more active controlling role, and it was clear that company profits were at a reasonable level.

Failures were also acknowledged, the main one being the absence of any plan or method behind the design of the network. As a qualified observer stated in that year of 1910, "It is this development with no method, without a pattern, without foresight, which has caused the gravest mistakes: the wide diversity of gauges [...], the construction of completely unproductive lines [...], the over-dense coverage in productive zones, and the neglect of other areas". The crisis which started in Europe with the Balkan situation in 1912, and was later extended by the outbreak of the Great War, meant that many of the optimistic forecasts of the Centenary would fall into oblivion. The depression reached Argentina in 1913. To dwindling economic activity was added the scarcity of materials necessary for railway development (coal, steel, etc). A drought aggravated the situation and the disruption of international trade led to an increase in the cost of living.

To the problems of falling company profits there followed the complaints of those who worked in them, who constituted one of the more qualified and disciplined groups of workers within the new working class which capitalism had created in Argentina.

Locomotive drivers and firemen had already formed their professional association in 1887, La Fraternidad (the Brotherhood), which in 1912 was the protagonist of a major strike which paralised part of the service for three months. The national government reacted by making its first attempt to act as mediator. The complaints, under the still favourable circumstances, concerned salary increases, limits on hours of work and broader provision of social welfare. From the point of view of the union the strike was not successful but it did lead to the preparing of a bill to create a pension fund for railway workers. The trade unions were not weakened, and in the same year of 1912, La Fraternidad joined the Federación Obrera Ferrocarrilera (FOF), Railway Workers Federation), which embraced the rest of the railway company workforce. The railway company workforce had constantly grown as the number of lines increased, and already exceeded 120 thousand people over all companies. Members of La Fraternidad amounted to ten thousand, which was about half of the total number of drivers and firemen. The economic crisis led to a general increase in the level of unemployment, which remained high from 1914 to 1916 and hindered the unions from going on strike again. However, in 1916 both associations signed a "solidarity pact" and when activity began to recover the following year they intensified their complaints.

In 1916 railway operations were in the hands of a dozen companies or groups of companies, which could be classified, based on the source of their capital, into British companies, French companies and State companies. Among the first were the most important broad-gauge companies, the BAWR, the BAGSR, the CAR and the BAPR. Also British, though less important and of dubious profitability, were the railways of the Mesopotamian region, the ERR, the ANER and their associated line the BACR, all standard-gauge, and lastly the narrow-gauge CCR. The French railways were the narrow-gauge SFPR and BAPGRC, and the broad-gauge RBPR. The General Administration of State Railways ran various lines of different gauges, and the province of Buenos Aires became again involved in railway activity with the narrow-gauge Provincial Railway, constructed using public funds.

These companies and groups were the result of a dynamic process which took place over the 30 years of this chapter's period, during which new stakeholders emerged or disappeared by being taken over or under pressure, or reorganised.

The Western and the Southern acted as a group even though they had not formalised their relationship. Between 1912 and 1914 they came close to merging, but approval of their agreement was hit by certain difficulties and opposition from the government of the Province of Buenos Aires, which continued to profess a railway policy contrary to that of the national government. On the other hand, their networks were adjacent but not interconnected, so the lack of a merger did not raise major problems. In reality they had acted in common since the Western had become a private company in 1890. The Southern had acquired the BAEPR in 1898, eliminating as a result the only intruder in its zone. Together the Southern and Western took charge of the small Buenos Aires Midland Railway (BAMR) metre-gauge line, a belated concession which the Province of Buenos Aires had inserted into their exclusive domain. In the final years of the nineteenth century the Southern had undertaken an out-of-the-ordinary piece of work. Based on an agreement with the national government, it constructed a main-line from Bahía Blanca through the National Territories of Rio Negro and Neuquen towards the border with Chile. By 1916 the BAGSR had grown to more than six thousand kilometres of lines and its nett profit was £2,834,164 in that year. It had paid 7% dividends continuously since 1899, although the crisis, due to the war, of the previous three years had reduced them to 4.5%. The Western had gradually extended its network from the middle of the 1890s, growing to three thousand kilometres in 1916. In the west it reached the Territory of La Pampa and the south of the Province of Mendoza. Its nett profit in that year was £1,419,685 and it paid dividends of similar value to those of the Southern.

The Central Argentine followed in importance. As we have pointed out previously, the BARR and the CAR, after having competed with each other to control the provincial areas of northern Buenos Aires, southern and central Santa Fe and the route to Tucumán, had merged in 1902. Beforehand they had acquired other lesser companies which operated in the region: the BANR, the WSFR and the SFCGSR. Until 1908 the merged company was known as the BARR, but from then on it became the CAR. In 1916 the network amounted to approximately 5,300km and its nett profit was £2,034,993. It serviced the provincies already mentioned and that of Córdoba, becoming established on its eastern side. After paying average or low dividends until the merger, from 1904 the new company paid 6% on its ordinary shares each year up to the advent of the war, when it was reduced to 4%.

The Pacific had set up a significant network involving the AGWR, TR, VMRR and BBNWR companies. It had established relations with the last two ever since they had been created, and its directors had been involved from the start of both projects. On the other hand, relations with the AGWR remained conflicted until the start of the twentieth century, with them competing ferociously until 1904. The AGWR had made an exploitation agreement with the TR. In 1907 the BAPR was able, by means of a working agreement with both, to include them in its group. In 1916 this network extended over 5,700km, and its nett profit reached £1,808,033. It served the northeast of Buenos Aires province, the south of Córdoba province, and the provinces of San Luis, Mendoza and San Juan. The BBNWR line reached the port of Bahía Blanca passing through the territory of La Pampa and the south of Buenos Aires province. The dividends paid by the BAPR varied somewhat. Starting low, they rose to 7% between 1905 and 1908, only to fall to 2-3% in subsequent years. The war crisis at the end of the period reduced the remunerations of its shares to zero. The exploitation agreements entered into in order to form the group network had become onerous and had a bad effect on the profits of the mother company.

The railways in the Mesopotamia had competed with each other. In the early years of the twentieth century the two largest, the ERR and the ANER, struggled for the right to control the EAR. In the end this line merged with the ANER in 1907. The ERR company then directed its efforts towards finding a way to reach Buenos Aires, which it achieved by setting up an agreement with the small Buenos Aires Central Railway (BACR). In 1912 all these lines came under the control of Percival Farquhar's syndicate group, but when the war demonstrated the financial failings of the group, the ERR and the ANER remained united, under the control of the directors of the ERR. Thus this standard-gauge network of nearly 1,800km served the two provinces of Entre Rios and Corrientes and the northern Territory of Misiones, and with government support was able to establish a border connection to the standard-gauge railways of Paraguay. Its profitability had improved, however the ordinary shares of both companies hardly ever issued dividends.

The BACR was a company formed in the 1880s with local capital. It had started as a form of standard-gauge light railway and was called the "rural tramway". Its route ran northwest from Buenos Aires with a branch to Zarate, a port on the River Parana. In 1906 it celebrated an agreement with the EER company to link their lines by means of a connecting ferry service across the Parana from Zarate to the port of Ibicuy in the province of Entre Rios. This required a reconstruction to heavier rail of the BACR line, for which it obtained funds in London by issuing debentures, the total amount being many times greater than its share capital. The BACR lines were 319km in extent.

Also funded by British capital was the metre-gauge CCR group. It consisted of the namesake company with its line from Tucumán to Córdoba and from there on to San Fransisco on the border with Santa Fe province; the CRR from San Francisco to Rosario; the Steam Tramway in the city of Rafaela; and a different ANWR (both names being the same in Spanish), this line running from Lamadrid to Tucumán. In 1905 the group was conceded an extension linking Rosario with Buenos Aires. These lines also fell under the temporary control of the Farquhar syndicate, during which a restructuring operation simplified its capital and reorganized its administration. The CCR group achieved exceptional profits between 1905 and 1909, based on financial maneuvres within the actual group, which permitted it to pay dividends outside the normal range, but the group as a whole was a weak and unprofitable enterprise. Its network of almost 1,900km served provinces from Buenos Aires to Tucumán via Santa Fe and Córdoba, with branches in Catamarca and Santiago del Estero.

There were three French companies. The metre-gauge SFPR, arising from the sale of provincial state railways at the end of the 1880s, had extended its line with a branch in the province of Córdoba in 1904. It worked lines over more than 1,800km. It had a capital of 45 million pesos, mostly consisting of debentures. The metre-gauge BAPGRC had inaugurated its 1,268km network, from Buenos Aires to Rosario and branches in the province of Buenos Aires, between 1908 and 1912. Its capital was also 45 million, of which 80% was in debentures. The last French conpany to emerge was the broad-gauge RBPR, which linked Rosario and Puerto Belgrano in an arc which crossed the British-owned lines running from the interior to other ports. Its length was almost 800km and its capital reached 35 million gold pesos, 75% in debentures.

The national State, after parting with most of its lines before 1890, had started to construct lines in isolated areas. In general, these railways were intended to foment activities in their areas, rather than to compete with the private companies. They did not make incursions into areas where private capital was disposed to invest, and in 1909 they were grouped into a single State company. In 1916 it covered the following lines, all metre-gauge except the last one: the Northern Central Railway (NCR) from the Bolivian frontier to Santa Fe, of 1,986km; the Argentine Northern Railway (ANR) in the provinces of Catamarca, La Rioja and northern Córdoba, of 1,438km; the Embarcación to Formosa Railway (EFR), of 298km; and the 913km of the broad-gauge Patagonian Railways.

The overall figures, extracted from the statistics compiled by the National Railway Board, summarize the expansion of the railway system during this period. From 6,689km in operation in 1887 it grew to 14,755 in 1897, to 22,126 in 1907, and reached 33,821km in 1916. The numbers of passengers carried at the same year set (1887, 1897, 1907 and 1916) were 8,199,051; 16,410,945; 41,784,834 and 64,829,930. The corresponding numbers of tons of cargo transported were 3,844,045; 11,100,000; 27,929,011 and 36,630,578. The capital invested grew from 11,577,625 pesos in 1887 to 508,216,315 pesos in 1897, to 775,964,416 pesos in 1907 and 1,342,204,563 pesos in 1916. For the same years, total gross incomes went from 19,516,585 pesos to 28,293,081 pesos to 87,970,346 pesos and 125,568,837 pesos. All the pesos in this paragraph refer to gold pesos, where at that time 5 gold pesos were equivalent to 1 pound sterling.

The whole network, which reached 33,800km in 1916, was divided as follows: 86% in private companies, and the rest in State lines, 61.5% was broad-gauge, 30.5% narrow-gauge (mainly metre-gauge) and the remaining 8% standard-gauge.

Shunting yard at Plaza Constitución Station (BAGSR) near the end of the 19th Century. *(Photo: Museo Nacional Ferroviario)*

Second Station building at Plaza Constitución after being extended in 1907. *(Photo: Museo Nacional Ferroviario)*

Southern Railway iron wharf at Ingeniero White. Demonstrates the feverish port activities of an export economy, circa 1910. *(Photo: Museo Nacional Ferroviario)*

First Class passenger coach constructed by the Southern Railway workshops in 1911.

MARIO JUSTO LÓPEZ

3 | From Equilibrium to Crisis in the Private Railway Companies 1917 – 1946

Expectations Raised by the Election Success of the UCR in 1916

On 12th October 1916 Hipólito Yrigoyen assumed the presidency of the Republic. This event was a novelty in the political system of Argentina. For the first time, after almost 50 years, an opposition party, the Unión Cívica Radical (UCR) had triumphed, and a president had been elected who was not favoured by the outgoing head of state. This was the result of the profound political reforms carried out by Roque Sáenz Peña and continued by Victorino de la Plaza when, in 1914, he took over the presidency after the death of the former incumbent. The UCR, established in the national political scene since 1903 under the leadership of Yrigoyen, had abandoned its previous abstentionist and revolutionary strategy following the inception of the new national electoral process in 1912. After partial successes in some districts, it managed to impose itself in the hard-fought elections of 1916. Now in power, the party and its new president had not presented to the people a programme for their government and had repeatedly declined to specify what public policies they would implement should they be elected to govern. However, its harsh criticisms of the previous regime, based mainly on their impediments to the holding of free elections, created a climate of uncertainty. It could well be supposed that these criticisms, couched in moralising tones, would extend into the ambit of economic policy and, specifically, to the consideration afforded to foreign capital, which had taken over of the provision of major public services like the railways.

To the uncertainty created by the new political climate in the sphere of the railway companies was added the economic crisis, which had started in 1912 and had been prolonged by the world war. Their activities were affected by shortages and price rises for fuel and spare parts, which originated mostly in Great Britain. This increased costs, and because of falling traffic and exchange rate difficulties, led to reduced company incomes. In addition, though the deterioration in the economic situation and an increase in unemployment led, for a while, to a decrease of pressure from the labour sector, resumption of the struggle towards obtaining better working conditions was only a question of time.

The railways, with their unceasing growth and tens of thousands of administrative and work force employees, had become one of the largest labour organisations in the country. The trade unions which had emerged were slowly growing in power and worker representation. The great railway strike of 1912 was not successful, but served as a training experience for the labour leaders and expanded their capacity to mobilise the workers. One of their claims, the creation of a pension fund for railway employees, was sanctioned by a law in 1915, which in order to set up the fund led to new charges on the companies. Another development, which we had mentioned in the previous Chapter, was that the two railway unions, La Fraternidad and the Federación Obrera Ferrocarrilera (FOF), had signed a pact in 1916 to unite their forces against the company managements. The fall in profitability due to the crisis, and the latent labour demands, served to magnify the uncertainty of the direction which the government might take.

Argentina had taken a step forward in defining its railway policy following the sanction of the Mitre Law in 1907. This, as discussed in the previous chapter, meant that it had finally opted for a railway system based on the operation of foreign private companies under the direct control of the national government. However, how far this control was to extend, arising from the interpretation and application of the norms of the Mitre Law and of the General Railway Law, remained to be specified. In 1911 Pablo Nogués had been appointed Director of the National Railway Board (NRB), and he had started to determine the grounds for establishing a companies, as in Great Britain or the United States. In Argentina, the medium which reported on new public works policies was the newspaper founded by Bartolomé Mitre, *La Nación*, which from mid-1906 published a series of editorials on this theme. These favoured public ownership of municipal services requiring small capital investment (such as street lighting). In the railway case, on the other hand, the editorial proposals moved towards strengthening existing state companies, by correcting errors they had made, by filling their posts with more competent staff, and by extending their lines into non-marginal areas with intent to operate there at a profit. Also proposed was a reaffirmation of the state's power to control private activities in order to assure good services and avoid excessive profits.These proposals should take into account the realities of the railways in Argentina, which manifested booming private companies funded by foreign capital which were keen to continue investing in the growth of their networks. It should also be taken into account that growth of the system continued to be a purpose of the government and society's desire.

President Figueroa Alcorta announced in May 1907 that he would present a bill proposing powers to intervene in the setting of railway tariffs, within defined limits, and to equalise, for existing railways and those which might be established in the future, their treatment with regard to tax exemptions. It fell to Congressional Representative Emilio Mitre to prepare a definitive document which was discussed in committee in August of the same year. Having received a favourable report from the committee, Mitre was concerned to emphasise that the initiative was in two parts: that relating to future concessions, and that which referred to existing concessions. The ultimate aim was to unify the regulations for them all. He also indicated that a fundamental reform of railway policy was being introduced, which was the creation of a tax by means of which, for the first time, companies would help defray public expenditure. Another important part of the rules was that it established government powers to intervene in the tariffs on the basis of a limit on gross company income of up to 17% of its capital as recognised by the State itself. Some Representatives in Congress objected to the limit and the tax valuation. But Mitre was able to wider range of controls. In the first place, with regard to recognition of a company's capital, the Director determined that the State had the right to set aside part of the capital issued, in proportion to the amount not destined towards actual investment. In second place, any change of fares and charges proposed by a company required the prior approval of the NRB before it could come into force. Both the former and the latter provisions would give the Board wide powers to inspect company accounts. In third place, the railway service was a public service and as such the companies were obliged to maintain it in operation, to operate it within certain parameters, to execute all operations under the supervision of the NRB, and to deal equally with all clients. If they did not comply with these obligations, companies would be liable to severe fines. This last point was especially relevant in the case of a trade union dispute, since a suspension of service because of a strike would not only imply a loss of income but also a failure to comply with the conditions of service. Until 1916 the ideas drawn up by Nogués had not been seriously tested, and until 1912 rising company income had prevented any complaints from the companies. After that, the sudden general crisis had meant that the great railway strike had not produced any major outcomes. In 1915 the Pensions Law had been sanctioned but not yet applied. The companies asked, at that time, for approval of a rise in fares and charges to compensate for major cost increases. Finally, no capital had been recognised since 1912 and the proposals by Nogués had neither been adopted nor rejected by the Executive, it being preoccupied with other matters. Consequently, it remained as a task for the new government to firm up the control policy which had been outlined.

The Railways During the Radical Presidences

In general terms it can be said that the Radical Party governments carried on the previous railway policy and continued specifying in more detail the state controls arising from the ideas of Nogués. He, for his part, continued as Director of the NRB for two more years. However, the way in which the Executive took forward the negotiations, discussions and demands fluctuated widely, which the companies interpreted as an alternation of periods of hostility with periods during which their rights were recognised. The changes of attitude can be understood by noting that during the presidency of Yrigoyen there were three successive periods of about two years: from October 1916 to early 1918; from then until 1920; and from that year until the elections in 1922. It became evident that the fluctuations were not capricious but were in response to election pressures. Before the congressional elections in 1918 and the presidential elections in 1922 there was no great predisposition on the part of the government to deal with company complaints, but rather to attend to the demands of railway workers and the interests of cargo shippers. Also to be taken into account is the effect of the increasing agitation caused by labour union groups, which culminated in an indiscriminate and bloody repression in early 1919, known as the Tragic Week. This escalation of violence, together with a fear of loss of confidence in the middle classes of the City of Buenos Aires, led the Executive to adopt a more favourable attitude towards the companies in the years 1919 and 1920.

The year 1917 saw a growing discontent within the personnel of the railway companies. The cost of living had suffered a constant rise during the years of the war. Unrest showed signs of reactivation and the unions, strengthened by their solidarity pact, decided to demand improvements for their members. Initially there were local strikes, originating in the local sections of the FOF, which mainly affected the State railways and the Central Argentine. The Minister of Public Works, Pablo Torello, who replaced the NRB Director in the role of mediator, failed in his attempt, and the complaints became more frequent in the belief that the President would support them. Finally, the two unions in common accord drew up a list of eleven demands, among them the sanction of a new retirement pension law in recognition of the deficiencies in the 1915 Law. They also declared that a general strike would start on 23rd September, which was complied with by a vast majority of the 120 thousand manual and office workers of the railways. The companies pointed that if they agreed to the requests of their workers, especially with regard to the proposed working conditions, they would have to increase their personnel by between 30 and 40%. They asked the government to act as arbitrator and for the time being they waited expectantly, given that there was no cereal crop to transport during this period of the year. If the strike had been delayed for three more months the damage suffered would have been much more serious. The first response of the national government was to do nothing. Some days later the Minister of Public Works tried once again to act as arbitrator, and once again failed. Violence broke out in the Tafi Viejo workshops (Province of Tucuman) of the State Railways and lives were lost. Then Yrigoyen decided to act in person. He decreed some improved conditions for railway personnel and convinced La Fraternidad and the companies to accept them, the latter with a promise that he would permit an increase in fares and charges. The FOF was sidestepped. As the strike persisted, though weakened, it was decided to provide railway services with military protection. The anarchist union, the FOF, felt itself betrayed and broke the solidarity pact, but in the end the strike stopped on 17th October, having lasted 25 days. There were repeated partial stoppages until May 1918 and the FOF continued to threaten another general strike. In all cases, the government showed itself to be against all these threatening measures and in the end requested and obtained from the Justice Ministry the arrest for insurrection of the general secretary of the rebellious union. Railway services returned to normal after that.

On the matter of fares and charges, the railway companies claimed that an increase was absolutely necessary. At first, they continued to sustain that such increases did not need to be previously permitted by the authorities, who only had the right to intervene when profits exceeded the 6.8% limit fixed by the Mitre Law. Pablo Nogués was affirming, on the contrary, that as the railways were a naturally monopolistic service, and because it was the mission of the government to control the reasonableness and justice of the prices for this public service, it had the duty to analize any suggested increase. For example, it might insist on examining the costs of running the service. In fact the companies had seen a fall in their incomes, in comparison to what had been the case until 1912. Costs had risen by 200% since then, whereas income had only increased by 140%, and profits were far below the maximum specified by the 1907 law. The BAPR had yielded 3.85% and the CAR 3.70%. The minor railways yielded far less, though the BAGSR and BAWR did better. However, the fact was that the government did not authorise any increase in fares and charges until the general strike had been resolved by means of concessions to the unions. Soon after this a rise of 22% was authorised, and an additional 10% in May 1918.

This moment can be considered to be the start of a harmonious relationship between the government and the companies, which was to last during the following two years. In these years President Yrigoyen took decisions which were interpreted by the railway companies as friendly gestures. By means of successive decrees starting in July 1919, the amounts of capital held by the companies from 1908 to 1912 were recognised using the dispositions of the Mitre Law. Although the Executive continued with the criterion determined by Nogués, who had resigned the year before because of differences in the way that the President wanted to manage the administration of the State Railways, this action unjammed one of those matters which could have been considered before the discussions about fares and charges. The total of capital effectively invested amounted to £158,370,857, whereas the total listed in the account books of the companies amounted to £181,414,498. The difference, which represented 12.7% of the capital of the companies, was not recognised, although discounting of some of the difference was permitted over a period of ten years. The companies appealed the 1919 decree, which suspended its application, and based on their own calculations continued to pay the 3% contribution. For a long time the Executive did not resolve the dispute, which was only decided, in favour of the State, by President Justo during the 1930s. Meanwhile, in August 1919, the Congress sanctioned retirement pension Law 10.650 for railway personnel. It had been drawn up under the previous administration, of De la Plaza, but was delayed in committee until Yrigoyen applied pressure on the legislators to convert it into law. This was received with approval by the companies. It gave them the obligation to contribute 8% of their salary costs to the pension fund, but they would be covered by an authorised 5% increment in fares and charges, and the regulations anticipated that any shortfall in the pension fund would be covered by the government. At the same time, also under pressure from the President of the Nation, the Congress sanctioned Law 10.657, which clarified the 8th Article of the Mitre Law and determined that tax exemptions applied also to municipal taxes, which had previously been denied. Finally, in early 1920 the BAGSR, the BAWR and the BAPR formed a new company, the Compañía Ferrocarrilera de Petróleo (Railway Oil Company), which was given permission to lease oilfields of the Compañía Petrolera de Comodoro Rivadavia, a permission which at the time would not have been granted to North American or British oil companies. Colleagues close to Yrigoyen, like Minister Torello, had advised the Directors on the Boards of the privately-owned railways that the President was "well disposed towards British capital and especially towards the British railways", as proved by the above measures. In return, the companies ceased to question the authority of the government to control their activities. Notwithstanding this, the companies realised that in their discussions with the government they had a common problem in facing up to the imposition and application of the Mitre Law, and set about creating joint arrangements for coordinating and negotiating their interests. As soon as in 1908, their joint arrangements barely agreed, they formed a lawyer's consultative committee. In 1918 the company General Managers had started to meet regularly. From 1921 the local Board chairmen did the same. This led to the formation of a committee of railway representatives and managers. Later on, in 1926, they would create groups to study the matters which most preoccupied them: labour relations, fares and charges, and a joint approach to certain railway technical problems.

These harmonious relations with the government coincided with a period of economic prosperity. The companies found themselves benefitting from a demand for the transport of stock which had accumulated because of the difficulties of obtaining merchant shipping towards the end of the war. The extended low level of imports had caused the value of the peso to rise against the pound sterling and this had led to extra profits from the exchange rate tax. For one year the dividends paid to holders of ordinary shares in the larger companies returned to the percentage levels paid before the war: 7% from the BAGSR and the BAWR, 6% from the CAR and 5% from the BAPR. Very soon, however, the railway business climate turned sour. Operating ratios continued to be high. The average in 1920 for all the private railways was 78.8% as against 65.9% in 1914. The Argentine commercial surplus was reduced and the peso lost value. The companies registered exchange rate losses. Cereal production fell owing to adverse climate conditions. This produced what came to be called the post-war recession, which diminished nett profits, caused the shares of the major companies to fall, and placed the minor ones in a dire financial situation. The companies, relying on the support of the government, requested a new increase in fares and charges. At this time, however, the reaction of the government was disconcerting. The acting Director of the NRB, Ariodante Giovacchini, seemed to accede to the request, as did Minister Torello. But surprisingly, following a real comedy of errors, the government ended up announcing that it would not authorise any increase and mounted a press campaign against the companies. Presidencial elections were due in early 1922, and government officials did not want to confront the shippers. It was not until August in the same year that a new table of increased charges was approved. The retiring president's last act two days before the expiry of his mandate was to designate a new NRB Director, Herminio Capdevila, who, like his acting predecessor, did not have any aptitude for the post. A little later, however, now under the new administration, this lack of ability would be made up for by the new Inspector General of Railways, Manuel F. Castello.

The new Radical Party President, Marcelo T. de Alvear, attempted to implement a different policy, with the aim of establishing a set of longer lasting regulations not subject to changing electoral circumstances. This became possible based, more than anything, on the recovery of economic activity, which permitted most companies to improve their profits. This did not mean that there would not be specific disputes or circumstantial problems or that the government would not pay attention to them. At the start of the new presidency, as the fall in meat prices on the international market, which had begun in 1919, deepened, Alvear's government put pressure on the railways to reduce their charges, without much success. In the face of complaints by La Fraternidad and the new Unión Ferroviaria (Union of Railwaymen) which was formed in October 1922, replacing the anarchist FOF, the Executive decided on compulsory arbitration. Later on in 1926, facing an international fall in the prices of rye, oats and wheat, the government imposed cuts in the charges for transporting these cereals, of five to ten percent and fifteen percent in the case of the Central Argentine. When a year later the Fraternidad demanded the imposition of a new, more favourable, salary scale, it received the backing of the President. But, above all from 1925, when Roberto M. Ortiz replaced the Yrigoyenist Eufrasio Loza as Minister of Public Works, there began a permanent action towards laying down a new general framework for fares and charges that eliminated the increases recently conceded. The year 1926 was a good one for the companies. On average, the four largest railways, the Western, Southern, Central Argentine and Pacific, paid dividends of 6.5%, close to the limit set by the Mitre Law as a recompense for the capital invested. Early in the following year, Manuel F. Castello, now acting as the interim NRB Director, expressed the opinion that the Southern could reduce its fares and charges by 10%, and soon after said the same to the Central Argentine. In June of 1928 a decree ordered the former company to reduce its charges, which were implemented after some complaints; and the same occurred in October to the latter company.

The re-election of Yrigoyen in 1928 signalled the end of moves towards establishing a new framework for fares and charges. Not wanting to see his ability to manoeuvre curtailed in his new administration, the old radical leader suspended enforcement of the decree issued to the CAR, required Castello to carry out a new study of the problem of fares and charges, and in the end did not raise the problem with other companies. In his brief second term, faced with emergencies provoked by crop failures and threats of strikes by the railway workers, he merely acted to ensure continuity of service and the provision of a police presence on the trains. In the face of insistent rumours that North American interests were seeking to purchase the British-owned companies, the president ratified his confidence in the existing companies, stating to the British Ambassador: "We are and always will be satisfied with British capital investment, which has never caused difficulties or hindrances". This judgement coincided with the general line taken with regard to foreign policy, manifested in, for instance, celebration of the D'Abernon-Oyhanarte Anglo-Argentine Agreement, signed in 1929, which however was never ratified nor put into practice.

Apart from their different styles and modes of action, the two radical presidents carried forward a railway policy which was broadly a continuation of the policy initiated in 1887 and gradually refined since that date. The policy had been defined in more detail after the Mitre Law had been approved, becoming a policy focused on the model of a railway system based on exploitation by private companies with state control.

The model functioned as a result of the activities of private companies. This meant that the management and administration of the railway system was the concern of the Boards of these companies and of the beaurocracy which, over time, had formed within their structures. It was also the case, in the face of the State's inaction, that their concerns included the planning of future extensions, the emergence of novel technologies and, most importantly, the procuring, as far as was possible in each case, of capital sums via the issuing of shares and bonds (debentures) in the financial markets. All this activity presupposed that railway operation was profitable and that the capital invested should be remunerated. Of course, as a public service, railway operations implied entering into relationships with hundreds of thousands of people, who in some cases had opposing interests to those of the companies. On one side, shippers and passengers who demanded better services at lower prices, and on the other side, railway workers, employees and labourers who expected better salaries and working conditions. The State, without losing sight of its aim to maintain and expand railway services, for which it accepted that the companies should be profitable, should also attend to the conflicting interests of customers and dependents. In the conflicts which arose, without favouring one side or the other and depending on the circumstances, it ended up acting as a referee searching for a balance which maintained the railway system model. But, in addition, the public railway service was a monopoly, and the socially costly idea of introducing competition between companies had fallen out of favour. This demanded that the government had to use its powers of control. It controlled investment by means of the mechanism of "recognised capital". It controlled fares and charges by insisting on the principle that they could not be changed without its agreement and, moreover, had to be reduced on demand. It controlled continuity and quality of service by means of the legal authority to impose fines. And finally, it controlled the profit on capital investment by limiting it to the rate fixed by the Mitre Law. Even though it had been this Law which had determined the rules of the model in 1907, its application until 1916 had not enabled it to be considered as completely defined. Discussions persisted about the interpretation of its rules, and the successive crises of 1912 and the Great War had altered the interrelationship of its provisions. It was the experience of the Radical governments in applying these rules, following the ideas of Nogués, which established the model as described above, more so than the styles of the successive Heads of State.

Within the railway policy thus defined, there persisted the affirmation that the system should continue to grow. The form and financing of this growth remained in the hands of the private companies, as we have indicated, but only in those areas where the service would be profitable. Outside those areas it was the responsibility of the State itself, through the Administration of State Railways. When Alvear's administration began, in a propitious economic climate, it was insisted of the companies that they should extend their networks. After certain misgivings, they submitted requests for new concessions, which Congress delayed awarding because of confrontations between the Radical factions. But in fact the temperate zone capable of easy agricultural development was already well covered by rails, and so the private companies added little to the system. Growth of the system during these years was mainly due to extensions constructed by the State Railways. However, this expansion was not problem free. Yrigoyen ordered the constructions without assigning resources, and the same happened during the first part of the government of Alvear. This, together with several accusations concerning transparency in his administration culminated in a scandal which led to the resignation of Minister Eufrasio Loza. From then onwards a new programme of investment began, together with an intention to improve the administrative process of the State.

The State lines, including the NCR and the ANR which had merged under a single administration from 1918, grew to a length of 5,370km by 1929. However, their gross receipts in that year was 23,963,936 national pesos.[4] significantly inferior to that of any of the private companies of similar size. Its performance was poor: for 14 years, from 1916 to 1929, it sustained losses except for negligible profits in three annual statements. In addition, the State operated the following branches: Formosa-Embarcación (298km) in the Territories of Formosa and Salta; the so-called Ferrocarril del Este (Eastern Railway) (409km) in the Province of Entre Rios; and the lines in Patagonia (1,267km). In 1923 to these was added the small Central of Chubut Railway, inaugurated in 1888, which in spite of initial hopes, had never achieved a good profit. Once more, the State was acting to rescue private capital invested in railways.

From 1923, the crisis and postwar recession over, the volume of traffic began a period of continuous growth, always allowing for oscillations caused by the incidence of the climate on the results of the harvests. The increments in the gross receipts of the more important railway networks clearly shows this. The Southern grew from a receipt of 132,616,100 pesos in 1924-25 to 149,674,128 in 1928-29, and this company's best year was 156,198,546 pesos in 1926-27. In the same period, the Central Argentine grew from

[4] From about 1900 until 1930 the Argentine peso had a value against the pound sterling which hardly varied: 11.45 pesos was equivalent to 1 pound.

132,505,114 pesos to 163,246,733 pesos; the Western from 54,450,331 pesos to 60,426,296 pesos; and the Pacific from 90,217,606 pesos to 104,629,627 pesos. Constant revaluing of the peso caused the virtual disappearance of the exchange conversion losses which in previous years had badly affected the annual results of the British and French companies. Profits also grew, for the same reason, and remained at significant levels. The BAGSR profit grew from 5.42% in 1924-25 to 5.83% in 1928-29 (with a peak value of 6.88% in 1926-27). In the same period, the CAR profit rose from 5.14% to 6.40%, the BAWR from 4.73% to 5.68%, and the BAPR from 5.06% to 5.78%. The minor companies, which had faced serious difficulties during the recession years, also benefitted from similar improvements.

The end of the recession did not lead, however, as had previously been anticipated, to a renewal of investment in an expansion of the railway system. During this period, the private companies either extended their lines by just a few kilometres or not at all. Among them the BAGSR stands out, growing from 6,085km in 1917 to 6,733km in 1929, as well as taking over the BBNWR (1,225km), previously owned by the BAPR. This last, for its part only grew by about 230km, from 4,280km in 1917 to 4,516km in 1929. The CAR and the BAWR built virtually no extensions. Instead, the private companies used their resources, sometimes in significant amounts, to improve their systems. In 1925 the Southern began the construction of a new Plaza Constitución station and in 1929 introduced the first diesel-electric train sets. The Central Argentine electrified its Buenos Aires suburban lines between 1916 and 1931. The Western did the same in 1923. In addition, to increase the demand for transport to and from the remoter areas of the fertile humid pampa, the companies created supplementary services for agriculture and livestock farmers. These included offers of free seed classification, the promotion of genetic studies of seeds, and even the setting up of a consortium for colonization. Development of farming technology in Argentina had fallen behind compared with that in other similarly placed countries. The railway companies, with the direct aim of promoting an increase in traffic, undertook activities which tended to increase farming production, substituting for the indifference shown by the government. Prominent examples were the experimental farms set up by the Southern in the valley of the Río Negro from which fruit production developed in the area, and the experimental farms set up by the Central Argentine in the province of Santiago del Estero to stimulate vegetable production under irrigation.

The general extent of the Argentine railway system on 31st December 1929 was as follows (with figures in brackets for 31st December 1916): the total extent of metre-gauge lines had reached 11,503km (10,394); that of standard-gauge lines was 3,007km (2,680); and that of broad-gauge lines was 23,039km (20,747). The State operated 7,344km (4,873) and private companies operated 30,205km (28,948). The whole network had reached 37,550km (33,821).

The Irreversible Crisis of the Privately-owned Railway Companies

The economic crisis which began with the collapse of the New York stock exchange in 1929 and which rapidly spread to developed European countries, had a deeply serious impact in Argentina, as might reasonably be expected. Industrial company production fell markedly, which promptly led to an increase in the level of unemployment not previously experienced, and decreased their purchasing power. For countries producing raw materials or consumers of industrial products, this meant that the volume and price of their exports tumbled. In 1929 the value of exports from the whole of Latin America had been 1.800 million dollars. In 1932 this fell to only 700 million. Latin American countries started to lack the funds required to service payment of their external debts and to pay for essential imports, and a chain of defaults began to erode their economies. Exchange controls were implemented and the gold standard was abandoned, where it existed.

Argentina was no exception. The collapse of export activity, agravated by a poor harvest in 1929, led to a steep decline in gold reserves. In December of that year conversion of the peso, reinstated in August 1927, was suspended after most of the reserves had been lost. This situation was made even worse because speculative funds exited the country and the imports did not decline as fast as exports sales. The value of the peso began to fall in February 1930, the price of grains declined even further and this led to a fall in fiscal revenue, caused largely by reduced customs duties and a pronounced deficit in the balance of payments. The cost of living rose, there was unemployment, and the salary payments of civil servants were delayed. The economic crisis was transformed into a political crisis when in September 1930 a coup toppled President Yrigoyen and revoked constitutional government.

The activities of the railways were badly affected by the recession. Traffic, especially cargo, declined. At the close of the June 1929 financial exercise, 33.3 million tons had been transported. In June 1933 this had fallen to 24.5 million. The gross income of all the lines had fallen by 200 million pesos from 1929 to 1934, while expenses were only able to be reduced by 100 million. The government opposed any staff dismissals and was reluctant to authorise any wage reductions. To all this was added the loss arising from the exchange controls, amounting to 30 millions in 1934. Also, in many cases the controls prevented the companies from obtaining the corresponding authorisations to transfer their reduced profits, which led to blocked credit balances and unpaid foreign debts. The average profit of the lines went from 5.71% to 1.82% over the same period, 1929 to 1934. The fall in profits (which had been 156 million pesos in 1929 and became only 80 million in 1934) meant that dividends on ordinary shares were not paid. The four large broad-gauge companies had paid 7% (8% by the Southern) in 1929 and from then onwards no dividend was paid on these shares (the BAGSR paid 1% in 1931) until they were wound up after the sale of the lines to the Argentine Government in 1947. Even worse, the companies felt it impossible to pay dividends on preference shares, bank loans, bonds, and to service debentures. This situation remained unchanged during the whole decade, though at certain times some of the most outstanding liabilities were settled. The companies found themselves having to plead in the courts for moratoria in order to avoid liquidation because of insolvency. Thus, for example, the Pacific signed an agreement with all its debenture holders together with those in the group which it controlled, the

AGWR and the VMRR, extending due dates until 1935. The Central Argentine signed a similar agreement with its bond holders, extending the due dates for three years. With regard to its debenture holders, it was able to service them for a while longer, until finally it was obliged to ask for a moratorium. Only the Western and the Southern were able, with difficulty, to continue to fulfil their obligations until the outbreak of the world war in 1939. At that time they also set up moratoria, and even before had stopped paying dividends on preference shares. It was even worse for the minor companies. It is not surprising, therefore, that railway bonds and shares were completely depreciated. The ordinary shares of the four major companies, which in 1929 were priced at about their nominal value, lost value on several occasions. The Southern went from 105% in 1929 to 22% in January 1933 and continued falling toward 8% in January 1940. For the Western the fall was from 97% to 15 and then to 6%; for the Central Argentine from 97% to 16 and 7%; and for the Pacific from 98 to 9 and 3%. This meant that the companies were unable to access their usual sources of funds, and were forced to turn to the banks for costly loans.

To the problems originating from the economic recession there was added the growing competition from the motor car. Present for some time in the United States and Europe, road transport had only recently become a serious threat to the railways in Argentina. A network of roads had not existed before the emergence of the rail transport system in the country. Even though its geography and ground surfaces did not offer any serious obstacles to the development of a road system, the traditional materials required for durable road construction were not easily available, as it was mostly necessary to transport them from distant locations. For these reasons, the country had not experienced much growth in this mode of transport. However, in the previous decade the fleet of motor vehicles had begun to expand. In 1920 it consisted of 49 thousand motor cars and two thousand trucks. By 1930 these numbers had risen to 358 and 96 thousand, but not much notice had been taken of this increase. The railway companies, in an environment of growing economic activity, did not see it as the emergence of a competitor. They were convinced that the phenomenon occurring in Europe and North America since the end of the Great War, of a continuous loss of traffic in favour of the new mode, would not be repeated in Argentina. On the other hand, the Radical governments, relying on traditional economic policies and committed to a transport mode based on the activities of the private railway companies, had continued to think that the country needed to grow its railway network, and had no plans designed to promote the construction of roads. But in the new scenario of low prices for agrarian products, the lower charges offered by the trucks, especially over short distances, together with their flexible ability to get really close to loading and unloading points, created a deadly adversary. When the companies found themselves checked by falling incomes and inflexible costs, the realisation dawned that they also faced the risk of slowly losing part of their market. For distances of less than 300km, truck charges were below that which any railway line could charge. For distances up to 600km they remained competitve, though not by much. On the other hand, initially in the provisional government following the coup, and more strongly in the new government of President Justo, there arose in official circles a change in policy which coalesced into plans for the construction of highways for road vehicles. In June of 1932 the Executive presented a bill for a highway administration law to Congress which was rapidly approved, and with its funding assured led to a significant increase in road construction. From then onwards, the percentage of road construction funding in the national budget continued to rise. In 1927 it had been 2%; in 1938 it became 6.4% and continued to rise. The result of this was the emergence of a network of paved trunk roads together with a considerable network of improved secondary roads, and the main ports in the provincies of Santa Fe and Buenos Aires gained easy access to these networks.

The Railways in Regard to the Bilateral Relationship between Great Britain and Argentina

Towards the end of 1931 the railway companies began to approach the authorities to request the adoption of measures that would help them recover from their difficult situation: a modification of the exchange control policy, coordination of transport modes, modifications in the regulation of the sector, and authorisation for the dismissal of personnel. During 1932 their requests became more insistent and led to demands being made not only in Buenos Aires but also to the Argentine ambassador in London. The responses were invariably negative, and the authorities showed indifference towards the problems being experienced by the companies, meanwhile favouring the emerging automotive transport mode, as previously noted. Once the Executive finally decided to develop a plan for the regulation of automotive transport, which the foreign companies took to be a favourable gesture, the Congress did not approve it, and the president made no effort to have it discussed. In the period following the crisis, the Boards of Directors in London persisted in dealing directly with the Argentine authorities, as they had always done, confident that the railway policy adopted by the country would not change and that foreign private companies would remain responsible for the provision of railway transport services. Their main effort concentrated on obtaining a modification of the exchange control mechanism in force since 1931. The committee which oversaw this, under the instructions of the Treasury Minister, Alberto Hueyo, prioritised servicing the public debt. Attention was then given to commercial interests; foreign investments in public services, such as the railways, remained in last place. The exchange rate which had to be paid was higher than that before the crisis, because of the depreciation of the peso. This is what generated the so-called "exchange rate loss"; but also, in many cases, permission to convert currency was not granted, which then led to funds being "blocked" in Buenos Aires.

When in early 1933 Argentina decided to negotiate a trade agreement with Great Britain, the British-owned railway companies thought it might be beneficial for them. Following the Ottawa Conference in July and August 1932, where Great Britain moved a step further towards the adoption of the so-called Imperial Preference policy to protect its economy and that of its Dominions and Colonies, the government of President Justo thought it advisable to initiate negotiations towards ensuring the continuity of

Argentina's traditional exports to England. In May 1933 an agreement was celebrated, known since then as the Roca-Runciman Pact, following negotiations during which both parties defended their particular interests. There was little in it for the railway companies, barring a clause specifying "benevolent" treatment for British investments in Argentina. This was no more than a vague promise carrying with it no specific obligations. What interested the companies was how the funds arising from the balance of payments of trading with Great Britain would be distributed in Argentina. In this regard, it was agreed that an annual amount of three million pounds would be set aside to deal with service of the public debt outside the area of the pound sterling. For the rest a list of priorities was established: in first place was servicing the holders of Argentine public bonds resident in the British Isles; and second was payments for imports from Britain. If there was any remnant, it would be used to unblock the funds which the exchange controls had caused to remain in Buenos Aires. Once again, remittance of the profits of the public service companies remained last in the queue. Regarding these, permission would be given for bank loan payments and for servicing debentures, and only afterwards for the payment of dividends to preference and ordinary shares. Finally, in order to solve the problem of the funds which had become blocked before the signing of the agreement, the Argentine government issued a loan, which became known as the Roca Loan, at 4% interest and 5% for redemption. The British railway companies subscribed 171,600,000 pesos, which at a preferential rate of 12.68 pesos to the pound (the current rate was 13.33) was equivalent to £13,500,000. Other companies providing public services, French, Swiss, Belgian and North American, obtained the same beneficial rate, which reduced the demand for foreign currencies in the local market. But the Roca Loan bonds were not easy to place on the London market in order to obtain cash, so the companies created a trust which accepted them for 20% in cash and 60% in savings certificates at 3% annual interest. In that way the larger companies were able to cancel their unpaid liabilities, service debentures and some preference share dividends, except in the case of the BAPR which was unable to settle all the interest due on its bonds. By November 1933, Argentina had modified the exchange control regime by establishing an official market, with a devaluation of 20%, at 15 pesos to buy and 17 pesos to sell. This market was used to sell currencies arising from traditional exports, and to tender for payment exchange permits stipulated by bilateral agreements such as the Roca-Runciman Pact. The amounts collected were used to finance the public debt and the agricultural price supporting mechanism. Those parties who did not obtain permits by tender would have recourse to negotiation in the open market for currencies arising from non-traditional exports (fruit and manufactures), from new external investments, speculative funds and maritime charter fees. In early 1934 the value of the pound oscillated around 20 pesos in the open market, a significant increase compared its value of 11.45 pesos before the crisis. Access by the railway companies to the official market was restricted. At first they were only given permission for the payment of income tax in Great Britain. Later on the payment of interest on debentures and bank loans was acceded to. Apart from this they were obliged to turn to the open market.

In regard to their other requests, the companies had little success. Though dismissal of personnel was not permitted, in some cases reduced salaries were allowed. For a time they continued hoping to benefit from some form of transport co-ordination scheme. However, while the plan to construct a road network continued to be favoured, the co-ordination project remained delayed in the Congress. In response to company insistence, the Minister of Public Works set up a committee which recommended the adoption of some solutions to the problems they complained about (alleviation of rigid exchange rate rules, avoiding the construction of roads paralleling railway lines, allowing the railways to set up door-to-door services, approval of the transport co-ordination project, regulation reform).Towards the end of 1935 the co-ordination project was approved by the Chamber of Representatives, but it would only be passed by the Senate in early 1937, although no concrete results followed from its approval.

In the mean time, the Argentine and British governments began to negotiate the renewal of the 1933 accord, which would expire in 1936. The UK government, which little by little was modifying its strategy of not intervening in favour of the companies, decided to insinuate that the clause specifying "benevolent treatment" should be replaced with one that offered a more productive attitude, above all with regard to the currency exchange regime. However, in the face of Argentina's negativity, the clause remained the same in the new agreement of late 1936. In the company Boards, the realisation was beginning to dawn that the Argentine government's attitude towards them would no longer be returning to that of the past.

Railway Policy during the Decade of the 1930s

From the company point of view, however, awareness of the changing situation was only gradual. On the other hand, partial recovery of the Argentine economy towards the middle of the decade gave some the hope that, as in the past, a crisis which appeared to be insuperable would come to an end given time. The recovery led to more lucrative operations, which created new challenges for railway managements facing them with scarce resources. At least in the four large broad-gauge networks, after the revival of 1934 until the new fall in agrarian productivity of 1937, several innovations were adopted based on two objectives: to increase the range of services on offer, and to reduce operating costs. Service provision improved, and the private company model was able to respond to the demands which had been placed on it. The main improvement offered was in the range of suburban passenger services, which was experiencing increasing public use because of population migration from rural areas into the industrial zones within Greater Buenos Aires. Of course, major works conceived in the previous decade were paralysed or cancelled, such as the construction of the Southern Railway's new Plaza Constitución terminus, the new Central Argentine station at Rosario, or the permanent Retiro terminus for the Pacific Railway. Neither was new rolling stock purchased, except for the reception of previous orders or stock manufactured in the country. Nor were railway tracks upgraded, though it should be recorded that many kilometers of main line tracks had been replaced with heavier rail during the 1920s. With the aim of reducing operating costs, a process of conversion to diesel motive power was started, for shunting duties, for trials on certain services, and by the purchase of a large number of passenger railcars from Hungary (CAR, BAPR), or Britain (BAGSR/BAWR). Some rail services were replaced by road services; locally produced fuel oil was replacing imported coal; older coaches were modernised and others improved; tank, refrigerated and ventilated wagons were constructed on existing frames, and others adapted for small-scale goods and parcel items. In order to compete with road services, long-distance passengers were offered air-conditioned day-time and excursion services which were faster and cheaper than night-time services. Attempts were made to introduce the following improvements: door-to-door freight services, in spite of the difficulty in obtaining authorisation; block cargo trains; shared use of freight wagons between the four major companies, even though this was against regulations; an experimental container service; and modernisation of signalling and communication systems. Two of the companies, the Southern and the Pacific, managed to set up road transport companies to offer certain services which would cost more to provide by rail. Of course, all these measures were partial, intermittent and insufficient. In many cases senior staff members of the companies were accused of being incapable of dealing with the new scenario, though of course it was all taking place in a hostile climate and without access to major resources.

Neither the complaints nor the efforts of the companies succeeded in changing official policy. As described previously, the government's continuing lack of any move to pass the bill which would regulate road transport, of conceding a more advantageous exchange rate, of moves to promote public works which favoured road transport over rail, and of declining to modify regulations which limited flexibility in the provision of railway services, added up to persistent indifference in the face of the problems affecting the companies. When in mid-1935 the British Ambassador ventured to raise some of the complaints with

President Justo, and in particular the exchange-rate problem, the response was unequivocal: the situation of the railways resulted from the innate competitive advantage of the motor vehicle. This official attitude was understandable, taking into account the direction which public opinion was moving. Already in 1931, during the presidential election campaign in November, the main competitor to Justo, Lisandro de la Torre, had seriously questioned the official policy, mainly on the ground that it was inefficient in controlling the private railway companies. As the candidate of the Progressive Democratic Party he criticised, among other things, the fact that in the previous decade the profits of the companies had been high and some had been able to pay dividends of seven or eight percent. Their tariffs had increased from 1917 to 1922, and the price of railway shipping charges had become very high, especially when compared to those of similar countries such as Canada. The companies had set up reserves which should now be used in order to confront the crisis. The National Railways Board did not adequately control the cost of their activities. They had made unnecessary purchases, and conversion to oil fuel operation had been slow and insufficient, leaving them tied to imported coal, an expensive fuel. Their senior personnel was foreign and this increased operational costs because they received long and expensive overseas leave, high salaries, and pension payments above those required by law. Their capital accounts were inflated, the most obvious example being that of the CCR. Also, the proportion of debentures they had issued was very high, which generated serious problems at critical times. During periods when the major lines had absorbed minor ones by means of leasing contracts, they had committed themselves to the paying of sums which were now impossible to find. Some characteristics of the country increased the cost of railway operation, such as seasonal agricultural traffic, but others could have been avoided, such as excessively luxurious passenger services which did not agree with the new spirit of the times.

These moderate criticisms from De la Torre (a native of Rosario) were soon followed by other, more aggressive comments from opposition groups against the foreign companies. The fact that the Roca-Runciman Pact had been set up motivated all the opposition sector, the Socialist Party, the Progressive Democrats and the Unión Cívica Radical (UCR), to emphatically react against the awarding of unfair advantages to foreign entities which were active in the Argentine economy. During debates in Congress from 1932 to 1937, concerning the transport co-ordination bill, the opposition adopted an irrational stance. They refused to discuss the bill itself and the need to discuss the public transport policy to be adopted. Their attack on the railways was solely because of them being foreign and on the government for attempting to regulate road transport in order to benefit foreign companies. The final result was a law which created a committee of seven people – five to be appointed by the government (Minister of Public Works, Chairman of the National Highways Board, Chairman of the National Railways Board, Chairman of the National Ports Administration and Chairman of the State Railways, and two from the private sector, one appointed by the road transport companies and one by the railway companies – which could not be interpreted as favouring the foreign companies. Perhaps the issue which most angered the opposition, and that was indirectly linked to the issues which concerned rail transport, was the debate and approval in September 1936 of the law which co-ordinated transport in the City of Buenos Aires and led to the creation of the Buenos Aires Transport Corporation. The opposition felt it had been swindled because the matter had been taken out of the Buenos Aires City Council, where the Socialists, with support from the Communists and the Progressive Democrats predominated, and taken to the national Congress. The road transport lobby, and especially the bus drivers whose anarchic activities had jolted the tram companies, mobilized themselves with support from importers of North American road vehicles. The debate simplified itself into a confrontation between national interests (the bus drivers) and foreign interests (the tram companies). So, for example, it was thought that the committee set up to study the problem, and which proposed the bill, had acted in defense of the interests of the Anglo-Argentine Tram Company (owned by Belgian, German and British investors). This was because it had affirmed that "the transport of a large mass of passengers can only be realized under conditions of security, regularity and the cheapest possible fare by the system of tramways or underground railways, with supplementary bus or coach services in areas not served by the system". The government's unwillingness to support the private railway companies arose mostly from the political influence of the opposition sector; however, a potentially much more serious influence was the emergence of a new current of thought which was being adopted by a wide circle of followers: nationalism.

Railway policies first established by the Buenos Aires provincial government, and later also by other provinces and the national government, and which from 1890 was consolidated entirely in the hands of the federal government, had not until 1930 attracted many objections. Of course there were isolated criticisms, manifested during some debate or critical moment. Shortly after the 1890 crisis or during the struggle to raise rates and charges in the 1920s, voices had been raised which criticized the foreign companies. But no proposal for an alternative policy had arisen and, in particular, construction of the Argentine railway system based on the participation of foreign investment, mainly British, had not been questioned. It had led to an accelerated expansion of the rails over extensive areas of the national territory, and to the formation of enormous companies with huge capital investments spread over thousands of shareholders, which employed more than a hundred thousand workers and administrative personnel. The opposition parties, the Unión Cívica Radical founded in 1891 and recreated in 1903, and the Socialist Party set up in 1896, had on the whole not raised objections. The former, when it took over the national government, in fact continued along the same path, as we saw previously, and it was during its three presidencies that the policy based on the activities of private companies under State control reached its maximum definition. The latter kept its criticisms of the railway companies enclosed within its more major criticism of the whole capitalist system. But all of this changed in the thirties.

Some antecedents can be found in events occurring years before. Motivated by the labour unrest which characterised the first Yrigoyen presidency, groups had been formed which advocated the expulsion of foreigners and the use of violence against trade union organisations. It was in 1919, around the out of control repression of workers and anarchist demonstations, that the first significant nationalist organisation emerged, the Argentine Patriotic League. The rise to power of fascism in Italy had led to emulation in Argentina. Among the initiators, participants and adherents of the revolt on 6th September 1930 which toppled HipólitoYrigoyen, nationalists predominated, and even the provisional president, José Félix Uriburu, could be considered to be one of them. But it was not until a few years later that certain doctrinal elaborations gave shape to the movement, with questions about economic policy, including railway policy, and an original stance in the matter of historical interpretation, known as "revisionism". This enabled a widening of its support base, until that time extremely reactionary and aristocratic. The signing of the Roca-Runciman Pact served as a pretext for the publication of a book by the brothers Julio and Rodolfo Irazusta, who had been supporters of Uriburu and like most of the nationalists were furiously opposed when presidential candidate Agustín P. Justo's platform triumphed against the fascist illusion of Uriburu, the General from Salta. The book, *La Argentina y el imperialismo británico* (Argentina and the British Imperialism), is considered to be the first broad and coherent manifesto of nationalism. It describes Argentina's past as a long submission to British interests, the only exception being during the time of Rosas (Governor of the Province of Buenos Aires from 1829 to 1852). Their denunciation is a doble one: against the external dependency; and against the ruling class, the "oligarchy", who had submitted the country to the necessities of international commerce and to British imperialism, satisfying its small-minded class interests and sacrificing the national independence. With regard to the subject of Argentina's railway history, the new doctrine found its strongest exponent in Raúl Scalabrini Ortiz, whose thesis developed during the latter half of the 1930s can be summarised as follows: the railways in Argentina were constructed by the British as part of their network of domination. This is why the lines were laid out solely to connect the interior to the ports, why the scale of fares charged was detrimental to local industry and commerce, and why importation from England of consumables and capital goods was promoted. Foreign capital had not been indispensable for the installation of the railways, as the country itself had had sufficient resources. The inrush of capital had been made possible by the connivance of the ruling classes and imperialist interests. In addition, the activities of the railway companies had not been subjected to any form of control. Many of the investments had been deceptive, consisting of appropriations of national funds. The running of the railways had been a source of fabulous profits for the British. The crisis denounced above has obscured secret profits arising from the lack of control. During the whole history of the railways all governments and companies had acted in the same undifferentiated way. The result was that the railway lines had served to consolidate foreign domination, mainly by the British, in Argentina.

Given that these ideas were on the rise, intermingled with the confused political system of the 1930s and with a government of doubtful legitimacy, it was not surprising that the authorities were very cautiously against making any decisions which could be seen as benefitting the foreign railway companies. It is probable that the inopportune conditions of the moment weighed more than the objective of setting out a new transport policy which favoured road transport over railways, to the extent that the latter were founded on foreign capital. This impression is reinforced if we look at what was happening to the state railways.

The State-owned lines had been extended during the 1920s, when the privately owned railways had grown very little. The government of President Justo had noted this situation, and had appointed Pablo Nogués as General Administrator. Nogués was a personal friend of the President, and had served with notable success as National Railways Board Chairman until 1918. Nogués exerted an enormous influence on the national government and made great efforts to achieve better efficiency and drive continued growth of the State railways. He received every necessary support towards pursuing this aim. The idea that State lines ran through marginal regions was abandoned, and the task of extending them to compete with the private company lines was undertaken in certain areas. There also emerged the idea that the State network should have its own access to the city of Buenos Aires. Following the general collapse in 1929 and 1930 the State Railways also found support from new economic thinking, such as the prescriptions of the interventionist policies of John M. Keynes and the example of the New Deal. The lack of access to Buenos Aires was presented as something which should be put right as soon as possible. It was proposed that the State Railways should construct a fifth direct main line between Buenos Aires and Rosario, parallel with the four existing lines, in order to have its own access without having to depend on the private lines which already served the region. Without it, the State company would not be able to influence the economic future of the country.

The result of all this, from the railway policy point of view, led to a contradiction: the State had lost confidence in basing railway activities on private railway companies with state controls whilst betting on the growth of road transport in the areas which the railways served, but in the mean time promoting expansion of the State-owned railways. Probably, it might have been more rational to proceed in the opposite manner: redoubling reliance on railways in the more developed areas, where transport was in much higher demand; and promoting road construction in areas of lower economic development, where the enormous cost of installing a railway could not be recovered. But the irrational opposition, the rise of nationalism, and dubious government legitimacy, prevented adoption of this latter way. As the idea grew in the opposition of the public that private railways were detrimental, that transport coordination was only meant for their benefit, that planning transport services mattered only to the British and not to the country, and that for the government of Great Britain the most important consideration was to keep the railways in the hands of British capital, public policy was being formed in an improvised, piecemeal manner.

The years 1937 and 1938 were bad for economic activity. Drought reduced agricultural production, international prices again decreased and tonnage transported by rail fell by as much as 50% in some cases. What has been described in the previous paragraphs, together with this new calamity, had its effect. All participants in the relationships which had formed around the railway companies, their Directors, and the British government officials as well as the Argentine authorities, became convinced that purchase by the national State was the only way to unblock the situation. However, ten more years would pass before this solution was adopted. Many factors led to this delay, which damaged the future of the railway system.

The Road Towards Nationalisation

The idea that Argentina should acquire the privately-owned railway lines, which towards the end of the 1930s was emerging as the only solution, had antecedents to support it. The most important and recent of these were the negotiations, which had just started and were rapidly concluded, for the purchase of two companies in difficulties. These were the Transandine and Córdoba Central railways. The first, opened in 1910 after overcoming numerous technical and financial obstacles, belonged to a company registered in London. It had been completed with the help of a State subsidy, it was always difficult to operate, and it had been incorporated into the Pacific group of lines. After the 1930 crisis, when the mechanism of working together with the Chilean section ceased to be viable, the TR interrupted operation until the Pacific group attempted to continue service. But in 1934 a landslide closed the line for several years and the English company did not initiate its reconstruction. Under these circumstances the national State acquired the line, incorporated it into the State's network of lines, and restored service after a while. The purchase was formalised in 1939. Much more important was the case of the Córdoba Central. It involved the whole of a railway network extending from Tucumán to the provinces of Córdoba and Santa Fe and down to the city of Buenos Aires. In part it was the outcome of several planning mistakes, such as when the State introduced metre-gauge lines in the 1870s, and later during the privatization and concession fever of the period in office of Juárez Celman, which resulted in poorly profitable lines. The crisis in 1930 overwhelmed this company. It was the first to be in difficulties when facing up to its obligations, including the payment of staff salaries, and its Board was the first to be convinced that it should seek help from the State in order to find a solution which would envisage continuity of service and the reimbursement of some of the capital invested. Discussions began in Buenos Aires as early as in 1934. After diverse negotiations the Executive made a purchase offer to the company in December 1936. The price would be fixed at £9,500,000, to be paid as £8,800,000 in public bonds at 4% interest plus £700,000 in cash. Certain sectors of opinion voiced their opposition, and the President did not push for approval of the respective bill. The delayed decision became more complicated because of growing labour unrest in the company. In early 1934 personnel had demanded that their pay be restored to the level it was before the cuts imposed in 1931, but the company refused. The government intervened and for a time took over payment of the difference. When this arrangement came to an end, the company remained intransigent. The unions declared partial withdrawals of labour, which interrupted services. In October 1937 the railway company, in an attempt to overcome the persistent conflict, proposed to the government a scheme which in effect consisted of a return to the purchase agreement. This was accepted. The State Railways would take over the running of services, the workers and employees would be absorbed into the same regime as that of the State company, the State would guarantee to the investors and creditors of the Córdoba Central a sum equivalent to the nett profit which the company had obtained in the 1936-1937 financial exercise, and would keep open the option to purchase pending consideration in Congress. It was agreed in principle that operation by the State would continue for one year, but this lease was soon extended to four years and the government committed itself during the period to pay 4% interest on the originally agreed purchase price, so that its annual financial obligation amounted to £380,000, against which it could deduct some £44,000 in respect of the cost of maintaining the line. The Minister of Public Works defended this decision on the grounds that it assured the continuation of an essential public service and "converted into reality a long-held wish with regard to communications: a direct connection from the provinces of the north and northwest into the city of Buenos Aires".

The operating agreement was a way to force acceptance of the option to purchase. This was the reason for some of the criticisms which it received: the President's term of office would end in February 1938, and he had taken upon himself a decision which should have been made by Congress. The obligations assumed were, in total, equivalent to those which would arise from the plan for the purchase. In the months that followed, steps to formalise the plan were carried out. In February 1938 a bill was presented which would ratify the lease, and Congress was also asked to approve the previous bill which authorised the purchase. The arguments recommending these measures also considered wider questions, beyond the case of the Córdoba Central Railway:

> [This operation] was not only the first step, the Executive was saying, of great significance for the development of what will be the orientation of our railways in the future, but is also an act of national importance and positive convenience [...]. Restitution to full control by the Nation of its essential and widely used public services is the policy that should be used in the future, if we wish to assure for collective benefit the basic principles of its economy in general and solid foundations for social peace and harmony.

Less than a year later, Congress assented to the plan and in January 1939 passed Law 12.272. The lines of the Córdoba Central, together with the tiny company it controlled, the Rafaela Steam Tramway, became the property of the State.

Immediately after having signed the first agreement with the Argentine government, the British Company took steps to implement the sale. An Extraordinary General Meeting in January 1937 authorised the sale and investment of the proceeds in bonds. Two months later it gained legal approval, required because it had ceased making interest payments since 1931. Immediately after approval of the law in January 1939, the Board undertook the task of again reorganizing its capital (the CCR's capital, last reorganised in 1932, had suffered from many manipulations after several restructurings), given that the price obtained represented approximately half of its nominal capital. The resulting scheme maintained the nominal value of the First preference debentures, renamed "A" preference debentures, a total of 8 million pounds, but their interest rate was reduced to 3½% and the holders would renounce past interest debts in exchange for £200,000 in cash. The remainder of the titles, the debentures with income rights and the ordinary shares for a nominal total of £6,168,355, were converted into new "B" debentures with the right to receive the amount remaining once the previous debentures had been sold. For the holders of these titles, this conversion implied an enormous deduction, which ranged from four to one (debentures) to twenty to one (shares). The total value of "B" debentures issued was £1,902,173. The newly reorganised capital approximated to the purchase price. In July 1939 an Extraordinary General Meeting approved the reorganisation and changed the name of the company to the Cordoba Central Trust Limited. The company was slowly wound up. Its capital was recovered from the titles issued by the Argentine government in completion of the purchase price.

Different factors had come together to make purchase by the government possible in this case. The rise of nationalist sentiments had played in favour, although it had also introduced obstacles. If the railway was the main tool of foreign domination, then the recovery of an important British-owned network, as was the Córdoba Central, was a meaningful step towards restoring the independence which economic links had damaged. Also, the purchase could have historical significance. In the nationalist literature of the time, the origin of that company represented a censurable act of capitulation. A nationalist magazine of the left affirmed in August 1937:

> A similar history, though even more shameful, is the sale of the Northern Central Railway, sold by tender in spite of the profits it generated, to the English company Hume Hermanos who a short time later transferred it to the Cordoba Central [...]. The

> astute English triumphed over corruption and the incompetence of governments. Better said, imperialism triumphed by imposing its own conditions.

But nationalism, on the other hand, was also an obstacle to the purchase, because its conspiratorial imaginings led it to believe that the government's acceptance of the price had been achieved as a result of bribes offered by the Córdoba Central, thus constituting a grave criminal offense. The State bureaucracy, especially that of the State Railways Board, was another force in support of the purchase and above all the influence exercised by its Administrator Pablo Nogués. There was already a tradition behind the aspiration to integrate the Cordoba Central into the State Railways, which have the metre-gauge in common. In that sense, the message sent to Congress by the Executive specifically stated:

> "After critical examination of the various plans which have been opportunely formulated for the resolution of the problem of linking the Northern Central Railway (part of the State Railways) to the Federal Capital, the Executive opts without hesitation for the CCR line to be used, with the State as owner. It judges that this is the most convenient solution, with regard to both technical and economic aspects. Even more importantly, it is a 'national' solution, because it satisfies the real exigences of the State network".

As we have already mentioned, concern for the preservation of the railway's services was another factor for consideration. The State argued that the situation the CCR found itself in risked suspension of its services with the detriment that this meant for all those who depended on this company for the transport of goods and people. Protagonist groups with real power had a decisive effect on the actions of the government. Shippers from different regions pressed for nationalisation to be accelerated. The labour unions looked towards the same aim, not in the hope of getting more advantageous fares and charges, but instead with the aim of achieving better working conditions and higher pay for its members. In this regard, the interpretation by the authorities of the position of the unions was very curious, in that they attributed to them a left leaning nationalist political stance. Thus, the bill presented to Congress in February 1938 affirmed: "The Executive has been able to verify that during the frequent conflicts provoked by the personnel of the privately-owned companies it has been increasingly difficult to lead the parties towards reasonable solutions, because the bulk of the workers feel that their economic situation is subject to foreign capital's ambition for profit".

The most common criticisms of the purchase of the CCR were those which referred to the high cost of the process or to the damage which the fiscal accounts could suffer if the State began to take over the unprofitable companies. But there was a general agreement, between both opposers and supporters of the government, as well as the authorities and the members of the Railway Company Boards, that the purchase of the CCR was the first step in the acquisition of all the lines. In one way or another, between 1936 when the first offer to purchase that railway was made, and in early 1939 when the purchase was legally ratified, the destiny of all the privately-owned railway lines was to be their sale to the State.

In the final months of 1937, during annual general meetings of investors in London to consider the balances of the accounts closed in the month of June, which were poorer than those of previous years, some of the Directors made public the idea that it would be advisable to open negatiotions with the Argentine government about the purchase of their companies. The Barings Bank commissioned an enquiry to determine whether the possibility of staggered sales might assist the government in Buenos Aires to decide. Following the renegotiation of the Roca-Runciman Agreement, the government in London had become convinced that the continued provision of public services by British-owned companies in Argentina was a factor which disrupted normal relations between the two countries. In the heart of the government headed by Roberto M. Ortiz (Justo's successor) there grew the idea that a gradual nationalisation was the way to proceed. This was firmly supported by Pablo Nogués, who suggested that Argentina could, as a first step, exchange British company debentures for bonds of the public debt. The Directors in London, represented by John M. Eddy, discussed this idea and made a counter offer on the basis of the possibility of forming a joint company, although in the end they could not get agreement because the Argentine government would not guarantee share dividends. In 1939 several bills for railway nationalisation were presented, but none emerged as significant. More important was the so-called Pinedo Plan in 1940, which among its provisions contemplated the possibility of acquiring public service company bonds and shares by using the credit surplus of the commercial balance of payments which the war and the various agreements celebrated with Great Britain had now rendered unavailable. But the outbreak of world war and the institutional fragility of Argentina were creating an unfavourable climate for taking forward the negotiations, which had shown themselves by their nature to be difficult. A five-year pause took place, and this further delay in reaching a decision was also damaging for the railway system.

The 1946, 1947 and 1948 Agreements

The outbreak of the war created new problems for the significant commercial relationship which Great Britain and Argentina maintained. The pound sterling became unconvertible and Great Britain began to accumulate negative balances of payments with various countries, which by 1945 amounted to seven times more than the US dollars and gold held by the Bank of England. When the war ended, Britain's exports had fallen to one third of its former level. Loans from Canada and the United States only covered the commercial deficit for a limited period. The continuation of the exchange control mechanism impeded for the time being any pressure on the reserves, while at the same time preserving a protected market. But it also indicated that the gold and dollar reserves in the Bank of England served as reserves for the whole of the sterling area. In addition, it was not possible to force those countries in credit to maintain their balances for an undefined period.

In spite of initial fears, which had led to the formation of the Pinedo Plan in 1940, the Argentine economy was not seriously damaged by the worldwide conflict. Industrial exports increased and opened up in the Latin American markets, including also the United States, as their usual providers disappeared. Even though these exports began to diminish in 1944, by 1945 they still represented a percentage four times as large as in 1939. The balance of payments showed successive positive outcomes. Although a more careful analysis of the circumstances indicated a rather mediocre panorama, the accumulated reserves, the capacity to produce food which the postwar market was desperate for and an intact production structure as a result of not having participated in the fighting, all this together made many believe that the country could look forward to years of accelerated progress. The economic indicators, however, should have called for caution. Agricultural production was stagnant, when not less than that of fifteen years ago. Industry lacked consumables and its export success was due to the temporary absence of more efficient competitors. The favourable balance of accounts was more the result of the impossibility of importation rather than the capacity to export. Between 1939 and 1945 the economy had only grown as much as that of Great Britain, in spite of the damage which had occurred there because of Nazi agression; it had grown less than that of Brazil, Australia and México, and much less than that of Canada and the United States.

Economic events had become inextricably mixed with political events. In the latter sphere, what Argentina had done was even less clever than in the economic sphere. The start of the war and the later involvement of the United States had left Argentina badly placed with respect to the rest of the Americas, where all the countries had broken off diplomatic relations with the Axis powers and had supported the nations of the Allies. On repeated occasions the country had opposed North American initiatives seeking the support of the continent for the war effort. Only after a diplomatic scandal, which demonstrated that the Argentine foreign service had been infiltrated by the Nazis, were relations broken with Germany and Japan in 1944. A declaration of war was made only once it was clear that Germany would be defeated. The de facto government which took over in 1943 had among its members and officials those who publically demonstrated their support for fascist and Nazi concepts. Each international policy move which implied a distancing from the complacent position existing with Germany produced acts of repudiation by the functionaries involved and violent reprisals against those in opposition who supported the change. In 1944 the second de facto government, headed by General Edelmiro J. Farrell, was not recognised either by the United States or by Great Britain.

The end of the war between April and August in 1945, the handover of the de facto government to a new adminstration following elections in February 1946, and the appointment of Juan Domingo Perón as President the following June, established the conditions which enabled Great Britain and Argentina to discuss those unresolved matters which had dragged on over the previous decade and had become more complex during the conflict. For the former, two matters were especially important: to reach an agreement about the accumulated balance of blocked sterling, and to maintain the possibility of continuing to purchase food without being able to achieve equilibrium in the balance of payments for more than two years at least. Less important than trade was the capital invested in public services, such as the railways. For the new Argentine government, a number of circumstances constrained its ambition to design a new policy. It had inherited a difficult international situation arising from the policies followed by the de facto government. Therefore it needed to reposition the country in the new external order which the outcome of the war had created. Peronism had received the internal political support of most of the nationalists and had adopted their discourse, so it was not clear what room for manoeuvre existed for Peron if he moved away from their position on external matters. The new government team was formed of people with very little or no experience of the process of government. Arising from this conjunction of factors were two initial errors of judgement: the economic situation was overvalued by considering that the country had more importance than it really did, and it was thought that a new conflict (between the United States and the Soviet Union) would immediately occur which would again benefit Argentina. Finally, Perón had based his popularity and electoral success, in large part, on the redistribution of incomes by raising salaries and wages, and an expansion of the internal market which the war had facilitated. It was vital for his political success that he not be diverted from this path. In the debates which had arisen on economic policy he had opted for a discourse which extoled an industrialist policy, directed by the State and opposed the expansion of the external market sector. The creation of the Instituto Argentino de Promoción del Intercambio (IAPI), the Argentine Institute for the Promotion of Trade, with Miguel Miranda as its Chairman, is the best expression of the desires and frustrations of the economic policy which he was trying to implement. With the end of the war, the international prices of agricultural produce had risen. The AIPT fixed the internal price for purchasing grain from the farmers below the international price, with the intention of financing industrial development from the difference obtained when the grain was exported. The consequences were disastrous for agricultural production. The cultivated area decreased, and there emerged a tendency to turn to breeding cattle, which required fewer hands, had become more profitable because of internal demand and was less affected by price controls. Even so, cattle production also declined from 1945 to 1950. The accelerated promotion of industrial retooling, using the returns captured from the land, was done inefficiently by means of purchases not based on any plans whatsoever. This policy worsened the commercial deficit in the balance of payments with the United States, which supplied fifty percent of industrial consumables in 1947 and 1948. In the mean time, the volume of exports from Argentina in 1946 was less than that in 1935 and in the best years of the 1920s. Fifteen years of stagnation, if not decline, had passed. Restoring its markets did not preoccupy the government because it did not envision commerce with the world as the engine of the country's development. Even though the commercial balance of payments was favourable until 1949, it then began to fall acutely. It was clear that the country was heading towards a deficit situation without being ready to cope with it.

As we previously saw, the British Government considered investment in Argentine railway companies was a hindrance to the normalisation of relations between both countries. In addition, several members of the diplomatic service, that were experts in Argentine matters, had a poor opinion of the railway company Boards and their Directors. Among them, only John M. Eddy, who had made his career in the BAGSR and who was a Director of many of the companies, was considered to be competent enough to face up to the challenges of the time. In 1945 the British government had decided to raise the question of these investments in the negotiations with Argentina. Eddy was in favour of trying to sell the companies, and had sounded this out with Perón and people close to him. The officials involved in railway matters who were advising the British Embassy in Buenos Aires therefore prepared an outline of ideas for inclusion in the negotiations to be started. It would have to be accepted that the value of the companies was less than the value of the capital invested. There was a consensus that it would be impossible to obtain a price higher than £150 million and that payment would be received in installments, probably over ten years. Discussions should start with a request for a higher price and no mention of spread payments. In any case, the officials were convinced that the railways should bring in the question of the blocked sterling. By the end of 1945 the balance accumulated in the Bank of England had reached £105 million and it was estimated that it would reach about £140 million by the end of 1946. Part of the balance should be used by Argentina to cancel a percentage of the price to alleviate the matter of the debt. The British wanted the compensation to be as high as possible, even though they doubted that the Argentines would agree. Great Britain could not cede too much because it would affect its position in similar cases with other countries. The new Argentine government had not determined its own position nor its policy with regard to matters of transport. However, the platform of the most organised party with Perón as its candidate for president, the new Labour Party, included as one of its central tenets "the nationalization of public services [...] as well as the adoption of all those measures which would take us towards the creation of the basis of our complete economic independence". The topic of the railways was expressly mentioned in the discourse of the nationalists who supported Perón, and he had let them know of his intention to purchase the lines. In any case, the idea had been around for some time, and no alternative way had emerged which would enable the rail network to exit from the dead-end it found itself in.

In the mean time, the railway system continued to be of fundamantal importance for the movement of goods and people. By 1945, the largest private company was the BAGSR. Its lines extended over 8,175km, an increase over the previous figure because of the take-over of the BBNWR. Its gross income was 177,412,019 pesos, and its return 2.05%. The figures for the other large companies were:

- CAR: 5.954km, 161,026,841 pesos, 3.19%
- BAPR: 4.459km, 116,370,276 pesos, 3.19%
- BAWR: 3.097km, 61,661,562 pesos, 1.63%

In total, private companies operated over 29,094km, and State lines over 12,942km. Thus the entire network extended over 42,036km. The increase in recent years had been due to the construction of branches and extensions of the State lines, and their acquisition of the CCR. Broad-gauge lines extended over 24,218km; standard-gauge lines over 3,262km; metre and narrow-gauge lines over 14,456km. The personnel employed on all lines during 1945 had been 142,162 people, of which 102,932 worked for the private companies.

This enormous railway system had urgent problems to resolve. It was faced with a situation which was unknown when most of the system was constructed: the emergence of automotive road transport. It was necessary to establish what role each transport mode would play in the country. After fifteen years of not being able to, the private railway companies needed to update their equipment and at the same time incorporate innovative technologies. To do this, they would have to find a new source of finance, the old one having disappeared after the system ceased to be profitable. Also, it was necessary to reorganise the administration of the railways as a whole, given that the traditional independent company administrations were no longer fit for purpose. The only thing that was clear in 1945 was that this restructuring could not be undertaken by the existing companies as originally constituted.

In June 1946 Great Britain sent a delegation to Buenos Aires, headed by the senior Treasury official Wilfred Eady, to debate the three matters which needed to be dealt with immediately: the blocked sterling balance, commercial trade during the following two years, and the destiny of the investments in the railways. At the same time, in July of the same year, Great Britain had come to an agreement with the United States with the aim of soon settling its monetary situation. In return for a loan of 3.500 million pounds it pledged a return to sterling convertibility. The British delegation found that Miguel Miranda, the Argentine negotiator, was an obstacle to the achievement of their objectives. As chief proponent for the time being of Argentina's economic policy, he stated that his government had no intention of purchasing the railways and that initially the only thing he wanted to discuss was the matter of the blocked sterling. The negotiations stalled until the end of August, when through the conciliatory mediation of the Minister of Foreign Relations, Juan A. Bramuglia, and the intervention of the President, discussion of all three matters set out by the British, taken together, was accepted. As the negotiations advanced, Bramuglia let it be know that it was Perón's wish to form a consortium between the government and the railway companies. That led to a move forward in this matter and the others as well. On 15th September the criteria for an accord were agreed, and two days later the agreement known as the Miranda-Eady Pact was signed. Once the guidelines were set for the gradual release of the blocked sterling and reciprocal commitments for the meat trade were determined, it was agreed in general terms to set up a joint railway company, to which the capital of each company would be allocated, in amounts to be specified later, and to which would be added an Argentine contribution of 500 million pesos. The new company would take charge of the railway operations, retrospectively, from 1st July 1946. The Argentine government committed itself to take the necessary steps to ensure a minimal financial return.

The pact received immediate and fierce criticism from diverse sectors of opinion. The newspapers affirmed that the British had received more than the companies had actually expected, and that the pact assumed by implication that the value of the railway companies was much higher than was reasonable and well above what the Argentine officials had actually estimated. The attacks by the nationalists, while at the same time demonstrating their complete lack of understanding of the British position, suggested that Perón was betraying the commitments they had assumed were agreed. Ricardo M. Ortiz said:

> Great Britain had a particular interest in maintaining the block on Argentina's sterling, perhaps not so much for the money itself, but rather because holding it maintained something essential: it avoided Argentina acquiring the railways. [...] It signified not letting the prey escape. While the railways remained in the hands of the actual owners, in whatever form that might enable their continuance, Argentina did not have any possibility of freely resolving the fundamental questions which affected its economic and social life.

Julio Irazusta, in a later publication, rejected the joint company because it would continue to be managed by foreigners and concluded that "the Miranda-Eady Pact was the most shameful handover made by the Argentine government in favour of the British".

Three of the Directors of the railway companies, among them being Eddy, immediately began discussions of the basis for the joint company and, in particular, the total amount of their capital which would be recognised and allocated to it as part of its capital. The positions of each side were some distance apart; Miranda, again the Argentine delegate, said that the amount he might accept could be 2000 million pesos, or 125 million pounds at 16 pesos to the pound. Eddy was not authorised to accept an amount less than 150 million pounds, so once again the discussions seemed to enter a position from which there was no way out. However, at the end of December, Miranda let it be known to the British delegation that, given the circumstances, he was unable to put to Congress a proposal for the formation of a joint company, even if the capital allocation was less than 2000 million pesos, and that whatever was agreed had to be presented in such a way that British capital was not involved. For those reasons he agreed to the purchase of all the private railway companies for the amount which he had always maintained they were worth: 125 million pounds. The surprised British, who had seen how public opinion and the opposition had treated all these matters extremely superficially, based on prejudices and without any real understanding of the situation, using the same discourse as that of the government officials but without grasping the problem of how to devise a new public transport policy, immediately accepted the purchase proposal, although they continued to debate the price. For the first time since the arrival of the Eady delegation, the British considered that they were in a stronger position, and for some reason, which they were not able to understand, the Argentine government had become "anxious" to buy the railways. A month later the positions of the parties became closer and on the 11th of February 1947 a new accord was arrived at, in which the Argentine government, through the AIPT, would purchase the assets of British companies for £135,500,000 (railways) and £14,500,000 (other assets), making a total of £150 million.

The new accord was much better received than the previous one. The official press affirmed that with it the chains of imperialism had been broken. A weekly peronist-nationalist magazine recognised that the price was high, but was justified because "it was buying liberation". The opposition only criticised the price, which was much higher than that which the government officials had previously announced they would pay. Only one traditional newspaper warned that there were serious doubts about the ability of the new authorities to manage what had been acquired. *La Vanguardia*, a socialist paper, pointed out a fact which would soon become important: the Central Bank had issued money which had as its guarantee the sterling balance deposited in the Bank of England. Payment for the railways, which was not an isolated operation because other public service companies were being purchased and public debt was being repatriated, would lead to a major decrease in reserves and generate inflation.

Beyond all this, both governments could express satisfaction with what had been achieved in the negotiations. Great Britain had resolved the problem of the blocked sterling, had caused troubling investments in British hands to disappear and, as a result of the United States loan which enabled convertibility of the pound, been able to face up to the trade deficit with Argentina. In turn, Argentina had acquired the principal foreign investment in public services by means of an exchange, since it was supposed that the purchase price would be covered by the unblocked sterling, funds of which until this moment only a tiny proportion had been available.

However, the anticipated arrangements which both governments had made towards taking on their commitments could not be carried out, and this had an impact on the fulfilment of the agreements. Great Britain found that convertibility of the pound was impossible to maintain; re-established in July 1947, it lasted only 20 days. Fears returned for the continuation of trade with Argentina in the future. Argentina, keen to accelerate the purchase of foreign companies, to recover debt bonds and continue importation of equipment, quickly exhausted the reserves of gold and foreign exchage which it had accumulated. This led to the negotiation of a third accord, in December 1947. During the series of meetings, Miranda made it clear that Argentina could not make use of the blocked sterling in the Bank of England because this had been converted almost entirely into the reserves which guaranteed the money issued by the Central Bank. On the other hand, he confirmed that Argentine government still wished to buy the railways. To solve the problem, he proposed that Britain advance a sum of money to the Argentine government. The British negotiators accepted this suggestion, because in that way they retained the agreement to sell, which was important for them, and by linking the advance with the probable negative balance of trade in 1948, they were ensuring the provision of meat and cereals for a while longer in spite of the weakness of their currency. Finally, on 12th February 1948 the "Andes Pact" was signed, named after the British ship in which many of the negotiations took place. With regard to the railway question, it was established that the British government would advance £100 million on the account of the balance of trade for the year 1948. In addition it would pay £10 million in recognition of an increase in the price of meat. At the same time the sum of £5 million would be debited from the blocked sterling and £35 million would be transferred from the current account which Argentina maintained in Bank of England. The sum of all these amounts, £150 million, would be credited to the railway companies in payment of the price for them that had been agreed a year ago.

On 1st March 1948 a public ceremony was held to celebrate taking possession of that which had been purchased. Its features explain why, in addition to the irresponsible actions of the opposition and the nationalist opinion formers, it had been decided to make the purchase instead of setting up a joint company. The occasion was marked by an extensive propaganda campaign over the whole country. The place selected for the ceremony was the Retiro Station of the Central Argentine Railway in Buenos Aires. In front of the station a platform was erected, on which was placed the first Argentine locomotive, *La Porteña,* a 2-2-0 tank engine constructed by E.B. Wilson of Leeds in 1856. Behind was placed the official podium, with as background an enormous poster on which was written the preamble of the so-called "declaration of Argentina's economic independence" formulated by Perón on 9th July 1947.[5] One of its paragraphs deserves revisiting: "the people and governments of the provinces and territories of Argentina decided to break the dominant ties of foreign capital in the country and take back government control of its national economic resources". On the new Central Argentine Railway office building, still under construction, on the corner of the Avenue of the Liberator (General San Martín), another large poster was displayed, this time with an image conceived as merging an industrial worker and a rural labourer, with a locomotive

[5] In a speech delivered on Argentina's Independence Day.

in their hands and the caption: "¡Perón delivers, now they are Argentine!" Two nationalist fantasies, tiresomely repeated by the official propaganda, were becoming general beliefs: that the purchase of the railway system strengthened the country's ability to make economic decisions and that exploitation of the railways was a simple task and thus the take-over of the companies would not lead to any problems. No one, either from within the official domain or the opposition, had thought to specify what tasks the State would be taking over after gaining control of the railway services. All remained hidden behind the empty phrase of "economic independence". In reality, the government was taking over a double task for which it had not prepared. On the one hand, it had become responsible for the continued operation of the railway system, at the very least in the way it had operated until then. On the other hand, it had to confront and decide on the problems which had plagued the system for fifteen years. In this sense, the purchase of the railways should have closed the previous phase of operation and opened a new one. The future should have receive greater importance than the past, and nobody seemed to understand this. The first actions of the purchaser indicated that improvisation was to be the most important characteristic of the new administration. The initial step consisted of destroying one of the most important assets which it had acquired: not a physical asset, but rather the organisational structure of the private companies. A plan was put in place to remove senior personnel from posts in the formerly private companies, solely on account of their nationality. An early retirement scheme was implemented which was rapidly taken up by 400 staff. In addition, contrary to the provisions of the February 1947 accord, staff who remained at their posts immediately began to be badly treated and deprived of their tasks. This was not the best possible way to start the new operational phase.

Soon after the British companies had signed the Miranda Eddy Pact, they set up in May 1947 an agreement about how to distribute among themselves the amounts that the Argentine government would be charged for the sale of their assets. To do this they began by listing the amounts of each of their capital holdings, as corrected by the application of the Mitre Law. This first distribution should then be modified by the sums obtained from the sale of their existing assets in Great Britain and from the settling of debts between the companies themselves. These last mainly arose from the way in which the larger companies had taken over control of the smaller ones. Since 1930, the annual payments arising from each takeover, basically a percentage of their capital, had not been made and thus sums of benefit to the smaller companies had accumulated. In round terms, the final price distribution became as follows: BAGSR/BAWR Group, £72,700,000; CAR Group, £40,500,000; BAPR Group, £35,600,000; Mesopotamian Group, £8,300,000. In April 1948 all the companies had resolved their liquidation value. In October of the same year they distributed the major part of what they received between their shareholders. As a summary of the distribution it can be said that holders of debentures, almost without exception, received 100% of the nominal value of their investment, plus the interest owed. However, other investors suffered serious losses. Taken together, they received only 33% of the value of their investment. Overall, £100 million in stocks and shares were not repaid, which represents 37.82% of the total capital issued by the companies. Paradoxically, investors in the larger companies were among those worst hit (for example, ordinary shares of the BAGSR only received 20% and those of the BAPR only 12.5%). This was the result of having to reimburse the takeover debts. In spite of what had happened over the last fifteen years, the capital invested continued to be distributed over thousands of small and medium savers. In no company did individual holdings of more than £10,000 amount to more than 10% of its capital.

The 1947/48 nationalisation ended the existence of the private railway companies and with them the presence of foreign capital, mainly British. This model for railway development had generally worked well. The Argentine had achieved a transport system of excellent quality which had been an essential catalyst for its economic progress. And it had done this without needing to resort to local capital, which could therefore be devoted to other productive activities. This model was formalised in the Mitre Law, giving the

State appropriate means for regulation and control, which were fully exercised from 1916 onwards, as we have seen.

However, the economic factors which sustained the operation of the private railways began to disappear after 1930, and profitability fell. Their access to markets for capital investment was interrupted and the network lost the capacity to remain up-to-date and to respond to the challenges it faced. This happened just as the rise in road transport was making it impossible for the railway companies involved to survive, given the amounts they were able to charge, whilst coping with all their infrastructure and operating costs as well as generating the profits which would enable them to attract more capital.

Until then the Argentine government had considered the railway to be a central feature of its economic policy, and in difficult circumstances had always collaborated with the companies in order to overcome any problems. This changed in the decade of the 1930s. The railway were left to cope on its own, and continued to operate for more than fifteen years under adverse conditions, transporting large volumes of cargo which, during the Second World War, reached levels never seen before. The same happened to passenger numbers, above all in suburban services. But it could not invest nor re-adapt in the face of the growth of road transport, which was starting to take away its most profitable traffic. The railway slowly deteriorated during these fifteen years.

Nationalisation should have been the start of a new policy which would recognise the railway's place in the transport system and should supply the means to enable its efficient operation. But the distortion of reality which had been produced by the rise of nationalism, imagining conspiracies and negating evident facts, became an obstacle to the design of this new rational and effective policy, as will be told in the history of the following decades.

In the 1920s and 30s the railways invested in powerful locomotives. A Class MS6a of the Central Argentine Railway, manufactured by Armstrong Whitworth in 1930. *(Photo: Museo Nacional Ferroviario)*

In 1931 the Central Argentine Railway completed the electrification of its suburban lines, Inaugural train manufactured by Metropolitan Vickers *(Photo: Museo Nacional Ferroviario)*

Elegant sleeping car of the Southern Railway, made by its own workshops in 1921. *(Photo: Museo Nacional Ferroviario)*

In the 1930s the railways began to incorporate diesel locomotives, Drewry shunting locomotive manufactured in 1939, on the Southern Railway *(Photo: Museo Nacional Ferroviario)*

The State Railways were greatly expanded during the 1930s. Train from Bariloche crossing the Río Negro Bridge at Patagones, circa 1935. *(Photo: Museo Nacional Ferroviario)*

JORGE E. WADDELL

4 | From Nationalisation Towards Plans for Modernisation 1947 – 1976

On 1st March 1948 the British-owned railways were taken over by the national government. The actual ceremony took place at the Retiro Station of the Central Argentine Railway, was organised by the government itself, and constituted a massive demonstration of public support for President Perón and his new policy of "economic independence". Whilst recognising this event as most important in terms of the size of the companies and the capital involved, it was only part of a process which began towards the end of the decade of the 30s and ended in 1951. Less ostentatious than taking possession of the British railways had been the taking over of the French lines in 1947, as these were of minor importance in the railway system and had performed poorly. The process of nationalisation culminated with the incorporation into the national State of three minor railways, one of which was the Buenos Aires Central Railway (BACR), a small private Argentine railway, constructed mainly with British capital and taken over on 14th May 1949. The other two were provincial companies that were both transferred to the national State in 1951: the Province of Buenos Aires Railway (PBAR) and the Corrientes Industrial Railway (CIR).

When the nationalisation process culminated in 1951, the national State became the sole protagonist of railway life in Argentina given that, in addition to its proper function of determining railway policy, it had inherited all other aspects of the railway enterprise. This was not a novelty in Argentina. There had almost always been State-owned railways, though of minor importance compared to the private railway companies. What was novel was that the State had taken over the entire network. It had become the only regulator, controller and administrator, different activities which when carried out simultaneously by the same entity would generate functional confusion.

The State Converts Itself into the Only Railway Impresario

Following nationalisation, a political discussion about the condition of the railways erupted. The government felt it had cheaply purchased a high-quality railway system, whereas the opposition considered that a very high price had been paid for a system close to becoming scrap. Discounting the actual terms of the political discussion, in reality neither position applied to the real condition of the system. Formed as it was from the networks of many different railway companies, its condition varied enormously. But we can say that the nationalised system, and in particular the four large Southern, Western, Central Argentine and Pacific networks provided an efficient service of a quality which had not declined. After the war they had made great efforts to restore the former quality of their cargo and passenger services. On the other hand, the smaller companies and those with financial problems had seen their services deteriorate. Overall, it could be said that the railway system, now monopolised by the national State, operated properly with acceptable levels of quality and efficiency. In spite of this, some serious problems had emerged, basically as a result of failure to renovate infrastructure and equipment following the financial crisis in 1930.

Although in 1948 the railway system still operated relatively well, there were two structural problems which had impeded it for the past several decades. These were the unplanned and duplicated nature of the lines in the system, and the diversity of their gauges. The first arose from the fact that most of the network had been constructed on the basis that it was beneficial to have different railways in competition with each other. So the network grew in a disordered fashion with redundant lines. Since all were now the property of the State, there was no point in them competing.

The railway network, with redundant lines in competition and using different gauges, also led to the installation of superflous structures, especially in large cities where each company had its own station, engine and goods sheds and shunting yards, which hindered urban development. All this duplicated infrastructure was under-used, given that the density of traffic in the railways of Argentina was always very low. Juan Pablo Martínez (the third author of this book) has identified four reasons for this over-provision in the railway network: (1) lines constructed by the State in marginal areas; (2) construction of secondary lines and branches for the exploitation of natural resources which later became exhausted; (3) construction of lines in areas already served by other railways; and (4) construction of branches solely as a speculation, taking advantage of the monopoly a railway possesses. All these cases might be justified at particular moments, but not necessarily over periods of extended duration.

With regard to the diversity of gauges, the problem had begun during the 1870s with the construction of the lines from Córdoba to Tucumán and from Concordia to Monte Caseros. On the completion of the processs of nationalisation, the Argentine railway network in public service was formed from lines with five different gauges. Broad-gauge (1.676m) was the most extensive and was that of the principal railways; standard- or universal-gauge (1.435m, called medium-gauge in Argentina), used mainly for the Mesopotamian lines; metre or narrow-gauge, almost always used for the former State Railways; and two smaller gauges, 0.75m for several lines in Patagonia, and 0.60m for the former Corrientes Industrial Railway.

As well as these structural problems, the railway system suffered from serious difficulties which had begun to emerge after the 1930 crisis: competition from road transport, and a lack of significant investment since then. Both the infrastructure and the rolling stock were showing signs of ageing. The main line tracks had been renovated in the 1920s, but the rest of the network remained constructed from light-weight rail laid on earth ballast. Locomotives and other rolling stock were similarly aging. Most vehicles were over 30 years old, and obsolete when of wooden construction. Almost all the steam locomotives offered low tractive effort. The age of the rolling stock and infrastructure required a high level of maintenance in order to provide good service conditions, which in turn led to the need for more personnel and higher running costs.

In regard to fares and charges for railway services, the policy of the new government was not to update them in the face of inflation. In real terms, this meant that income fell by an amount calculated to be approximately 50% between 1946 and 1952. With regard to salaries, the pricipal service cost, in the same period they had risen by about the inflation rate, which generated a significant imbalance between income and expenditure. In addition, the effective fall in charges was stimulating the demand for railway services, both goods and passenger, and especially for urban and suburban services. In order to meet these demands, the railway resorted to over-working its infrastructure and rolling stock, which increased their deterioration and maintenance costs.

When the final balance sheets of the private railway companies were closed on 30th June 1946, the result had been a surplus averaged over the group. From then on this never happened again. The fall in real terms of fare and charge income plus the rise in salaries, together with the increased costs for maintenance of the infrastructure and obsolete rolling stock, soon generated an operating deficit which it was never possible to reverse. It remained the greatest problem for the railway network throughout the second half of the twentieth century.

In summary, reorganisation of the network, by facing up to the redundant lines, to the unification of the different gauges, to the setting up of an efficient state company and to the adoption of measures aimed at solving the other problems which afflicted the railway system, all awaited the formulation of a new policy for the railway sector, in line with the foundational aims of Peron's government. However, little was done.

As we have pointed out, the railway network needed to be reorganized. On the 1st of January 1949 a decree was issued creating the new organisation, but which consisted only of the assignment of new names (of historically important Argentine presidents and army generals) to the old companies. The BAGSR became the Ferrocarril Nacional General Roca (FCNGR); the BAPR became the Ferrocarril Nacional General San Martín (FCNGSM); the former State lines became the Ferrocarril Nacional General Belgrano (FCNGB); the CAR became the Ferrocarril General Bartolomé Mitre (FCNGBM); the ERR and ANER together became the Ferrocarril Nacional General Urquiza (FCNGU); the BAWR became the Ferrocarril Nacional Domingo Faustino Sarmiento (FCNDFS); and lastly all the lines in the region of Patagonia became the Ferrocarril National Patagónico (FCNP).[6]

In the nationalist gospel of the 1930s, which had been adopted as the basis for Peronism, an important affirmation was that the country's railway system had been distorted into fans of lines converging on the ports, and particularly the Port of Buenos Aires. Therefore, as a consequence, nationalisation created the expectation of a reorganization of the system. Let us see what was done about this. Immediately following nationalisation there were about 20 railway administrative units operating in the country, most of them organised into five major groups. One of the largest groups, by reason of its extension and increase of traffic in recent years, was the State Railways Administration, which owned the vast ANCR, the Eastern Railway (ER) in the region of Mesopotania, the line from Viedma and San Antonio Oeste to Bariloche with its branches, the three isolated Patagonian lines and the line under construction from Pedro Vargas to Malargüe. Of highest economic importance was the South-Western group, which included the BAWR and BAGSR networks, the BAMR and the BBNWR. The BAPR administered the Buenos Aires and Pacific railway, the AGWR and the VMRR. The CAR only controlled itself. The ERR and the ANER formed a separate group. In addition there was the French railway group: RBPR, SFPR and BAPGRC. Another company was the BACR, whose operations were coordinated with those of the Mesopotamian railway group.

[6] These renamed networks will from now on be called the Roca, San Martin, Belgrano, Mitre, Urquiza, Sarmiento and Patagonian Railways, respectively.

As we have already said, the reorganization started with the giving of new names to the companies as they already existed, although with some modifications.

The creation of the FCNP appeared to anticipate a political will to construct a large network in the Patagonian region, but it did not happen. It grouped together the three small sub-systems centred on Puerto Madryn, Comodoro Rivadavia and Puerto Deseado, which were not connected and had a variety of gauges. When the line from Río Gallegos to the coal mines at Río Turbio was constructed it was not included in the remit of the Patagonian railways, but instead was operated as an industrial branch of Yacimientos Carboníferos Fiscales (YCF, State Coal Company). After a few years, in 1956 the Patagonian Railway disappeared, and all its lines were incorporated into the Roca Railway. All the standard-gauge lines were formed into the Urquiza Railway, including the ER (the State-built Eastern Railway), the ERR, the ANER, and the BACR, acquired in 1949.

The broad-gauge lines were organised on the basis of the leading British companies, but with some redistributions between them. The RPBR was divided between the Roca, which took over the sector lying south of Capitán Castro Station, and the Mitre, which took over the rest. The latter permuted some branches with the San Martin: the Mitre remained with the La Carlota-Villa María section, which had been controlled by the BAPR; the Junín-Pergamino and Rufino-Venado Tuerto corridors, which had been part of the CAR, moved to the San Martín. Also the ex-BBNWR was redistributed between the Roca and the Sarmiento: the sections south of Darregueira were allocated to the Roca and the rest to the Sarmiento.

The metre-gauge lines were formed into the Belgrano Railway, with a total extension of 14,500km.This heterogeneous system consisted of the ANCR, the SFPR, the BAPGRC and the BAMR. The Transandine was initially allocated to the San Martin, but was moved to the Belgrano in 1951. The Province of Buenos Aires line, transferred to the Nation in 1951, was annexed to the Buenos Aires Midland line to form in 1954 the Ferrocarril Nacional Provincia de Buenos Aires (Province of Buenos Aires National Railway). This had an ephemeral life, as it was dissolved in 1957 and its constituent lines returned to the Belgrano Railway.

Thus the State reorganised the broad-gauge network into a geographical shape which sought to ensure that each railway existed in an exclusive zone, avoiding penetration by any branches of other broad-gauge railways. This was not a positive move. In the narrow-gauge case, the small railways were absorbed into the structure of the very large ANCR. In the broad-gauge case, the railways were well established and so able to resist change and conserve their autonomy. On the other hand, the ANCR clearly predominated over the narrow-gauge lines.

In spite of ideological affirmations, the reorganization never set out to correct the alleged defects of the Argentine railway system. Quite the opposite: it made them worse. The reorganisation of the broad-gauge lines weakened the attraction of the ports of Rosario and Bahía Blanca, and made the port of Buenos Aires even more attractive. The strong position the government was in when it acquired the British lines was squandered, and from then on the railway structure crystallized: when succesive administrations tried to initiate changes, they were impotent to do so.

When taking over the assets of the British companies it was established that the lines would for the time being continue to be run by their senior staff. Only a month later a provisional special committee was created, consisting of the Treasury and Public Works Ministers and the Presidents of the Central Bank and National Economic Council, to administrate the acquired networks and to plan investments. But the only concrete changes imposed on the railways were of a cosmetic nature: such as, for example, replacing the name of Retiro station with that of Presidente Perón. Shortly afterwards a Transport Ministry was created, when the Constitution was reformed in 1949, authorised to administer the railways and to coordinate the different transport modes. Among the immediate measures taken by the Ministry were: designation of a central committee for the purchase of railway equipment and supplies in London, exemptions from customs duties for those purchases, and free railway transport in certain cases.

In early 1950 Ferrocarriles del Estado (State Railways) was created, with the intention of introducing "an organisation to coordinate public service on the railways recovered for the national economy, with the object of realising all the elevated purposes which the Executive had taken into account when it nationalized this public service". Towards the end of the same year, each of the railways acquired the category of a State-owned Railway Company, all grouped under the heading of "Empresas Ferroviarias del Estado" (EFE, State-owned Railway Companies).

In 1952 the Empresa Nacional de Transportes (ENT, National Transport Corporation), was created, which incorporated all the nationalized transport companies of whatever ambit: aerial, terrestrial, marine or fluvial. The railways became part of the ENT, which aspired to unify the exploitation of the different forms of transport under a single State enterprise. This resulted in failure, since the ENT did not have sufficiently strong powers to organise itself into a truly effective entity, and was limited to identifying the deficit balances of the various transport enterprises it comprised.

With regard to government administrative structures relating to the railways, there existed the old General Railways Board which had been renamed as the National Railways Board, but following the creation of the Transport Ministry its powers became overshadowed by this new entity. In short, the State was the architect of railway policy, the controller of its services, and of the entity which provided them. Since the responsibility for these functions were distributed between the Transport Ministry, the National Railway Board, the National Transport Board, the National Transport Corporation and the different railway networks, the end result was confusion and and excessive bureaucracy. Many of the functions of these new structures were overlaid between them, which in practice neutralized them and led to policy conflicts, making the whole organisation inefficient. In reality, the railways continued functioning as autonomous enterprises, operating under the organisational inertia they had before nationalisation.

As for as railway operations went, the results obtained were not very encouraging. The personnel employed constantly increased.

It had varied with the amount of traffic when it was in private hands, between 154 thousand people in 1929, 130 thousand in 1936 and 158 thousand in 1947. By 1954 it had reached a record 204 thousand, and it continued to rise in the years which followed: 210 thousand in 1955, 214 thousand in 1956, 218 thousand in 1957. It is true that traffic had increased but an analysis of this increase leads to an understanding of the reasons behind the railway crisis, which was unravelling and would become worse in succeeding years. Cargo traffic had stalled, if it did not fall. In 1925, 35 million tons had been transported. This figure had fallen to 30 million by 1940. When the war ended it had recovered back to 35 million. But in 1954 the total transported was only 31 million and continued to fall. However, this figure, when expressed in ton-kilometers, achieved in 1954 the maximum of 15,000 million obtained by the private companies. This phenomenon might be explained by noting that competition from road transport had removed shorter-haul traffic from the railways. But to this should be added, as a decisive factor, the policy of concentrating all traffic through the port of Buenos Aires, closing down other ports and obliging merchandise to travel unjustifiably longer distances. In contrast, passenger traffic had exhibited a constant increase. The main reason for this was the enormous population which had concentrated around the city of Buenos Aires in a process of internal immigration, leading to an astronomical rise in suburban traffic. This process had begun during the existence of the private companies, and grew during the war years, when an accelerated industrialization programme attracted inhabitants from the interior to Buenos Aires in great numbers. It then became a serious problem to resolve, and it grew worse during the initial years of nationalisation. Other factors which influenced the growth in passenger traffic were the lack of government action in the construction and repair of main roads, difficulties the middle class had in purchasing motorcars, and the expansion of social tourism, which began to move great numbers of people to various places during the summer season. In 1941 the percentage of passenger as against cargo transport, measured in traffic units, was 24.2%. By 1947 it had risen to 35.8%, and in 1954 to 45.5%. Passenger traffic requires more personnel than cargo and this justified, in part, the previously noted rise; but it is also much less profitable, especially if it is impossible to increase the fares because the government policy is to keep ticket prices low. The same happened with cargo charges, for economic if not social motives. The result was the emergence of a deficit; the first, in 1947, was not revoked but allowed to multiply. The figures that follow are not easy to compare because inflation began to erode the value of money but it can be mentioned, for example, that in 1947 the deficit amounted to 117 million pesos, which had in 1955 grown to 1.400 million and in 1956 to 2.500 million. Politically motivated fares and charges instead of subsidies had made the State enterprise lose all sense of efficient operation.

One of the measures most criticised during the early years of the national administration of the former British railway companies was the policy of dismissing British staff members. When a company's owners change it is logical and natural that management staff should leave and be replaced by staff answering to the new owners. However, in the case of the railways it not only beheaded the enterprises, but the government went even further, attacking middle management, technical staff and against anything else of British origin. Using various mechanisms, such as early retirements, awards and other encouragements, the government policy was to "wipe clean" the former companies of "imperialist" elements, according to the nationalist propaganda of the age. The few professional staff who resisted and stayed in their railway posts became so disheartened at the manner of their treatment that they felt forced to retire.

This policy of replacing foreigners with Argentine employees was disastrous for the railways. In the first place, because most of those dismissed had held technical posts, and were engineers and railway transport specialists of great experience, especially those in the technical office team of each railway, where the future of the line would have been formulated. Thus the government threw away all the know-how gained from the experience of more than eighty years of railway development. It separated itself from those who really knew about railway activities. But an even graver mistake was substitution of the foreign technical staff by inexperienced

Argentines who were appointed to important positions solely because they belonged to the ruling Party, or were friendly with the President or his immediate collaborators. The result was the replacement of a technical elite which understood its trade, by a group of good government supporters who, although they might be well-intentioned, were not technically competent. The treatment of railway employees by the government was reprehensible. Partisans were rewarded and given unjustified promotions, but those who were not supporters of the Party were proscribed or moved to inhospitable regions. The railways, as a large part of the government administration along with other State enterprises, became a place of witch hunts, espionage and persecution against those who were not supporters of the governing Party.

In any case, insufficient investment was devoted to maintaining the tracks and rolling stock already affected by the 15 previous years of neglect during the private era, in an adequate state of repair. Even less were technical innovations installed in order to modernise the system. In 1947 there were 3,919 locomotives and 80,000 wagons; by 1954 the numbers had barely grown, to 4.135 and 83.400. Their use without requisite maintainance had increased by almost 20%; for locomotives the average distance run between repairs went from 48,800km in 1947 to 59,700 in 1953. Ten years after nationalisation, a feeling of frustration had replaced the initial optimism. As Ricardo M. Ortiz recorded in 1957:

> The country had gone through a trial stage with regard to the running of the railways, and it would not be correct to say that this stage had generated excessively favourable results. It had not led to the acquirement of the necessary materials in proportion to what the development of the country needed, neither had it managed to protect and encourage a local industry to achieve the execution of its destiny, nor had it professed any desire to solve the problems presented by the idiosyncrasy of the network, such as the diversity of gauges and the resistance to traffic coordination at junctions. And finally, nor had it devised a necessary and effective instrument of government capable of mobilising the Nation as a whole behind the progress of its railways. The frustrations produ-

ced by this mal-administration has led to the railways falling out of public interest and support.

The Modernisation of the Railways during the Perón Presidences

From the start of the 40s decade, there was a marked increase in the demand for passenger rail services, especially in the Buenos Aires metropolitan area. Until the 30s most of the demand had been within what has been called the Greater Buenos Aires cordon; i.e., between 15 and 25 km from the terminal stations, but by the 50s the increased demand had extended towards an outer cordon of between 25 to 40 km. Service provision had to be redesigned to satisfy this new demand, which implied a significant increase in train mileage and the need for more rolling stock. To begin with the need was covered by taking over some of the coaches used in longer distance services, but this was not sufficient. This led to a marked overuse of rolling stock and its corresponding additional maintenance costs. The demands on motive power and coaches reached the point where obsolete stock had to be brought back into use to meet the demand.

With regard to cargo traffic, though there was no marked increase but rather a standstill as a result of the macroeconomic situation the country was in, the most important modification announced by the government was a change to the regime for wagon distribution. This is a sensitive matter for any railway company, since how the wagon stock is distributed over the network can lead to its better utilisation. During the private company era the only criterion used was the priority of the request for wagons. Starting in the 30s, when the companies began to run out of sufficient rolling stock to meet the demand for cargo services, certain steps were taken towards optimising the distribution of their wagons, especially with regard to what was called "common wagon use" by the broad-gauge British companies. In addition, the government began to make decisions regarding the allocation of wagons to certain traffics, based on national economic needs.

The Peronist (Justicialist) Party proposed to change the whole system by establishing a "New Justicialist Wagon Regime", which in the end did not mean a change from the previous method but rather a reformulation of what was already happening under a new name. It did not lead to better utilisation of cargo services. In any case, the demand for cargo transport stalled, there was no shortage of wagons, and it was noted that most of the wagons were antiquated and obsolete. And even though there was no increase in the transport of cargo, it was evident that a new type of wagon would need to be obtained. For this reason a so-called "New Justicialist Wagon" was designed to overcome the shortage of useful wagons. In reality it was a copy of wagons already available. Only one was constructed.

With regard to passenger coaches, where the problem was more serious, especially in the suburban services, the Werkspoor factory in The Netherlands was contracted to manufacture 450 coaches for the broad and narrow gauge lines. The coaches were constructed from a design drawn up during the war by the four major British companies in order to unify passenger rolling stock. These new vehicles, which began to enter service in 1952, alleviated the situation by replacing the more antiquated stock, and even though the majority were allocated to long distance services, the coaches thus replaced were transferred to suburban services although they were not really appropriate for that purpose. Also, in 1951 a stainless steel Budd train was purchased from the Cheseapeake & Ohio Railway in the United States. But there were only 12 coaches, destined for a restricted luxury service. As for the narrow-gauge lines, the policy was to continue the practice of manufacturing coaches in the workshops at Tafí Viejo and Alta Córdoba, where vehicles mainly for the Belgrano Railway suburban services were constructed; it is also worth mentioning the construction of an air-conditioned luxury consist for tourist service. Regarding goods wagons, some covered wagons were constructed, and the acquisition from Canada of 1.542 flat wagons should be emphasised because of the valuable service they provided. Tank wagons were also constructed. But just as for passenger coaches as for goods wagons, the numbers of vehicles thus provided fell very short of the those required for service expansion and renovation, and so only served to aleviate the situation for a short time.

It can be said that the most erratic policy pursued was with regard to the provision of locomotives. To start with, the policy of the Peronist administration remained the development and construction in the country of a narrow-gauge diesel locomotive for the Belgrano Railway, an idea conceived by the State Railways. However, in 1948 IAPI negotiated the purchase of 145 narrow-gauge locomotives, after which the national manufacturing project was set aside.

There also were moves towards the manufacture of broad-gauge diesel locomotives in Argentina. Pedro Saccaggio was put in charge of this project. He was a retired senior BAGSR engineer, who had designed locomotives based on his experience in the Southern during the 20s and 30s, which included that of the first locomotives to be built from his designs. Two prototypes were made, called *La Justicialista* and *La Argentina,* and were exhibited all over the country as examples publicising the technical achievements of this new stage in Justicialist Argentina. To manufacture them in quantity the Fábrica Argentina de Locomotoras (FADEL, the Argentine Locomotive Factory) was created, with Saccaggio in charge. Although the plan was for more than 700 locomotives, a contract was agreed for the manufacture in Italy of 280 diesel engines. But, on the other hand, IAPI purchased 81 locomotives from Baldwin and General Electric in the United States, which demonstrated yet another example of official policy contradictions. The FADEL project, which during the three years of activity had only produced three locomotives and some body shells, was abandoned following the military coup in 1955. At the same time, resulting from the agreement with the government of The Netherlands, diesel locomotives were being built in the Verkspoor factory; however, these proved to be rather unsatisfactory.

Another contradiction which emerged in Peronist railway policy concerned the type of locomotive for future use. At first sight it would appear that the new State administration had adopted the use of diesel locomotives; however, there were large purchases of steam locomotives for both narrow and broad gauge lines between 1948 and 1951, and in 1953 steam locomotives were bought for the standard-gauge Urquiza Railway.

The government had also financed a project to construct a state-of-the-art steam locomotive in Argentina. The prototype, developed by Engineer Livio Dante Porta, emerged in 1951. On the basis of the results he achieved, the government contracted him to develop improvements for other steam locomotives in current use, and his work became known internationally.

To conclude, what the government did towards the development of locomotives, both nationally and by purchases from abroad, not only reflected the dual nature of its policy, but also showed its inability to define whether the future should involve diesel or steam traction. Over and above this, it should be noted that the government's introduction of diesel locomotives was important and was a first step towards the complete dieselization of the railways, which would only be achieved thirty years later. But the large scale introduction of diesel locomotive was not accompanied by an adequate maintainance policy. Workshops dedicated to diesel traction were not built; only old steam locomotive sheds were adapted to carry out the minimum necessary maintainance. Thus, in a short time, between five and seven years, half of the diesels introduced during this period had fallen out of service.

The erratic technical policies of the railways during the Peronist period led to a range of experiments. The new railway managers, who mostly ignored the know-how accumulated during the several decades of Argentine railway development, and without taking into account international best practice, began to do stupid things. One of these was the project to convert road omnibuses into railway service vehicles. In other parts of the world these had been experimented with during the 1930s, and promptly discarded. Here, omnibuses and small railcars that were adapted and constructed in railway workshops of all kinds, resulted in resounding technical failures. None of these vehicles lasted in service for more than a year. Another experiment involved the design of a light railcar, but only one prototype was built. Also, the well-known Spanish Engineer Alejandro Goicochea Omar was called upon to experiment with and develop a TALGO train, but no more than a trial was done with a prototype goods wagon. Neither did Peronism pursue a coherent policy regarding diesel railcars. There were experiments with vehicles constructed in the country, as previously mentioned, but at the same time diesel trains were purchased from the Ganz company in Hungary, based on an investigation which had been carried out by the BAPR.

Regarding development of the railway network during the Peronist administration, the discussion always had a clear stress on the need to improve the existing network, and to extend it. Usually cited and pompously inaugurated were several extensions to the network, including the branch to Socompa in 1948, and the branches to Pinamar and Rumi Punco in 1949. The government of Peron capitalized on all the publicity for the inaugurations of all the extensions. The most important of these was the branch to Socompa in the Province of Salta with its connection across to Chile. However, this branch arose from the completion of a work plan established in 1940 by President Ramón S. Castillo. Of the other two branches, the one to Pinamar on the Atlantic coast of the Province of Buenos Aires did not imply any need for construction, as the plan was to install a railcar service over an old line which had been constructed thirty years previously for the transport of firewood. The Rumi Punco branch was a tentative start on part of an incomplete section of an unfinished line from Catamarca to Tucumán and which was never constructed. Also inaugurated, in the Province of Chubut, was a passenger service over the few kilometres from the City of Comodoro Rivadavia to the Rada Tilly seaside resort. Neither was this a new project, but rather consisted of running a rather decrepit railcar over a line constructed twenty years before, during the development of the City's port. As we have seen, all these Peronist extensions of the network were previously conceived projects or the rehabilitation of existing lines, but in no way were they new, substantial extensions of the railway network, with a single exception. This was the project for a line parallel to the Andes range from Malargüe in the south of the Province of Mendoza to Zapala in the Province of Neuquén. Only a few kilometres were constructed, which never entered service.

The Argentine railway network, designed by private companies without any planning guidance from the State, was ill-proportioned and had some flaws which prevented it operating in a unified manner. There were redundant lines which lacked interconnections. To remedy this last omission, a few junctions were constructed: in Colonia Alvear (Province of Mendoza) the San Martín and Sarmiento lines were linked, and in Santa Isabel (Province of Santa Fe) two San Martín and Mitre branches were joind. In both cases only a few hundred metres of rail were required.

Peronist railway policy did not represent a significant change from that of the private companies in the past. Passenger service diagrams remained as before. However, new express services were introduced. In 1949, an *El Huemul* service was inaugurated between Buenos Aires and Bahía Blanca; in 1951, an *El Marplatense* service between Buenos Aires and Mar del Plata. These were no more than publicity stunts rather than real improvements. *El Huemul* ran only once per week, and *El Marplatense* carried tourists for only three months in the summer. Some trains were renamed with titles alluding to the regime, such as *New Argentina* and *Eva Perón*, etc. Another innovation during these years was the introduction of cross-network services. In 1952 direct trains were inaugurated from Mendoza to Rosario and Córdoba, from Rosario to Mar del Plata, and Mendoza to Bahía Blanca. The object of these services was to break the centralism of the Federal Capital and to link together important cities in the interior. But they were extremely limited, fell to one or two services per week because of poor demand, and did not represent any significant change, only the substitution of direct diesel trains where there already were connecting steam services.

As we have pointed out, no real railway planning emerged following nationalisation. The inertia in the system allowed the railways to continue to function as they had before. There was no attempt to seriously study the problems of the railways, nor to formulate proposals for their alleviation and for convincing service improvements. This could be argued to the contrary by mentioning the two quinquennial plans, published in 1947 and

1952 by the Perón government, which featured the railways. In both plans, however, though with marked differences in respect of the railways (and generally in all the themes), the plans do not contain other than vague generalities, in the style of "the railways should be efficient" or "the railway services should be at the service of production". The second quinquennial plan, even though it continues to formulate wishful thinking generalities like the first one, contains rather more precise railway policy ideas concerning rationalisation of the network and simplification of its infrastructure.

On 23rd July 1952 Minister of Transport Maggi signed Resolution 306/52 in which was established a study plan for the construction of new railway lines in many parts of the territory of Argentina. The proposals, with few exceptions, were very vague and illogical. It spoke of complementing existing lines with new ones, but these would need to be new narrow-gauge lines, even when the existing lines were broad- or standard-gauge, which would aggravate the diversity of gauges. This was particularly egregious in the case of the Mesopotamian region, where there already was a single gauge (standard), but nevertheless additional new lines were required to be narrow-gauge.

In early 1955, Resolution 499/55 of the Transport Ministry approved the plan for the restructuring of the lines accessing Buenos Aires. Among the basic principles in this plan there stands out an idea which often recurs in the policy for the railways: that they should be removed from the central zone of the capital. This meant that cargo terminals would be taken out of the city, and passenger stations would be moved close to the city limits, although how this should be implemented was not very clear. This plan never actually materialised, since it was formulated only months before the government fell, but it implied the notion that the railways would be prevented from participating in the urban transport market in favour of other means, particularly buses and cars.

As for an in-depth study of the network and its services, there was no serious intent to carry out a systematic investigation, as we have repeatedly emphasised, even though it was obvious that many services were over-provided for, especially on secondary lines with very low traffic densities. Some services were withdrawn and replaced by buses. In the Greater Mendoza area, between 1949 and 1950, services that still existed on suburban branches were removed, and in Patagonia the local service between Puerto Madryn and Trelew was replaced by a new bus route. Regarding uneconomic branch lines, in early 1955 two were closed in the Province of Santa Fe: one from Rafaela to Coronel Fraga and Josefina, part of the old Rafaela Steam Tramway; and another from Humboldt to La Pelada on the SFPR. Both lines were relatively unimportant and costly to operate; their closure demonstrates the start of a preoccupation with the latter point which in some way anticipates what would become a central theme of railway policy during the following decades.

Nationalisation had been fully supported by the two railway unions. Based on that, the unions adopted a subordinate role towards the ruling party. Notwithstanding this, an important event occurred in late 1950 and early 1951. Inflation was significantly depreciating the salaries of railway workers, and unease reigned. The union leaders denied the situation and refused to petition the authorities. Although no one expected it, the unease exploded into a violent railway strike without the support of their leaders, who remained on the government's side. In the face of this situation, and surprised by the strike, the political authorities threatened an intervention by the armed forces, a measure used previously in the history of the railways, but which was all the more significant given that it occurred during a Justicialist government. The conflict ended after arduous negotiations, and cost the resignation of the Minister of Transport, Juan F. Castro. This event marked a prominent demonstration of the fortitude of the railway workers as a group which would play a leading role in the history of the railways in the immediate future.

A Rapid Succession of Modernisation Plans

The military coup which occurred on 16th September 1955, called the Revolución Libertadora, inherited a complicated panorama within the railway system. The previous government did not, or could not, face up to the need for a coherent policy aimed at modernising and optimising the railways. It had presented a number of statements and declarations of intent which in no way changed the continuing decline of the sector. Deferred maintenance, and rolling stock and rail obsolescence, were pressing problems. The situation had been aggravated by the significant increase in passengers which occurred between 1956 and 1960. But the central problem of the railway sector, which went beyond its specific ambit, was the financial deficit: the balance between income and expenditure indicated that it was extremely loss-making. Not only was this a problem for the railways, but it transcended them, because it had become the main fiscal policy problem and so affected all national economic policies. The Revolución Libertadora attempted to draw up plans to reverse not only the lack of modernisation but also the deficit problem.

The new government decided to place the railways in a new institutional framework, a task which had been unresolved since 1948 and which had led to totally unsuitable and inefficient railway organisation. From nationalisation until 1956, the various railway lines had functioned as autonomous companies grouped into inefficient bureaucratic administrations like the National Transport Corporation, within the organisation chart of the Ministry of Transport. In 1956 it was decided to create a new State-owned railway company, to be in charge of the exploitation of all the lines, called Empresa Ferrocarriles del Estado Argentino (EFEA). This new entity meant that there would be uniform administrative criteria over all the network, and would permit the separation of railway operations, administered by the new public enterprise, from the authority fixing and applying policy for the sector, which would remain the Ministry of Transport.

The EFEA was led by a Board and its Chair. Engineer Dante Ardigó was designated the first Chair; he was a manager of vast experience after a long career in the old Southern Railway. Nationalist writers criticised this nomination as the abandon of a national railway policy and the handing over of the railways to imperialist spokespersons. Apart from these far from reality ideological diatribes, this brand-new company had to take on the challenges facing the railway: obsolescent, old-fashioned, inefficient, lacking rolling stock and with a huge operating deficit. As a first step, it was decided to reorganise the network. Two of the administrative units created during the Peronist government were eliminated. The Patagonian railways were made part of the Roca administration, and the Buenos Aires Provincial's transfer into the Belgrano Railway was finally confirmed. In that way the eight Railways were reduced to six. In addition the word "Nacional" was removed from the formal names of the Railways.

Other measures were also taken towards making the exploitation of the railways more uniform. A single criterion was established for numbering and identifying locomotives, railcars, and later on all passenger coaches, given that until then each Railway had used criteria inherited from the private companies. A common painting scheme for all railway vehicles was also established. New technical regulations were drawn up and brought into effect, to replace those of the private companies which still remained in force.

The new railway administration was concerned about obtaining rolling stock, and especially locomotives, to replace the obsolete fleet of steam locomotives and continue the policy of dieselising the whole network, which had begun some years before. Locomotives were purchased from the Alsthom, Alco, General Electric and General Motors factories. 1957 was the centenary of the inauguration of the first railway in Argentina, and this event was celebrated with an important railway exposition in Palermo (a northern suburb of Buenos Aires), where the new locomotives were exhibited together with other projects and advances. On the theme of the modernisation of the lines, we should note concerning the Sarmiento Railway suburban service that remodelling of the Once de Septiembre terminus had begun, that new Japanese electric trains had been purchased, and that automatic colour-light signalling had been installed on part of the line. The need to acquire locomotives and motor-coaches in large numbers quite quickly led to the mistake of buying a great variety of machines of different types, makes and technologies. This was done without previous investigation and it generated a diversity which was very onerous to maintain because of the lack of standardisation.

The creation of EFEA, which had positive effects by centralising coordinated operation of all the railways in a single entity, also had negative effects which were accentuated as time passed. The tendency of the Company to appoint too many senior managers, the uncontrolled growth of its central administration, and the never resolved tensions between the new governing body and the Boards of the six constituent lines (Mitre, Roca, etc), generated turbulence in the running of the railway network, although the effects of this would emerge a few decades later. In addition, the new organisation was essentially a bureaucratic entity, very far from being a company in the modern sense.

With regard to the exploitation of the railways, a marked increase in passenger numbers was observed during this period, whether long-distance, urban or suburban, reaching 622 million per year in 1958. This led to two immediate effects; on the one hand, the need to increase staff numbers, given that passenger services place major demands on personnel; and on the other hand, an increase in the deficit, as the passenger service was already making a loss, and there was no policy of raising ticket prices in line with the increased costs of operation. Also, in order to satisfy the passenger demand, it became necessary to overwork the rolling stock, and especially locomotives and other traction units, with consequent neglect of cargo services, where demand had not changed.

When Arturo Frondizi took on the Presidency of the Nation in 1958 a new and more encouraging stage opened in Argentine politics. The discourse of the new government was marked by its emphasis on development. The idea was that by means of energetic public policies the Argentine economy would be transformed away from the stagnation and dependency in which, according to the government, it found itself. This policy basically consisted of consolidating and shoring up some key sectors of the economy, those which when developed would break recessive tendencies and provoke significant growth of the economy, which would then act as a stimulus on all other activities. Among the basic sectors considered to be strategically important were the oil and automotive industries. The government therefore boosted these two activities, which achieved successful results in a short time. Argentina achieved self-sufficiency in oil and many automotive companies were established. However, it was clear that support for the oil and automotive industries necessarily had a negative effect on railway operations. If the use of road vehicles is encouraged, and there is a policy for the development of fuel for these vehicles, evidently this policy will tend to reduce the participation of the railway in the transport market, which in any case had already been happening during the past three decades.

The government argued that the railways should modernise and transform themselves for the demands of the Argentine economy, but this was not happening because they had been designed for an age when the only activities were agriculture and cattle raising. Railway transformation was almost an obsession for Frondizi and his collaborators, and the policy established was called the "Transport Battle"; a policy which would generate strong reactions in various sectors, not least from the unions, and would remain constant throughout his administration.

As we have seen previously, in spite of the passage of ten years and of experiments directed at changing the railways, there had been little significant change since nationalisation. Most of the infrastructure and rolling stock remained obsolete, and the new equipment introduced had been unable to reverse this situation. The financial state of EFEA had tended to worsen owing to the permanent railway operating deficit, a deficit which no government dared to correct, and which constituted a heavy charge on the economy as it was the main component of the overall fiscal deficit. Any policy for fiscal rationalisation inevitably had to attack the problem of the railway deficit, which could be attempted in several different ways. In 1959 a report prepared by the Comisión Económica para America Latina (CEPAL, the United Nations Economic Commission for Latin America) was issued, on the state of the railways in Argentina, and possibilities for their development. This report set out the harsh reality of the sector. The state of the network and its rolling stock were of an age and unsuitability such that a proper and acceptable service could not be offered. The diagnosis of the CEPAL report was based on the lack of modernisation and the minor role of the railways in the transport market.

Regarding how to approach the transformation of the railways, Frondizi did not have a clear policy, and various methodologies were tried out during the different stages of his government, characterised by an almost constant instability. In the initial stage railway policy was planned by the Transport Minister, López Abuin, who, in line with the CEPAL report, maintained that the problems of the railways could only be solved by means of a long-term transformation and modernisation process incorporating new operational techniques. López Abuin's policy coincided with a time of economic expansion during Frondizi's early years as President, and it began with significant modernisation projects, incorporation of rolling stock (continuing the acquisition of diesel locomotives), and the installation of new operational technologies such as automatic colour-light signalling. The idea of long-term modernisation had become established, but the resignation of López Abuin, victim of one of the many crises in the Frondizi cabinet, put an abrupt end to this stage.

As part of the incorporation of new rolling stock, we should mention that during this period contracts were signed for the acquisition of railcars from FIAT in Italy and the firm of Ganz Mavag in Hungary. The policy for the construction of diesel locomotives, which had been initiated by the government of Perón with the FADEL project, was reformulated; the accords with FIAT about the use of their existing and future diesel engines in a new type of lcomotive was renegotiated; and there was particular concern about the development of a national railway industry. In that sense, an accord was agreed with FIAT to install two industrial plants in Córdoba city, one for the manufacture of engines for locomotives and the other for the construction of passenger coaches and railcars, which formed the basis of what came to be called FIAT Materfer, the main provider of passenger rolling stock for the Argentine railways during the next three decades.

The second stage of Frondizi's railway policy was led by Engineer Álvaro Alsogaray, the Treasury Minister. The economic expansion having effectively come to an end during 1959, Alsogaray undertook a revision of the fiscal accounts and elimination of the deficit. As we have already noted, the railway deficit was the main cause of the Nation's deficit, and the Minister took steps to solve that problem. Although Alsogaray's proposals coincided to a great extent with López Abuin's plans, he was aware that there were no genuine resources to sustain a long-term recovery model, and, even if there were, the expected results would arrive far too late for the Argentine economy to survive in the face of the parlous state of the operational deficit. Alsogaray's policy consisted of, on the one hand, tariff increases, and on the other hand, reduction of operating costs. To achieve the latter, he proposed transfering to the private sector certain peripheral railway operations, such as restaurant cars and tearooms, cleaning, rolling stock maintenance, printing, cargo loading and unloading, etc. The idea of Alsogaray and Constantini, the Minister of Public Works, was to leave to EFEA only the actual operation of the railways, while all subsidiary tasks should be transferred to the private sector. Implementation of this transfer began, but it generated much tension with the railway unions. In April 1961, during one of the recurrent political crises, Alsogaray resigned and a new railway policy was installed.

The third stage of Frondizi's railway policy followed on in 1961 and had as protagonists Roberto Alemann, the Treasury Minister, and Engineer Arturo Acevedo, Minister of Public Works. In this stage, the railway deficit would be dealt with by means of a drastic and immediate reduction in the size of the Company. Lines that did not cover their operational costs would be closed and a large number of railway personnel would be made redundant, steps which began straight away, provoking the worst union conflict in the history of the railways in Argentina and which was one of the causes of the fall of the government in 1962.

Right from the start of the Presidency of Frondizi, the relationship between government and railway personnel was not a good one. The transfer to the private sector of some peripheral activities did not go down well. Added to the permanent salary discussions and the plans to reduce personnel, this generated a very strained atmosphere of recurring strikes. But when Arturo Acevedo announced in 1961 that drastic measures would taken with regard to the railways, and then after the first few lines were closed in June, this agravated the conflict. The railway unions proposed alternative plans in negotiations with the government, but Acevedo was inflexible. One of the most irritating points, especially for La Fraternidad union, was the introduction of new railcars, which could be driven by only one person instead of requiring the driver and firemen of a traditional locomotive. This was the spark which in the strained climate of the relationship with the government set off the serious conflict known as the Great Railway Strike of 1961. Towards the end of October a two-day strike took place, and in reprisal the government decreed the closure of various lines and workshops, which immediately detonated an indefinite strike.

This show of force caused the government to militarize the railways, in order to establish requisition of staff and other serious measures. The unions resisted and the conflict continued for forty days. However, total stoppage lasted for only ten days as the government was able to implement emergency passenger services using the armed forces. The strike was violent, with acts of sabotage and the use of force in several places. On the 10th of December, Cardinal Caggiano was able to mediate an agreement which permitted the return of some of the staff who had been dismissed, the restoration of services by the railway employees, and a promise to reach a consensus on salaries and re-equipping of the railways. It was also established that a revision of the branch closure policy was required, to enable a case by case analysis of the possibility of reopening some of them.

The question was: who won the 1961 strike? The government considered itself to be the winner, but it ended up terribly weakened by the conflict and did not survive more than three months longer. The unions also believed it was their victory. However, the closed branches were not reopened and many of the government's policy proposals which the unions had objected to were not withdrawn. Massive reappointment of railway staff who had been let go did not happen and the policy of personnel reduction continued in place. The 1961 strike was an inflection point in the history of the railways. The absence of the railway during forty days, and especially of the suburban services, led to the emergence of a whole alternative system of informal automotive transport which would compete with the railway. Passengers and cargo transported after 1961 drastically decreased. And thanks to the official publicity presenting and justifying government policy, public opinion formed the idea that the railway was obsolete, unfit for purpose and that, all things considered, there would be no major problems if it ceased to exist. It was true that the poor quality of the service backed up the official publicity, but the result from then onwards was that public opinion lost all interest in the railways.

Probably one of the most discussed themes of recent railway history in Argentina, together with the nationalisation in 1947, was the so-called Long-Term Plan drawn up during the presidency of Frondizi. Faced with the deteriorating situation of the railways, the poor perspectives they presented and the permanent rise of the railway deficit which was putting the fiscal accounts in jeopardy, in 1959 Minister Alsogaray contracted with the World Bank an overall study of transport in Argentina, which would diagnose the situation and formulate proposals for the following ten years. A team of North American and Argentine technical experts was formed, led by Thomas Larkin, a Colonel in NATO who had specialised on the theme of transport.

The Larkin Plan constituted the most ambitious plan of those produced in the 60s decade. It was finished and presented to the public in February 1962, during social and political circumstances which led to its immediate abandonment. The Great Railway Strike had only just ended, during which the unions had resisted any intent to reduce the number of railway employees. And in March 1962 the Frondizi government was overthrown by a military coup. The plan had been called the Long-Term Plan because in effect it aspired to set out railway policy over ten years. The study had started in October 1960. The overall idea was to reduce the extension of the network by closing unproductive branches, amounting to 21,000km in all, half of the total network, in two stages. The obsolete rolling stock, all steam locomotives, 70,000 cargo wagons and 3,000 passenger coaches, should be withdrawn and their scrap value used to pay for the purchase of half the new replacement diesel locomotives. Twelve workshops out of a total of 28 should be closed, and fifty or sixty thousand employees should be dismissed. The investment required would be 1.400 million dollars.

The plan was ambitious for two reasons. Firstly, because it contained an integrated study of transport in Argentina, including railways, roads and shipping. Something that had never been done before, and would never be done again. Secondly, because it set out a ten-year action plan, financed from internal and external sources. For that time, given the political and economic instability which had become chronic in Argentina, it was too soon to formulate plans over such a long timescale. In the Plan we can find a very good description of the technical and economic state of the Argentine railways and a series of recommendations. In terms of the reality of the situation the railways were in, it cannot be faulted. Nobody was unaware of this reality, which consisted of an ageing network, mostly obsolete rolling stock, an excess of personnel and an extremely negative income-expenditure relationship. What did generate controversy were the proposals in the Plan, which pointed to a restructuring of the railways based on a smaller network, fewer employees, operational modernisation and concentration of service on profitable corridors and traffics, leaving to other modes, automotive especially, the task of replacing the services withdrawn by the railway.

With regard to the redimensioning of the network, the Plan proposed the closure of about one third of the lines, based on its investigation of the whole network and an assessment of the future needs of the Argentine economy in the years ahead. The proposed reduction was to be significant; by the end of the period of the Plan one third of the network would be closed. The branch closures would be done in stages over five years, and only after paved roads had been constructed to replace the railway. The Plan recommended that special care be taken to not imply a reduction of the transport offering in each zone when lines were closed, and for that reason they had to be done in a staged manner. As for the reduction in staff numbers, it was obvious that as the network contracted and its operations modernised there would be a surplus of employees. Their numbers would need to be reduced, and this would be achieved using a variety of methods: voluntary retirement, early retirement, dismissal, the formation of employee cooperatives, and in other ways.

As far as the modernisation of railway operation was concerned, the Plan established the need for rationalisation and purchase of modern rolling stock. All steam locomotives would be eliminated and replaced by diesel motive power, and all wooden coaches and wagons would be replaced by steel rolling stock. The network would also in large part be renovated, and it was anticipated that new technologies such as automatic colour-light signalling would installed in order to speed up the movement of traffic.

An important detail in the Plan was to do with a modification of the way trains were to be run. There should be various categories of trains, both passenger and cargo: expresses between the principle population centres, in combination with local trains serving smaller centres. It was anticipated that running trains in this way would lead to a better use of rolling stock and reduce operational costs. Workshops and material stores would also be reorganised and appropriately specialised. Special attention was to be placed on the tariff structure, which should be matched as closely as possible to the actual operating costs. Three sources for the financing of the Plan were identified: external credits, mainly from the World Bank itself; contributions from the government; and the funds obtained from the sale of the materials arising from lifted rails and scrapped obsolete rolling stock.

For some of those involved, the Larkin Plan signified the beginning of a long-term policy for the railways; for others, it was the start of ills to come. Also, there were insinuations that it was an anti-railway plan. Arising from the conspiratory visions so common in Argentine history, the Plan was thought to conceal an intention to do away with the railways so as to replace them by automotive transport, in which the car, truck, petrol and oil companies would be directly or indirectly involved. Actually, the formulation of this plan took place during a period in which there predominated the idea that the railway was an obsolete technology, something which had been repeated by the nationalists since the 30s. It was also true that, in general, all the world's railways were going through restructuring processes roughly similar to those proposed in Argentina. For that reason we do not believe this conspiratory vision. What can be affirmed is that this railway reorganisation plan was made during a government which did not defend the railways, especially given that certain influential men in the presidential circle were taking an anti-railway stance.

Another talking point is the fate of the Larkin Plan. When it was presented in 1962, the Frondizi government was hanging on a thread, and it fell a few days later to be replaced by a weak, constrained government incapable of making decisions. The Plan never got going and neither were the resources it required ever obtained. And although the line closures made in 1961 were ascribed to the Plan, they never followed from its recommendations, but instead arose from the dynamics of the government's confrontation with the unions. Proof of this is that the closures were made before replacement paved roads were in place and that in some cases the Plan had specified they should be retained.

Changes of Course with Poor Results

The government of Arturo Umberto Illia, when he was elected President in 1963, inherited the railway problem, which remained basically unchanged: the operational deficit and the lack of service modernisation. However, at this time the economy in general experienced strong growth, which abated the constantly recurring financial crises, and this led to important improvements for the railways, resulting from the provision of new rolling stock initiated by the previous government. The complete set of Fiat and Ganz-Mavag railcars entered service, dieselisation of Roca Railway suburban services was finished, the Mitre Railway suburban line to Tigre was modernised with new Japanese electric multiple unit coaches, and long-distance services were improved by a provision of Japanese and Fiat Pullman coaches. New cargo wagons were also purchased. The workshops at Spurr (near Bahía Blanca) were finished, the first in the country designed for the repair and maintenance of diesel-electric locomotives. It can be said that this was a period of railway service expansion. The passenger service offer improved considerably following the change of attitude at the end of the Frondizi government.

Still pending was a permanent solution to the matter of the lines closed by Frondizi. These closures had led to regular reopening demands, mainly from the railway unions. In 1964 the Illia government decided to reopen some of the lines. This policy, which from one point of view could be seen as contrary to that in place since 1960, was nevertheless limited in scope and only applied to a few lines of high political importance, such as the former Buenos Aires Provincial Railway from La Plata to Olavarría. In spite of the reopening of this and other lines, it was only to run on-demand goods trains using very few personnel. No decision was made on any of the other lines closed by Frondizi. They were not reopened, nor were they definitely closed and the tracks lifted. The symbolic act of reopening some lines, although unnecessary and inconvenient for the railway company, was actually not an abrupt change of policy, but rather an attempt to emphasise the difference with respect to previous policies, and to placate the railway unions.

The Illia government charged the Consejo Nacional de Desarrollo (CONADE, the National Development Board), an organisation created by Frondizi, with the formulation of an action plan for the railways, within a general plan for economic development. This plan, which emerged in 1965, basically consisted of a set of speculations about the transport requirements of the Argentine economy and a succinct project for satisfying these requirements. It did not differ greatly from the Larkin Plan's concept for the establishment of an efficient, economically viable railway company, making use of modern technology with an suitable tariff regime aimed at a gradual reduction of the operating deficit. The plan emphasised that an increase in freight transport would arise from the sustained growth of the economy, forseeing that by 1970 the railways would be carrying 34 million tons. In order to satisfy this demand, rolling stock would have to be adapted and added to. But the reality was that by 1970 only half of the predicted increase in freight was reached. At the same time that the CONADE plan for the railways was formulated, the Transport Ministry presented its own plan, which though it objected to certain points in the former plan, was actually not very different.

Notwithstanding the intention to differentiate its railway policy from that of Frondizi, the Illia government followed some of the Larkin Plan recommendations. For example, express passenger trains with very few stops were established on the main routes, with improved passenger accommodation. Thus were born *El Aconquija* to Tucuman, *El Aconcagua* to Mendoza, *El Cerro Catedral* to Bariloche, and the *Estrella del Valle* to Neuquén and Zapala. In 1965 the complete dieselisation of the Sarmiento Railway was finished, finally eliminating steam propulsion and making it the first railway to achieve this objective.

Following the institutional crisis which toppled the Illia government and the appointment to the presidency of General Juan Carlos Onganía in 1966, the Army gave its full attention to the railway system. The strong man placed at the head of Ferrocarriles Argentinos (FA, the new name given from 1965 to EFEA, the State-owned Railway Company) was General Juan Carlos De Marchi. He held contradictory views on railway matters. For the first two years of his administration he increased the number of services, especially for passengers, even though it led to rolling stock being over-utilised, which immediately caused severe difficulties. It was the diesel-electric locomotives which suffered most, and by 1967 and 1968 a large number of them were out of service. Many old steam locomotives had to be reconditioned and put back into service hauling various passenger and goods trains.

During the second stage of De Marchi's headship of FA there was an abrupt change of policy. He imposed a significant reduction of the railway services on offer, and especially of passenger services. Between 1968 and 1970 this led to the elimination of passenger trains on many secondary lines, and on other lines, in order to avoid objections, services were reduced to only one train per week. On the other hand, services on main trunk routes were increased. The so-called "Flagship Trains" appeared, which were faster and more comfortable than standard services from Buenos Aires. The *Arrayanes* to Bariloche, the *Tucumán Express,* and the *Libertador* to Mendoza, among others, began to run and were very well accepted by the public. Thus the policy for passenger services was to discourage traffic on little-used lines, while increasing and improving services to stimulate traffic on trunk lines.

In 1967 there occurred two important changes in railway policy. In the first place, a decree was issued which reorganised FA, creating within it a "Central Office" which would take over many of the administrative activities of the various railway lines. This office began to grow in an undefined manner, competing with the Boards of the six lines, and in this way creating yet another bureaucracy which would conspire against efficient operation of the railway system. In the second place, with the aim of reducing the operating deficit, in early 1967 the government ordered a significant increase in both passenger and cargo tariffs, arguing that they needed to be raised to offset inflation. Although this had been absolutely true since the late 1940s, the practical result of this measure was a rapid fall in the demand for both passenger and cargo services. Mass cargoes traditionally carried by the railways, such as milk, fruit, and farm animals, were lost for ever or minimally called for. During this period the annual tonnage of cargo carried fell below that transported in any year since 1900.

In 1968 and 1969 the World Bank carried out a study which concluded with a set of recommendations which ended up in the Plan de Mediano Plazo (PMP, Medium-Term Plan) of 1970. In this Plan the elimination of steam traction was again proposed, via the purchase of 535 diesel-electric locomotives. Partial rolling stock renovation was anticipated by means of the purchase of 125 coaches for the electrified lines, together with 470 trailer coaches. Also contemplated was the modification and repair of 2,000 cargo wagons per year over a five-year period, which was the limit for execution of the Plan. Regarding the network, the plan proposed to improve some of the track to permit faster services and to close 9,000km of line. The anticipated total budget was 840 million US dollars, to be partially funded by the World Bank. However, the Plan was only half completed. As the newspaper *La Nación* wrote when it was announced, "the indecision and the continuing formulation of plans which are not carried out seems incomprehensible".

Unlike previous plans, the Medium-Term Plan was formulated by FA itself. Three consultancies were contracted: the Fundación de Investigaciones Económicas Latino-americanas (FIEL) for the economic projections; a North-American company to advise on modifications to the administrative structure; and finally a French consultancy to take charge of planning for the modernisation of railway operations. Implementation of the 1970 Plan began immediately, with a loan from the Banco Internacional de Reconstrucción y Fomento (BIRF, part of the World Bank). In summary, the Plan provided for, among other things, the establishment of a supernetwork of trunk lines with feeder lines. The guidelines provided for a reorganisation of FA, centralising the administration and doing away with the administrations of the six constituent lines, which would be replaced by four regions: the Southwest Region formed from the ex-Roca and Sarmiento lines; the Central from the ex-San Martín and the Mitre; the Northwestern from the ex-Belgrano; and the Northeast from the ex-Urquiza. This reorganisation was put into operation on the 1st of January, 1972.

The Medium-Term Plan, following on from the concerns of its predecessors – the 1962 Long-Term Plan and the 1965 CONADE Plan – became preoccupied with overcoming the eternal problem of the operating deficit. For this reason it determined that FA should cease to operate any economically disadvantageous lines, but that if the government decided to keep them in operation it should financially compensate FA for doing so. The Plan was also responsible for promoting improvements to the flow of information within the administration of the FA by proposing the establishment of a modern computing centre. All these innovations generated some opposition in the middle administrative levels of the FA. For example, it was never possible to computerise the movements of cargo wagons because it went against existing corrupt practices for assigning always scarce wagons to shippers in the long-established goods-yard movement offices.

Starting work on the implementation of the Plan implied the renewal of many kilometres of line and the manufacture of coaches and wagons. It was decided that all of these should have couplings which could be replaced by buckeye couplings, as a first step towards doing away with the existing couplings, so as to permit heavier tonnage trains. The policy concerning traction, aimed at the elimination of steam locomotives, was to incorporate 280 new diesel locomotives. A study was carried out to determine the best choice of manufacturer, and General Motors was selected as offering the most effective locomotives for the railways of Argentina.

The policy of running high-speed luxury passenger trains on principal trunk routes was the main attraction offered by FA. However, this policy could not be sustained because of its high cost, and by 1973 these trains had their permitted speeds reduced because neither the rolling stock nor the infrastructure could maintain the scheduled timings.

In 1973, when Juan Domingo Perón began his third government term, a Triennial Plan was announced which, just as in the case of his two five-year plans in the years 1946 to 1955, only contained vague formulations about railway policy of no real significance. When this new plan reached the railways, it was to nullify most of the previous government's attempts to modernise the system. In effect, execution of the PMP was terminated, marked simultaneously by closing down its finance from the World Bank. In March 1974 the recent regionalisation of the system was revoked, and the six main Railways were re-established. Plans to incorporate new rolling stock and renovate the infrastructure were abandoned.

The railway unions were given unaccustomed participation in the administration of the system, and this led to a stage of total politicization and internal factional fighting, reflecting similar behaviour to that happening in the government itself. As an illustration of this, we can report that authority to control ticket prices was given to the Juventud Peronista (an organisation for younger members of the Party, which confronted union leaders, sympathised with political groups in other countries (eg, Cuba) and supported violent political action). The different internal currents within Peronism pushed towards taking over the railway system, which entered an anarchic period. In an attempt to remedy this, the presidency of FA was handed directly to the unions, in the person of Cesáreo Melgarejo, leader of La Fraternidad. Many unproductive practicies which had started to be eradicated under the PMP were re-established and the personnel roster began to grow vertiginously. Proposals to combine the Retiro termini and other works which had been initiated were set aside.

During this period FA had a policy of increasing expenditure. For political reasons, passenger services which had been withdrawn as uneconomic and unnecessary were restored. Given that bus routes had replaced these services, this measure was not only useless but also counterproductive, since it increased the system deficit. Maintenance programmes were neglected, and it followed that trains began to be delayed owing to the bad state of the track and of the overused rolling stock. Passengers and freight continued to be lost, and the government was incapable of reacting because of its internal contradictions.

While José Gelbard was Economics Minister, the Corporación de Empresas Nacionales (CEN) had been created. This was a Commission formed to supervise all the non-military State-owned companies, and was made up of persons linked to the Confederación General Económica, a union business forum affiliated to the governing Party which debated a wide range of economic and labour questions with the government, and with the Confederación General del Trabajo (General Confederation of Labour Unions), on an equal basis with the latter, at least in theory, The CEN, on behalf of business people, should give the public corporations guidance directed more towards efficiency and less towards the securing of political ends. It claimed that they should be profitable, and if they could not be because of the imposition of political or social costs, there should be explicit compensatory payments.

The creation of the CEN led to confusion in the government administrative sphere, as it appeared to be a superpower with greater authority over enterprises than the State Ministries upon which they depended. The latter would be responsible for announcing policies for transport, energy, etc, but the CEN would direct the implementation of these policies, in the ambit of each enterprise through the corresponding sectors of the CEN, one being transport. However, inflation began to rise again once the agreements on prices and salaries had been broken owing to the so-called "Rodrigazo" crisis. This was named after the measures taken by the then Economy Minister in the government of Isabel Perón, Celestino Rodrigo, which caused hyper-inflation and paralysed the financial activities of the public corporations. In the railway sphere, towards the end of 1975 CEN increased its pressure on FA by setting up a working party on the railways, which dedicated itself to a systematic and critical examination of the FA budget in tense working meetings with the senior managers of the enterprise. Representatives of the Ministry of Transport also attended, but the meetings were controlled by the CEN. This process did not move forward, however, because the Isabel Perón government was overthrown in March 1976 and the Armed Forces took power, setting up the so-called Process of National Reorganisation.

Conclusions

The thirty years which lie between 1947 and 1976 constituted a period marked by crises in the various models applied to the running of the railways. By 1947 the private company model for the railways had failed. The companies were economically ruined and any possibility of reviving them was illusory. To avoid their collapse, the logical and inevitable way forward was nationalisation and operation by State-owned companies. By 1976 this model had also failed. The State in Argentina had shown that it lacked the capacity to continue operating the railways. All the problems that the Argentine railway system suffered from in 1947, by 1976 not only remained unsolved but had become significantly worse.

These thirty years of railway crises can not be examined independently without taking into account the situation which the country was experiencing. In the second half of the twentieth century Argentina as a country lost its way. Successive political and economic crises made worse by mutual feedback generated a long retreat. The Argentine government had been incapable of avoiding being a victim of major internal conflicts in its society, when not the cause of them. The State as an institution had not been able to carry out even its most elementary functions. Given the failure of the Argentine State to establish a stable and sustainable country, the railway system could not be expected to have had a different fate. The State crisis accelerated the crisis in the railways, which in turn aggravated the general crisis in the State.

Nationalisation of the foreign-owned railways opened up the possibility of starting a new railway policy. However, it generated a great polemic about its advisability and the price paid for it, a controversy aggravated by the political confrontation of that time. This led to the great discussion being on the act of nationalisation itself, rather than on the future of the railways. Nationalisation should have been the starting point of the new policy; however, both the government and public opinion limited themselves to criticizing or defending the purchase without thought for the future. The new policy exhausted itself in the act of taking over the railways, which was marked by much publicity but little more than that.

Another failure of the State was to not have given the railways an efficient management structure. Initially a number of different forms of administration were tried out, but in reality these were the structures that had existed in the companies before 1947. The network was not organised into a single State-owned company, from a legal point of view, until EFEA was created in 1956. This new organisation, which went through name changes and significant modifications of its internal structure, lasted for nearly forty years but was never capable of transforming itself into a real company, even though it was one in the legal sense. It never had real autonomy, nor a stable technical bureaucracy, nor leadership capable of achieving its objectives, nor a flow of funding to ensure its functional independence. The State company lost sight of any commercial vision for the railway business, and in fact transformed itself into another organ of the State bureaucracy, impotent in its march toward ruin. There were various attempts to give it a more commercial character, but these either never took off or were ineffective. Nor was it free of constant changes in senior personnel motivated by changes in the political situation, and this conspired against the possibility of any long-term development process.

Following nationalisation of the network and the State becoming the only protagonist of railway activities, the development and control of service functions were inevitably fused. Thus the controlling government offices, very small and lacking serious resources, in fact became subordinated to the various State-owned railway companies, which because of their size, economic capacity and multiple human and technical resources imposed themselves on the government offices. The controlled dominated over the controller. The same happened to the main strands of railway policy. In many cases the State company (the FA) determined them, when this should have been done by the technical offices of the Ministry of Public Works. The relationship between those responsible for railway policies and the companies was not a peaceful one. The reality was that whoever was politically in the best position imposed themselves, blurring the complicated and ineffective structure of the State organisations which were supposedly governing railway activities.

With the railway monopoly in the hands of the State, many practices which the old private companies had devised as palliatives against the critical situation they had been in were abandoned, like door-to-door freight services, or the original container service inaugurated by the Pacific Railway, or combined rail-bus passenger services. The railway turned within itself and ignored other modes of transport, without taking into account that those were the very modes which were taking away their traffics. Instead of linking with those other modes in order to form an integrated transport system, the railways chose to remain apart without realising that they were already in weak position with regard to competition with the automotive transport mode.

The State also did not realise that it was necessary to have an integrated transport policy. Prior to nationalisation, the private companies had pleaded for transport coordination; that is, for a single policy in the sector which would avoid competition between the different modes under unequal conditions, a policy which they thought to be absolutely necessary. Following nationalisation, when the coordination would have been relatively easy to achieve as almost all transport was in the hands of the State, it did not happen. There was a railway policy, an automotive transport policy, a ports policy, and none were in any way linked. For example, the ports and the railways, that necessarily must coordinate their activities, and in fact had done so before nationalisation, had to report to different organisations with their own distinct policies, which greatly obstructed the flexibility of the limited relation between the trains and the ships, which was naturally detrimental for the railways. The same thing happened to the policy for roads. When new highways were being constructed and investments in the rail network were being made there was no coordination between the government departments involved that could lead to a common vision and the avoidance of wasted resources.

With regard to policy for the purchase of rolling stock, it can be said to have been anarchic. In the case of locomotives, 1.500 diesels of many different models, manufacturers and tecnologies were bought during the period. This variety conspired against the recommended standardisation of rolling stock units, already made use of before nationalisation. Purchases were generally made in a hurry, in response to urgent needs. Attention was paid only to matters of finance and credit, with no consideration of whether the units would be suitable for the use to which they would be put on the railways of Argentina. Consequently, a large number of locomotives were, because of their characteristics, not being put to good use or going out of service soon after purchase, a significant waste of funds. This problem was not as serious in the case of passenger coaches and freight wagons as the purchases were relatively minor, but standardisation was again neglected. The acquisition of motor coaches and electric multiple units for the suburban lines, which was a separate story because they had a different type of coupling, led to problems of incompatibilty with the regular rolling stock. Apart from this, we can say that the country made a serious effort to modernise its rolling stock, but without doubt this effort could have been more effective and better used.

Only towards the end of the 70s decade were technical norms and a degree of uniformity established for use in future vehicle purchases, but by then twenty years of erratic policies had passed.

The railway network had regressed during the period. In 1947 its lines extended over 42,578km, which by 1977 had fallen to 36,930km. This quantitative decrease was caused by the closure of some uneconomic lines and branches. Measured in kilometres this decrease is not significant, but in qualitative terms the network was in a much poorer state than in 1947. With the exception of some main lines which had a major upgrade at the end of the 60s, the rest of the network suffered from serious problems difficult to remedy: light-weight rails and earthen ballast. This meant that antiquated steam locomotives had to be kept in service on all these lines, because their light traffic did not justify replacement with heavier rails and gravel-stone ballast. It was obvious that once these locomotives were scrapped these lines would have to be closed, as indeed many were. The problems of deferred maintenance had also been significant. Extensive tranches of the network and especially crucial infrastructure such as bridges, viaducts and culverts, were in an unsafe condition which limited the carrying capacity of the tracks, that in Argentina was always quite low.

During the period there were no large extensions of the network. Even previously proposed projects which would have served useful purposes, like the southern transandine crossing (Zapala to Lonquimay in Chile) or the transpatagonian railway, were deferred. However, from the 40s the Argentine government invested enormous quantities of money on the construction of railway lines in Bolivian territory. The excuse was to generate traffic for the Belgrano Railway network, though this did not conceal the actual intention of countering the influence of Brazil, which was also constructing lines in Bolivia. Thus projects were delayed and maintenance deferred while economic and human resources were deployed in a foreign country, on works of a utility which is now doubtful.

We can summarise exploitation of the railways during the period as follows. Cargo transported in 1975 amounted to almost half of that carried in 1947, the railway having lost its share of the transport market to road haulage. In terms of tons per kilometre the loss was smaller, as short-haul cargoes constituted much of the loss. But also the kind of cargo transported tended to be high-volume primary products, which were difficult for trucks to cope with, such as gravel, cement, cereals and oily foods, petroleum, and timber, for which rates were necessarily low. Higher value freight, such as general cargo, parcels and packages, and refined products, was almost entirely lost. In other words, not only was the amount of cargo carried significantly reduced, but also it almost exclusively involved low-tariff primary products.

Passenger numbers went up and down, the best years being towards the end of the fifties. The numbers varied differently between long-distance and metropolitan region passengers. Over the period the result was unfavourable; that is, fewer passengers were carried in 1975 than in 1947. However, a multitude of passengers commuted on the suburban services of the metropolitan region; so many, in fact, that it would have been impossible to substitute enough buses to replace the railway services. Finally, there was a very marked fall in long distance passenger numbers. In spite of great efforts made at the end of the seventies to improve services and retain passengers, the results were disappointing. It proved impossible to break the decline in long distance passengers, who massively opted for coach and aeroplane travel, as these modes were developed and highways were paved.

The decline in cargoes and passengers transported during these thirty years can be explained by, among other factors, the marked fall in the quality of the railway service. In general, the comercial viability of services had decreased, because journey times had increased and punctuality had fallen. In addition, dining car and sleeper service was degrading. At the end of the 60s and the beginning of the 70s coaches with wooden seats were still in use and not heated. There were few air-conditioned coaches, used only for certain high-category services. It can be said that in 1970 one travelled under the same conditions as fifty or sixty years before, but probably more slowly and not to the timetable. Therefore it was difficult to retain passengers in the face of competition from automotive transport, which easily adapted itself to changes and offered a level of comfort and speed far superior to that of the train.

Cargo services also suffered from a significant degradation in quality. Punctuality disappeared and journey times lengthened. The lack of maintenance and defective locomotives obstructed the orderly running of services, and since the running of passenger trains had priority over cargo trains, any breakdown of the latter condemned them to long waits in the goods yard sidings without locomotives. Added to this, robbery of goods from the yards was endemic and increasing. Shippers of fish and other perishable cargoes which required punctual delivery left the railway and moved to road transport using trucks.

A constant concern during these thirty years was the tariff problem. Railway fares and charges, from the effects either of inflation, or of political decisions, or of competition from other transport modes, were always having to be set below the actual costs of operation. Over the whole period a specific policy was to keep passenger fares low, and especially so on the suburban lines. This policy, which in the long term led to the destruction of the system, also generated an implicit subsidy of property development in Greater Buenos Aires, which expanded rapidly, impulsed by the low fares into the center of the city. Freight charges were kept low in order to compete with road transport, which continued to increase its market share. The major shippers constantly threatened that they would transfer their goods into trucks if charges were increased, which set an impassable tariff barrier. In addition, the bureaucratic administrative structure of the State-owned railway conspired against flexible tariff setting. Without doubt the railway should have had some autonomy in the setting and modifying fares and charges, to adequately reflect actual costs and changes in the transport market. The system of tariffs regulated by the Ministry of Transport and uniformly the same over the whole network, prevented a proper approach to this problem.

The other constant concern over this period of thirty years is the operating deficit which, apart from ups and downs, continued to rise. Measured in terms of the relation between income and expenditure, the exploitation ratio was 1.2 in 1947 and became

2.7 in 1975, more than double. This means that for every peso of income in that year, 2.70 pesos were spent. The deficit had to be covered by the National Treasury, and it therefore impinged on the Nation's fiscal accounts. The State-owned railway company had permanently to negotiate with the authorities for additional tranches of funding to cover the deficit. This, apart from being a severe drain on the fiscal accounts, also made it impossible for the railway company to operate independently. This permanent need for funds to cover the deficit took resources away from improvement and maintenance works.

The railway industry in Argentina deserves a separate paragraph. The continual demand for railway equipment generated a considerable industrial sector providing a wide range of manufactured items, including goods wagons, coaches and even locomotives. But this industrial sector was only possible because FA purchased anything that it manufactured, at any price, arguing that this would stimulate railway manufacturing expertise in the country. The result was to have created a parasitic industry, which was not competitive and depended totally on the State-owned company. As in the case of most Argentine manufacturing industry, it was incapable of becoming competitive and if for some reason demand from the railway ceased, all railway industrial activity faded away and almost disappeared, which demonstrated its weakness.

The railway unions also contributed to the decay of the system. In 1947 there were two unions, La Fraternidad for drivers and firemen, and La Unión Ferroviaria for all other railway employees. Traditionally the railway unions had been very fierce supporters of the rights of railway workers. The politicization of all unionism in Argentina also reached the railway unions, and gradually were coopted into the majority party. They ceased to act on behalf of their members, the workers, and acted in response to the interests of the party grouping to which they belonged. During this period the two original unions were joined by two more, the Asociación de Señaleros (Signalmen Union) and the Asociación del Personal de Dirección (Senior Staff Union). In general, the unions opposed, more or less strongly, any move towards modernisation of railway operations. This was possible not only because of their strength as a movement and the severity of their strikes, but also because of their position in the FA. Formally or informally, the unions were installed within of the management structure of the railways. They occupied managerial posts and in 1975 they were even given overall control of the State-owned company. It is thus that, by holding senior positions in the formal and informal decision structure of the railways, they also can be held responsible for the poor results of railway operation over these thirty years. It can be said that in general the railway unions favoured having more members in the short term over supporting the transformation of the railways into an efficient and sustainable operation in the long term.

Finally, we must ask ourselves what role public opinion occupied during this railway period. The nationalists, ever since the 30s, had maintained an anti-railway stance, which was gradually adopted by public opinion. The railways ceased to appear in the newspapers unless there was an accident or a strike. There predominated the notion that the railway was an obsolete transport mode from the past which should be replaced by modern modes using motorcars and aeroplanes. In this context, what happened on the railways hardly mattered; public opinion was indifferent if not hostile, so it was difficult to take measures leading to the development of the railways.

To summarise, during these thirty years the railway, whose role was the transport of goods and people, suffered a significant decline in all its aspects; which might explain, all things considered, why it became aimless and defenceless in the face of innumerable contradictory short-term influences. Passengers wanted cheap fares, shippers low charges, suppliers high prices, workers better remuneration, unions more members, politicians free rail travel and railway jobs for their friends, and governors and mayors all over the country wanted to take over lands occupied by the railway. And the railway, in one way or another, satisfied all of these desires at the cost of its own existence. Everybody took advantage of the railway to the disadvantage of the railway. Nobody was capable of being the champion of an efficient railway system, useful to the people of Argentina.

In the 1950s diesel railcars were acquired to replace steam-hauled passenger trains. Ganz diesel railcar on the Urquiza Railway. *(Photo: Museo Nacional Ferroviario)*

In order to "dieselize" the Argentine railways a large variety of locomotive types and models were purchased. General Electric locomotive manufactured in 1953 for the General Bartolomé Mitre Railway. *(Photo: Museo Nacional Ferroviario)*

National manufacture of diesel locomotives was not successful. An improvised attempt resulted in the GAIA locomotive, of which 280 were made between 1963 and 1970. *(Photo: Museo Nacional Ferroviario)*

Electric coaches for the General Urquiza Railway, manufactured in Argentina under a Toshiba license. From 1955 onwards, coaches from Japan were acquired for modernization of the suburban lines. *(Photo: Museo Nacional Ferroviario)*

An ancient locomotive on the General Belgrano Railway, hauling a goods train made up from a variety of old cargo wagons. At the end of the 1970s, this was an anacronism. *(Photo: Museo Nacional Ferroviario)*

JUAN PABLO MARTÍNEZ

5 | A Traumatic Period of Reforms 1977 – 2006

The next period in our history of the railways in Argentina starts in 1976, a year in which a new rupture of the institutional order took place, with enormous political, economic and social consequences. It occurred at the most dramatic moment in the modern history of Argentina, when the country was in a situation of quasi-civil war during which acts of violence by factions operating illegally happened every day, while the State seemed incapable of responding effectively and with due regard to constitutional order. In March that year a coup established a military government, the so-called Proceso de Reorganización Nacional (National Reorganisation Process). Certain civil rights were rescinded and the dictatorship used very drastic means to prosecute the fight against armed opposition. Exhaustion of this regime, due to the collapse of the economy and the disastrous Malvinas (Falklands) War led to the re-establishment of democracy in 1983.

The democratic system re-installed that year achieved a valuable reconstruction of institutional practices, but was unsuccessful in facing up to the economic and social situation inherited from the dictatorship. Weakened politically, the Partido Radical (Radical Party) government of President Raúl Alfonsín was unable to avoid a grave economic crisis which culminated in the 1989 hyper-inflation, and caused an anticipated transfer of government to President-Elect Carlos Menem, who successfully overcame inflation, realized an ambitious if controversial economic transformation, and survived two successive mandates, although this was followed by a new phase of instability.

The large Argentine railway system could not fail to suffer from these political changes. During decades of public administration, all aspects of its activities had deteriorated, in spite of transitory periods of reform and apparent recovery. At the start of 1976 all its indicators were negative and tending to worsen. Previous attempts to reform the railways had not lasted long. The most profound reforming endeavour, the Larkin Plan, was never implemented, in spite of the incorrect attribution to it of the untimely 1961 line closures. The later Medium-Term Plan 1971-1975 had suggested similar proposals for rationalisation, but except for measures taken during the early years of the former military administration, some of which were cancelled after 1973, it remained a dead letter. With governments of variable origins and tendencies, the powers that be had not managed to impose a permanent reform on the activities of the railway, even when they had actually proposed doing so.

During the decades that began in 1976 matters would happen differently. In 1976 the dictatorship moved rapidly and energetically to impose strict reforming measures which, despite all previous experience, were typically traditional and did not have a decisive impact.

Although in December 1983 democratic government was re-established, railway policy did not experience the drastic change that it might have expected. This was because the original railway policy of the military government had been diluted as a result of political changes during its regime, and because railway policy at the beginning of the democratic administration showed a marked continuity with that of the previous government. In effect, during the Radical government, which undertook the first stage of democratic political life between 1983 and 1989, railway policy applied a sequence of three approaches which, with hindsight, led to the outcome which would occur at the end of this period. Thus in 1989 the new government abandoned traditional railway reorganisation measures and with unexpected conviction launched itself down the route of privatization by means of concessions, which after a few years would put an end to the large State-owned railway system which Ferrocarriles Argentinos (FA) had been.

This sub-period of privatisation, starting in 1989, in its turn went through markedly different phases. The apparently successful initial phase was interrupted by the great economic, social and political crisis of 2001. It was succeeded by a phase of great uncertainty over the future of the concession system, while the country went through the point of deepest recession and the external debt crisis. From 2003 there began an economic recovery phase which was reflected towards the railways, although in different ways depending on the privatised concessions involved.

Railway Policy Aspects of the Military Government

When the military government was installed, management of railway policy passed from the CEN to the Ministro de Economía y Trabajo (Minister for Economy and Labour). The latter in turn delegated this function to the Secretaria de Transporte y Obras Públicas (SETOP, Secretariat for Transport and Public Works). To lead FA, the military government appointed a retired officer who had occupied senior posts in the military administration of the railways which had ended in 1973. It might have been thought that this appointment would leave railway policy totally in the hands of the armed forces, or at least keeping FA under their control; but that did not happen. Due to the president of the Nation having great confidence in the Economy Minister, the SETOP was able to take over railway policy with energy and total authority, and impose it on FA.

SETOP devised an action plan which involved a return to the rationalization measures recommended fifteen years before in the Larkin Plan: closure of uneconomic lines and branches, withdrawal of little used passenger services, closure of redundant workshops, withdrawal of steam locomotives, and other measures. One of the first measures undertaken was the withdrawal of a number of passenger trains on secondary lines and the closure of stations which, because they lacked commercial activities, did not justify being kept open purely for operational reasons. Between

1976 and 1980 some 560 stations were closed, and passenger services were reduced by some 18 million train / km, about 30% of the previous total; almost all of this reduction was suffered by intercity trains and local services in the interior of the country. Some of the train withdrawals were purely a formality, because they had actually ceased operating some time before, but nevertheless continued to appear in railway timetables. This was the case, for example, of the railcar which ran between Comodoro Rivadavia and Colonia Sarmiento, which had ceased running to after it had been impossible to repair a mechanical breakdown in the modest local workshop, and the absence of a physical link to the rest of the Roca Railway network impeded its replacement by another unit.

Dimensioning the Network

The two most troubled matters were the closure of uneconomic lines and the rationalization of workshops. For the first, after some very tense situations in early 1977, a coherent working arrangement was created between SETOP and FA. The latter would carry out the required technical and economic studies — as they could count on a group of competent and experienced professional staff — which would then be assessed by a SETOP technical committee in order to avoid any divergence of objectives. The results and conclusions of the study were then passed to the Board of FA, for them to determine whether the line under study was uneconomic or not. In the former case, FA would apply to the government for permission to proceed to the closure of a line. A committee of SETOP officials would then visit and travel over the line and make a recommendation authorising either closure and lifting of the track, or just closure. In this way some 5,500km of line were closed between 1976 and 1980; much had already been out of use, because either there was little demand for service or the poor state of the track prevented the operation of diesel locomotives, which were heavier than the old steam locomotives.

Decisions to close lines continued to be made, in a way which was often irrational in many cases. Sometimes only closure was authorised, as in the cases of the Patagonian lines from Comodoro

Rivadavia and Puerto Deseado, where the rails were not taken up because the Ministry of Defence continued to regard them as important for military purposes. In other cases there was a lack of strategic vision. Such was the case of the line from Avellaneda to La Plata, of the former Buenos Aires Provincial Railway. Following removal of its passenger service, the Monteverde – La Plata section was closed. This did not take into account that the line provided reserve capacity for the completion of the suburban network in the south of the Metropolitan Region. Towards the end of the military government, the Municipality of La Plata was allowed to lift part of the track located in the southwest limits of the city in order to widen its ring-road. Years later freight services between Avellaneda and Monteverde ceased, and the line slowly deteriorated, its infrastructure demolished, finally built over, and now almost irrecoverable.

Line closures were the measure most criticized in the years that followed. They were blamed for the decay and death of hundreds of small villages in the interior of the country, which is undoubtedly an exaggeration, if not entirely wrong. The truth is that the so-called uneconomic lines and branches did not generate sufficient demand for transport to be able to cover a reasonable fraction of the marginal cost of keeping them in service. Some had been laid in order to exploit an activity (eg, mining) which later ended, but which had attracted a population related to that activity. Others were redundant lines laid by the private railway companies during the period of unrestricted competition, or by the State at national or provincial level; in these cases the lines had an insignificant zone of influence, its stations historically generated little cargo, and their relatively late construction had not led to many significant centres of population. When these redundant lines found themselves faced by road competition, their scarce traffic fell even further, their operation became even more uneconomic, and their stations offered little or no goods movements.

In many cases, the decline of the villages was accelerated because they were left on the margins of the paved road network. In the Province of Buenos Aires, new paved roads had been deliberately and mistakenly constructed far away from the railway villages. Being far from the paved road, they ceased to be convenient places for establishing grain elevators or bringing together commercial activities connected with rural produce. The running down of railway activity and the decline of the villages were parallel processes which reinforced each other.

When line closures were imposed, it was the culmination of a process which had been evolving over several decades and passenger services, if they still existed, only had a secondary role in satisfying the needs of the population. For that reason, it is more correct to state, finally, that lines became inactive because activities in their immediate region had been in decline for a long time, and not to the contrary. That this was really the case is supported by a recent statistical analysis of objective data relating to about 700 villages, the conclusion of which is that their demographic evolution, and their transformation into "ghost villages" in particular, can not be attributed to the railway policies launched in 1976.

Workshop Closures

Workshop closures were also controversial. Following a report from Misión Sofrerail (a French consultancy), it was known which workshops would remain in the future and which would close. Some were small and ancient, and others provided services condemned to extinction, like the repair of steam locomotives throughout the network. Towards the end of 1977, SETOP and FA had determined which workshops would stay open, but FA presented its draft 1978-1982 Medium-Term Plan, proposing that the condemned workshops would be closed only during the final year of that period. This met with an energetic reaction from SETOP, which ordered the immediate closure of Strobel, Santa Fe and Cruz del Eje, steam locomotive workshops already being run down. The measure was carried out, and qualified personnel were relocated to nearby workshops at Paraná, Laguna Paiva and Córdoba, respectively. These inopportune measures all had obviously painful personal impacts and some had serious consequences on the economies of the places affected. The problem was reproduced, on a smaller scale, by the withdrawal of steam traction, which gave rise to the closure of many loco depots over the whole system.

Later the same measure was applied to the Tafí Viejo workshop. This had been the great workshop of the former Argentine Northern Central Railway, which grew to employ three thousand workers and staff. Its two main activities had been the repair and servicing of steam locomotives, and the construction of several hundred passenger coaches.

Avoiding the social impact of workshop closures was almost impossible. A human factor which had impeded FA from carrying them out was the effect on the hundreds of families concentrated in the location of the workshop which depended on its employees. This factor was less significant if the workshop was implanted in a large city, where the displaced workers could easily be absorbed by local industrial activities; but this was never the case in medium or small size towns or villages, where the workshop was the largest employer. For understandable reasons, the larger and better equipped workshops were located in big cities or close to them, and it would not have been logical to close them in order to shift their activities to small establishments which anyway lacked the infrastructure required to absorb eventually significant transfers.

As in the case of line closures, it fell to FA to implement the adjustment measures demanded by SETOP, an ungrateful task because it involved carrying out painful measures in a peremptory manner, which could have been done in an orderly way during the previous five-year periods. The consequence of what has been described was that personnel numbers fell from 155,000 in 1976 to 97,000 in 1980, a figure which with ups and downs would remain fairly steady during the following decade.

Attempts towards Structural Reform

The policy applied by SETOP had certain positive components which could serve as a basis for the future development of the railways. These were incorporated in the 1971- 1975 Medium-Term Plan, where SETOP categorised the lines as follows:

- Buenos Aires suburban network.
- Interurban (Intercity) passenger network.

- Primary inter-regional network.
- Secondary network.

This categorisation took note, above all, that the projected investments should be assigned in accordance with the character and function of the lines. The intercity lines did not form a genuine network, but rather formed a star which radiated from Buenos Aires towards the major cities of the interior, thus defining corridors which would have higher speed and more frequent services. These lines coincided in part with the "super trunk network", an unhappy expression in the 1971-1975 Plan document. Policy for the intercity trains was that they would exist on these routes, where at least one daily high-capacity passenger train was required. This implied a policy of leaving lower demand cross-country routes to omnibus services. A detail to note is that the Interurban (Intercity) Network did not include the metre-gauge network; it was admitted that on a gauge of one metre it would not be economical to run trains at the maximum speed required to achieve a competitive journey duration. But this deficiency was made up for by providing bus services between Tucumán and Salta or Jujuy, and from Corrientes to Resistencia, the only significant urban centres not reached directly by the intercity passenger network.

The primary inter-regional network was the main cargo system, formed of the lines which, according to SETOP, should be considered the basic mesh of the Argentine system. All the inter-regional connections provided by the railways were included in this category; for instance, Mendoza-San Juan-Córdoba, Rosario-Bahía Blanca, etc. As passenger services on these lines were not forseen, line speeds could be lower than those of the intercity network: 70, 50, or 40km/hour depending on the importance of the traffic.

Concerning the Buenos Aires suburban network, 700km of lines were identified upon which the predominant activity was the movement of commuting passengers. The policy on this network was to intensify services by means of technological improvements and specific investments. SETOP pushed FA to pay serious attention to the business of suburban trains, which it perceived as one of the bastions of the future railway, perhaps the most secure of all.

If FA was not always happy executing the policies determined by SETOP, it made the subject of suburban trains its own. Responding to the policy enunciated for the suburban lines, in 1980 FA created at its heart a new office, called Gerencia de Línea Metropolitana (GLM, Office for the Metropolitan Line). The aim of this strategy was an intelligent one. Never before had there existed in FA any move towards the creation of service entities in response to the railway market or its clients. The metropolitan market was a very important one, and though FA had many technical specialists – rolling stock, timetables – they were relegated to operating functions, whereas the market did not exist at the organisation level.

It was necessary to create a group oriented towards market and client services, and to that end a start was made by taking away from the Belgrano Railway the southern metropolitan sectors, which had always been the Cinderella of the railway, and assigning them to the GLM, which began to function with the lines from Buenos Aires Station to 20 de Junio and from Puente Alsina to Libertad. The new office, dedicated exclusively to this novel sphere of action, was soon successfully reorganising services; thus it was that the suburban sectors of the Northern Belgrano, Urquiza and Sarmiento Railways were incorporated into the GLM. The process was too gradual, however, and four years from the start, transfer of the suburban sectors of the San Martin, Mitre and Roca Railways still remained to be done. In 1985 the GLM was abolished and the suburban lines were transferred back to their original Railways. We shall return to this theme.

Another vigorously launched policy was electrification. Plans to electrify the suburban network of the Roca Railway went back as far as the fifties. In 1972 a contract was signed with a Japanese industrial company to carry out, among other projects, the electrification of the Roca suburban network. In 1973 a Japanese-Argentine consultancy group prepared the basic engineering plans, but the government froze the project. In 1977 FA decided, with the agreement of SETOP to revitalise it, although it had to confront much reluctance from the Ministry for Economy and Labour, which feared it would not be profitable and pointed out that it would massively increase the country's debt. Finally, it was decided to partially implement the project by electrifying the lines from Constitución to Glew and to Ezeiza. leaving the line to La Plata for an unspecified later date. The work started in 1981 and the lines were inaugurated in November 1985.

The electrification technology parameters had been determined some time ago: single-phase alternating-current at a frequency of 50Hz and a voltage of 25kV; decisions which been imposed on the Japanese contractors by FA. These parameters were compatible with a scenario in which the long distance main lines would also be electrified, a policy which FA had made its own with a resolution from head office which approved the Plan Básico de Electrificación (General Electrification Plan). This proposed the electrification of the lines from Buenos Aires to Mar del Plata and to Rosario, and several other routes almost all coinciding with those on the intercity network list defined by SETOP. In this sense, there seemed to be congruence between the two policies, as electrification could be considered as the technological interpretation of the SETOP policy for intercity trains. Even in spite of the changes of authority which took place during the 80s, the Transport Secretariat never accepted the Electrification Plan, arguing that it was not supported by techno-economic studies which might have shown its feasibility. A bill promoted by FA declared that the Plan was of national interest, but it was never signed.

In 1982 FA created an Electrification Office to which it entrusted the project underway on the suburban Roca Railway and investigations for the electrification of other suburban and intercity lines. The policy of FA was to find international partners for these projects and it opted to find them in Eastern Europe, a choice founded on the possibility of realising these electrifications by means of non-financial goods exchange agreements, which were more possible to obtain from countries with centralized economies. Negotiations were started with Russia for the Retiro-Rosario line; with Czechoslovakia for a section of the San Martín Railway; and with Hungary for the northern suburban sector of the Belgrano Railway. In 1985 FA postponed electrification to Rosario and reassigned to Russia the section of the San Martín Railway with the signing of an agreement by which Russian technical staff would undertake the total electrification project. But the direction taken by railway policy from 1989 led to the permanent abandonment of these electrification projects.

The Railway Policy of the Military Government is Diluted

The military government had defined a very inflexible policy, which was imposed on the railway system during its four initial years. From 1981, however, the military regime entered a period of instability which culminated in the institutional exit of 1983. During its final three years the original policy was never explicitly repudiated; it remained in the paperwork, but FA was no longer required to impose unpopular internal measures which the declining regime was now unable to support. Gradually, the epicentre of railway power shifted away from SETOP towards FA. The latter left aside those rationalization schemes which had been endorsed but were still pending, and oriented itself towards a policy of increasing output and investment, with a strong emphasis on technological modernisation, such as electrification.

The Railway Policy of the Radical Government

Towards the end of 1983 the Radical Party was elected to govern the country. It would last for a little over five years during which it is not possible to speak of a railway policy, but rather of three policies in succession. It might seem surprising that the one applied during the first year and a half would not involve a break with the immediately previous policy, but rather continued with it; whereas the privatization policy that President Alfonsín unsuccessfully sought to establish during the last year and a half of his government ended up as a preliminary of the drastic reform which would arise during the next government.

First Phase: 1983-1985

The initial phase was peculiar in that the management group during the last year of the Process were confirmed as the managers of FA and gave a continuity to the policies which were applied in this phase. Tensions appeared between the FA management and SETOP about the recurrent theme of the railway budget. Soon it became clear that it did not support FA's investment plans and questioned the rationality of certain policies, such as that of electrification.

Second Phase: 1985-1988

In mid-1985, the government intervened in the management of FA, replacing senior managing teams and imposing a focus which gave more attention to the political requirements of the governing Party. At the same time, a decidedly more conciliatory position was adopted when negotiating with the trade unions, whose influence had started to grow. The new focus led to a revision of the course taken by FA in the previous ten years, favouring the re-establishment of certain powers for the different Railway Boards (Roca, Belgrano, etc) to counteract what was seen as the excessive centralisation of the FA main Board. Suppression of the GLM, demanded by the unions, was a consequence of this new political course. For the first time there began a timid policy of re-establishing passenger trains withdrawn years before. In any case management of railway policy had begun to drift into the hands of FA in spite of the formal position of the Transport Secretariat, so much so that this was not immediately perceived by the Subsecretary himself when he was appointed to administrate FA for a few months. At the same time, FA began to suffer from the effects of a phenomenon that, though not unknown, emerged with unprecedented force during this period: demands for railway land from political pressure groups. Following nationalisation, there had existed a permanent pressure from provinces and municipalities to get their hands on highly valuable railway lands in strategic urban locations of all the large cities in the country. Municipal and provincial authorities had drawn up ambitious plans for these rail-urban locations, but only a few had moved forward. In Rosario a main line diversion and joint station for the Mitre and Belgrano Railways was planned, and the land expropriated for its construction, but because funds were never available the land was squatted on. There and in other places, including Buenos Aires, railway yards which had been abandoned out of use were quickly taken over by shanty towns, called *villas*, as in the pioneering case of Ingeniero Brian on the left bank of the Riachuelo in Buenos Aires. However, until the 1970s these invasions were few and far between, although inevitable given the existence of a poorer layer of society in a strongly middle class country with a satisfactory average income level.

Paradoxically, following the re-establishment of democracy, illegal administrative actions actually increased. In various cities of the interior, conflicts between politically opposed provincial and municipal governments – such as in the case of Rosario, among others – gave rise to actions ostensibly aimed at regulating the shanty towns, but in practice were instruments of political pressure.

The case of the so-called Villa 31 in the Retiro area of Buenos Aires deserves to be mentioned. This shanty town had established itself on land belonging to the railways and to the Port of Buenos Aires. The earlier shanty village on this site had been displaced during the military government, and the lands had remained permanently empty until towards the end of 1985. One night in October or November of that year trucks arrived carrying thousands of people, who started to occupy the lands near Retiro Bus Terminal and the recently constructed storage sheds of the San Martin Railway. These occupiers were not homeless people, as they brought with them their furniture and home equipment, including panels for erecting prefabricated houses. The ground had been previously parcelled out using stakes and strings which indicated the plot to be occupied by each family. The senior management of the Railway was immediately informed, but the government did nothing to stop the intrusion, (which it might have facilitated), giving tacit political approval to the settlers.

Later on the occupation advanced into other areas and the San Martin sheds, still not in use, were gradually dismantled until they disappeared. At present Villa 31 is home to more than 40 thousand people, has multi-storey buildings which do not meet health and safety standards, all of which constituted an insurmountable obstacle to the development of the Bus Terminal, the Railway and the Port. In subsequent years under successive governments the Villa was allowed not only to expand but also to infiltrate along the verges of the railway tracks, which led to all kinds of future problems, with no sign from the public authorities that they had a duty to defend the rights of all sectors of the community.

During the so-called political phase of the Radical period, all the indicators of FA activities deteriorated and its budget continued to be a discordant theme. A new actor entered the scene, the Directorio de Empresas Públicas (DEP, Corporation of Public Companies), which was a recreation of the previous decade's CEN. Within DEP there began to grow a new power centre which would collide with FA management. Late in 1986 or early in 1987 the DEP asked Engineer Manuel Madanes to draw up a plan for the railways with the objectives of reversing FA's tendency towards decline and rationalising its operations. Madanes surrounded himself with a group of experienced managers, and produced a plan by the middle of the year which came to be known as the Madanes Plan. The measures he recommended implied a new reduction in railway staff, to about 65,000 employees, a matter regarded as inconceivable by the Unions. At the end of August 1987 it became unofficially known that Madanes might become the new president of FA, following the congressional mid-term elections in September of that year, from which the government hoped to emerge strengthened and with the energy to undertake a new phase of railway rationalization. The Unions prepared themselves for the clash and at that time a flurry of posters was stuck up in the environs of railway buildings, opposing the imminent imposition of the Madanes Plan which, to give it a bad name, was presented as a reincarnation of the Larkin Plan, a false and misleading claim as the circumstances were very different a quarter of a century before.

Politics frustrated these prospects. The Radical Party lost the elections and the Madanes Plan was archived. President Alfonsín decided to change the course of his government, to be more in accord with liberalisation and privatisation measures establishing themselves elsewhere at this time, and which were gaining a certain consensus in the opinion of the public. Rodolfo Terragno was named Minister of Public Works and Services and took on the policy of opening up to private capital those sectors which until then had been reserved under exclusive State control. Terragno proposed that Telefónica de España go into partnership with ENTEL (the Argentine State-owned telephone company), that Scandinavian Airlines do the same with Aerolíneas Argentinas, and that these foreign partners (paradoxically, public companies) acquire control of the Argentine State companies in order to manage them efficiently. This new strategy was directed by the DEP, whose management had aligned itself with the new course of the government. But in spite of the energy applied by the Minister, the government could not get this policy through Congress because of the resolute opposition of the Justicialist Party which, entrenched in the Senate with its traditional nationalist positions, stymied the intended strategy for the telephone and airline companies.

Third Phase: 1988-1990

During the final phase of the Radical government a plan was conceived, known as "Ferrocargo" to enable the involvement of private capital in the railways. But before explaining what this was about, it is convenient to go back in time to trace the background to the idea of railway privatisation starting from the National Reorganisation Process.

It is useful to go back several five-year periods in order to understand the slow start of the forceful ideas which finally came to be imposed. Until 1976 there was a consensus held by almost all the members of the railway community that a straight-forward privatisation was not possible. Everyone agreed with the statement that "all over the world railways make a loss". The North-American experience, which was the exception, tended to not be considered as an option, if only because little was known about it.

The military government announced a peripheral privatisation policy, which consisted of resorting to the contracting out of all those activities considered not to be essential for railway operation. This concept was thought to be applicable to heavy rolling stock repairs and mechanized track maintenance, and the private sector was encouraged to significantly re-equip itself, in view of the anticipated rise in investment that was about to take place. FA's current workforce would continue to carry out day-to-day maintenance, in response to operational needs. These ideas were only partially applied.

In the rolling stock case work was contracted out for the renewal and remodelling of coaches and engine replacements for diesel locomotives. The objective behind these major interventions was that much of the rolling stock was out of use because of serious faults which, owing to lack of timely repairs, had suffered cannibalisation and become a temporary source of spare parts which would keep better stock in operation. There came a time when the cannibalised stock, further ravaged by being abandoned in yards, could no longer be repaired by FA workshops, and therefore were contracted out for rehabilitation or reconstruction, which sometimes included elements of modernisation. In this way, the cost was able to be presented as an investment, which in fact was no more than deferred maintenance. Throughout the eighties there were several significant stock restoration contracts of this kind with private factories. This policy had served to maintain a local industry which faced an uncertain future when completed refurbishments, especially of the passenger coach fleet, and service rationalisation made new contracts almost unnecessary.

Regarding actual operation of the railways, few thought that this might be viable in private hands. Nevertheless, trials were attempted. Already in 1977 SETOP had worked with FIAT-Concord on a new equipment scheme, whereby the manufacturer would undertake the provision of service and maintenance of the units, at its own risk. A railcar service between Buenos Aires and Mar del Plata was explored by this firm but not agreed, as the profitability of the scheme was problematic. At this time the manufacturers were saying "the truth is that our business is to manufacture, not to operate".

In 1979 an economic study of the Embarcación-Formosa branch showed that it was not cost-effective. The passenger trains were especially not, but in this case the service was really useful because of the non-existence of a paved road along the greater part of the branch. SETOP conceived the idea of a concession with a private company for the railway service. It selected Atahualpa, a bus company based in Salta. The concession also provided the rolling stock – Ganz-Mavag railcars of which the Belgrano Railway had many – and the service began in 1980. Even though the provision of this service violated all solidly established preconceptions, this solution was possible because in the prevailing political climate opposition from the Trade Unions could not manifest itself. The service continued until 1985, when the contract terminated and was not renewed. There are different versions for why this was, including that Atahualpa had not satisfied its contractual obligations to FA; on the other hand, operation of the service had perhaps been subtly sabotaged.

From 1985, the Radical government began to pay attention to calls for more private participation in public services. These calls came from right-wing politicians and influential people in the public eye. An official with the rank of Secretary was put in charge of the matter and coined the phrase "privatisation of growth". The concept was that the public companies would maintain their fields of activity, but the market would be opened up so that private companies would be able to participate in its expansion. In that way, an eruption of private activity would not mean the destruction of employment in the public companies.

This concept led to some out of the ordinary applications in the railways. In Tucumán a local service which had been withdrawn during the Process was restored by giving a concession to a company in the area. The rolling stock and train crews were provided by FA and invoiced to the concessionaire, which only provided the sale of tickets, meaning it controlled the takings. The contract terminated after a few months, when it became clear that the takings were not sufficient to enable the concessionaire to meet the invoices from FA. Also, a concession to provide a service to Bariloche was given to a tourism company, which chartered a luxury train provided and operated by FA; the concessionaire would commercialise the service and provide for on-board dining. This service was also ephemeral.

Another strategy used to involve private participation in railway activities was an incentive for shippers of cargo. The idea was to suggest that they invest in locomotives and wagons which FA could not provide because of growing rolling stock shortages and lack of investment funding. A scheme was set up for the exploitation of private wagons, together with a similar one for locomotives. A few wagons were purchased by an iron and steel company, but nobody wished to buy locomotives. The private sector had no interest in tying up an investment in the railway for which it would not be fully responsible. This being so, the few attempts made to involve private companies in railway activities did not appear to have a future, for lack of sustainable long-term results. The conditions which FA was coping with during the 1980s led, towards the end of the decade, to individual privatisation iniatives becoming transformed into complete overall projects.

Among the privatisation antecedents there was a project formulated a few years before, about the former Rosario-Puerto Belgrano Railway (RPBR). At nationalisation, this had been divided between the Mitre and Roca Railways; later it had been reunited for inclusion in the Mitre Railway, and finally it was again divided. Its commercial activity was scarce and mostly concentrated near the Rosario end. When passenger trains on this line were withdrawn in 1976, the section between Almirante Solier and Timote became almost inactive. The RPBR had been a French investment with little economic purpose, given that its route crossed twenty other lines but had junctions with only very few of them. Nevertheless, the presumption existed that this line might convert itself into an important constituent of the national network once the junctions had been constructed. In 1975 FA had investigated a link between the stations at Orellano (on the ex-BAPR, originally named Germania, which remains the name of the village itself) and El Peregrino (on the ex-RPBR) in order to provide a direct route from the Junín area to Bahía Blanca. But the operational capacity of the link, according to the traditional regulations then in force, would have required a connection several kilometres long between the two stations, or alternatively the installation of a signal-box in the "middle of nowhere". Both of these alternatives were expensive, and the project was dropped.

At the beginning of the 80s SETOP had signed an agreement with an Italian state entity which sent a technical mission to look into ways of modernising the suburban railways of Buenos Aires. For reasons which we are not aware of, a study of the RPBR line was also included; it seems it was thought possible that it could be separated out from the national network and given a concession for its revitalisation by an investment group. The report of the Italian mission did not come up with many concrete recommendations, but it created a favourable expectancy about the future of the RPBR. In the renowned economics column of a newspaper the following words, approximately rendered, appeared: "Italian investors are interested in the Rosario-Bahía Blanca line, which has a formidable potential for exporting grains from the two major ports which it links". Responding to these prospects, in 1987 local consultants prepared a study for private exploitation of the RPBR's Bahía Blanca-Timote sector for the mass transport of grains. But from 1985 long stretches of the RPBR had flooded south of Capitán Castro, which significantly weakened the prospects of the project.

However, the company concerned asked other consultants to deepen the study. They recommended broadening the project to include the whole length of the RPBR line, but considered that it was very important to include contributions to traffic fed from the lines which crossed the RPBR, for which it would be necessary to construct the junctions which the State had omitted to provide for nearly 40 years. The consultant's analysis also included the Bahía Blanca- Darregueira-Huinca Renancó line, the mainline of the former Bahía Blanca and North Western Railway (BBNWR). This was one of FA's most active lines, because it carried the major part of the freight shipped to or from the commercial Puerto Ingeniero White (Puerto Belgrano was a naval port). In contrast to the RPBR, the ex-BBNWR had junctions with all the lines which crossed it, giving access to a large hinterland served by a fairly dense railway network. A conclusion drawn from these studies was that linking railway business with port operations was advisable, and the company concerned sought to take up a strategic position in the Bahía Blanca area, which was blocked by the Administración General de Puertos (Argentine Ports Authority) to maintain the State monopoly, which in those years was weakening in the face of the emergence of private ports on the River Paraná north of Rosario.

While a few private companies cautiously examined the possibility of setting up isolated railway contracts, Minister Terragno charged the DEP with the preparation for privatisation of several State-owned companies. Early in 1988 the president and board of FA were replaced, and they began investigations and negotiations which could lead to private investors being attracted into the railway business. In addition, Decree 1842 was promulgated, which allowed private investors to initiate new development activities in spheres hitherto reserved to the State or to public companies. The private investor could propose a new activity or business they would be in charge of and adequately publicize; if the State did not expressly object, they could implement the proposed activity. There would be public consultations to discuss such proposals, and State companies which would be affected by them had the right to be heard.

In the railway case, the DEP launched the Ferrocargo Project. The plan was that FA would remain responsible for railway infrastructure and control running the trains, while the operation and commercialisation of the cargo service would be assigned to a company with a majority (51%) of private capital and 49% from the State, provisionally called "Ferrocargo". The State would retain 29% of the capital of this new company, and the remaining 20% was allocated to its staff. During 1988 FA and DEP worked on this idea. If it had been successful, the process would have continued with projects called "Ferrotur" and "Metropol", relating to intercity and suburban passenger services, respectively.

In spite of not having progressed beyond the concept stage and the well-founded objections raised against it, the Ferrocargo project was productive because it drew the attention of a group of private Argentine companies, convened by the Minister, towards opportunities in the railways. In the end some private companies became involved (Loma Negra and Techint) and others tried to be (Materfer, Román and Sideco). Ferrocargo was ultimately unsuccessful because it was a pioneering, intrinsically complex project, with many weaknesses which made it vulnerable to criticism from those who would prefer to maintain the *status quo*, all of which contributed to the growing weakness of the last two years of President Alfonsín's government.

However, a new actor was entering the scene: public opinion. This had been moving towards a posture more distant from nationalisation and, responding to the actions of influential social sources, was taking up an attitude more favourable towards privatisation. That was why the first reaction against Ferrocargo would not constitute a frontal and inflexible opposition, nor a tough ideological clash, but rather it would present itself as a positive alternative proposal, generated by a coalition of the railway unions, the associations which linked the works contractors and railway suppliers, and certain privileged client companies which had access to the increasingly scarce FA provision for freight transport. Eventually, while Ferrocargo continued to be a sort of State secret, the coalition informed the president of FA that a plan existed for the revival of the Argentine railways, the preparation of which, they said, brought together the efforts of sectors which traditionally had remained isolated and sometimes in conflict with each other.

With keen expectancy, there took place in the FA assembly hall a presentation of the document which later came to be called the Trade Union Plan. It was not a new document, as it had been prepared at least a year before for one of the railway unions and it consisted of the reiterated proposal that an increase of public investment in the railways was the answer to all the problems. But it had been updated with a brief mention of the participation of private capital. The document had proposed that the grossly insufficient annual contribution at the end of the 80s from the National exchequer of $100 million be increased to $400 million. But then in apparent sympathy with the new context created by energetic ministerial policy, it included an equivalent amount sourced from external credits or bilateral agreements and, as a novelty, private investments, although actual projects were not specified. The Trade Union Plan was a proposal destined to take away the initiative from the government staff, who until then had worked with maximum discretion on the Ferrocargo project, though as we have seen some details had filtered out.

A second obstacle arose from the private sector itself, created by companies which set out a different course of action based on Decree 1842. A company published a notice in a newspaper declaring that it was interested in exploiting the southern sector of the RPBR line. This was a problem for Ferrocargo because the proposal used the legal framework created by the government itself (Decree 1842) in order to attract private company participation, but the proposal concerned only part of the network, whereas Ferrocargo applied to the whole network. Given this example of a specific initiative, other companies followed the same procedure, declaring their interest in the same line and in one case also including the Bahía Blanca-Huinca Renancó line.

The public presentation imposed by Decree 1842 took place, and each group expounded the advantages of their proposal in the presence of their competitors. After everyone had spoken, it was clear that the various proposals, all pertaining to the same stretch of railway, were not easily comparable, so the president of FA communicated to the Minister that it would be advisable to define a common basis for the purpose of soliciting tenders, from which the best offer would emerge. In that way the public sector had itself generated a potential privatisation process for a sector of the National network, which seemed to be much more concrete than the Ferrocargo project. In the mean time, the latter had been brought to a standstill: towards the end of 1988 it was considered for the first time by the Board of FA, and though it was not rejected, it received a number of observations and suggestions for changes which indicated that Ferrocargo would not be able to overcome the obstacles of those who opposed it.

While Ferrocargo languished, an FA working group began to prepare a tender document to give a concession for the ex-RPBR and ex-BBNWR lines, with the following special features: the concessionaire would be the exclusive exploiter of the ex-RPBR line, and its trains would be able to run over other FA lines by paying a toll. They would also be able to run services on the ex-BBNWR line, in this case in competition with FA and being charged a toll, since FA would continue to maintain the tracks and control traffic on the line. In this way a "shared exploitation" scheme would be created.

February 1989 unleashed the hyperinflation which was to end the Alfonsín government. In the presidential elections of May 1989 the Justicialist Party candidate, Carlos Menem, was successful. He should have taken over only in December 1989, but the crisis in the government led to the resignation of Alfonsín, and Menem was sworn in as President in July 1989.

Privatisation: New Railway Policy in 1989

While the first privatisation attempts were as set out above, the situation of FA had otherwise worsened. Traffic units (tons/km) had fallen from 23.300 million in 1979 to 19.100 ten years later. In spite of the electrification of the Roca line, suburban traffic was 100 million smaller at the end of the same ten-year period. Long-distance passenger traffic had grown by 10%, but cargo traffic had fallen by 25%, because FA policy during the second half of the 1980s had favoured the running of passenger services, which disadvantaged cargo services because the availability of locomotives was ever decreasing, falling from 844 at the end of 1979 to 603 as 1989 ended.

Menem took over in the midst of the hyperinflation crisis and the supreme objective of the new government was to interrupt this destructive process. The new president announced an unexpected alliance with those political parties which proclaimed a liberal orthodoxy, and with groups emblematic of economic strength. And to stabilise the economy and reduce the enormous deficit in the public sector, the government adopted a policy of privatising all major State-owned industrial and public service companies, and dismantling the huge public machine created since 1930.

Law 23.696, on State Reform, was promulgated in August 1989, to support the new policy. While this proposed the sale of most public companies, in the case of the railways it opted for a form of concession where the State would retain possession of the assets. The reason for this decision has not been documented. Perhaps it took into account that even though FA was a hugely loss-making

State company, it owned land of immense value. For that reason any buyer of the railways would be very tempted to close down its services and make a fortune by selling off the railway lands. In any case, the public ownership of the railways had been a taboo objective of the new governing Party, only comparable politically to ownership of the public oil company. Thus this the apparently timid form of concession favourably assisted privatisation (at least in the short term) because it helped to avoid the initial political obstacles that a straightforward sale had supposed, and helped to get the process under way.

The new policy emanated from the highest government level, but its strategies and aims were still not defined. To take it forward, a working-party was formed in the Ministry of Public Works and Services, which investigated the scarce antecedents of recent railway privatisations, and especially the experiences collected during the Ferrocargo initiative, with those who had driven it also being consulted. A first question to resolve was to decide about an FA proposal, involving a "framework decree" which should regulate law 23.696 in the railway sphere. FA proposed opening access to private activities by means of multiple specific concessions, somewhat similar to the scheme applied in Great Britain in the mid-1990s. This anticipated, in effect, extreme horizontal segmentation of activities using diverse types of concessions:

- Concessions for the operation of services on FA infrastructure by paying a toll, and using rolling stock rented from FA or provided by the private concessionaire.
- Concessions for track maintenance, paid for by a charge on the operators running trains on the track, whether it be FA itself or a private company.
- Locomotive and wagon concessions, for which the concessionaire would receive part of the FA fleet together with the corresponding maintenance installations. The concessionaire would rent the fleet to the operating companies, FA or private.
- There would be additional concessions, such as "express" freight services on fast passenger trains, cereal branches, etc.

It is not necessary to enlarge on the complexity of such a scheme, which could not ensure an investor had even a minimum degree of control over their investment, entirely dependent as it was on the actions of the other participants. In any case, it would lead to all kinds of disputes between the different concessionaires and between these and FA. It is evident that neither FA nor any other State government level had the capacity to control the numerous concession contracts that the scheme would have generated. The scheme promised to be very comprehensive, labour intensive and implied a considerable risk to the State; additionally, it was highly likely to perpetuate the corrupt practices which had ruined the State railways. Although not having exactly the same characteristics, the privatization of the British railways was inspired by similar ideas and deserved the same criticisms, which were justified by what came to pass.

Faced with the proposal for horizontal segmentation put forward by FA, the ministerial working-party proposed the form of privatisation which would in the end be imposed, which was established by Decree 666 on the 1st of September 1989. Article 4 of the Decree set out the form FAs concessions would take:

> Execution of Law No. 23.696 provides that the form of concession to be used by Ferrocarriles Argentinos (FA) is Concesión Integral de Explotación (CIE, Integral Development Concession lines or sectors of the National Railway Network, The object of this form of concession is that the concessionaire takes on the commercial exploitation, operation of trains and care of stations, maintenance of rolling stock, infrastructure and equipment, and all other complementary and subsidiary activities.

The objective of this provision of Decree 666 was to leave in the hands of the company holding the concession the management of all the various technical, commercial and economic aspects of the business. In each network conceded there would be a concessionaire, responsible for the coordination of operations and maintenance of its network, this without prejudice to trains of other network concessions being allowed to run on its lines on payment of a toll or by virtue of a specific agreement.

In this way it was expected that all technical and operational activities, control of the labour force, and investment decisions would all be efficiently integrated, and under single strategic management for the achievement of commercial objectives. This uniquely focussed control of daily operations hoped to achieve maximum efficiency in the coordinated working of the different services, and would sharpen the capacity to respond more rapidly to daily operational events.

The second key element of Decree 666/89 was the provision in Article 9 for initiating modifications to the operating regulations until then in force, and to enable future concessionaires to propose these changes so that, in the words of the Article, "they would permit new methods of technical development, arising from technological evolution, which would make possible the achievement of a more economical and efficient operation of the system". The ministerial working-party was not unaware that achieving viable concessions depended on the inseparable combination of improved operating regulations and a more economical development; but there did not exist any clear idea of how far these changes should be taken, nor how important they would be as soon as they were applied to cargo concessions and to every other aspect of the privatization process. Finally, Article 10 of Decree 666 recommended that the Ministry of Works and Public Services should privatise the "Rosario-Bahía Blanca Corridor", an idea which had been under consideration for nearly a decade, as has been explained.

As can be seen, the text of the Decree sets out a wide range of actions, which collectively are frankly incoherent. This was so because the bill prepared by the State-owned company FA simply had Articles 4 and 9 added to it. In this way it gave the appearance of having overcome the contradictory points of view of those who favoured privatization and those who wished to obstruct it, by linking them together.

Implementation of the New Policy: Initial Steps

In compliance with Decree 666, in November 1989 the first cargo network was established with the Rosario-Bahía Blanca Corridor concession. Assuming that the interest shown the year before in the RPBR – entire, in part, or together with the Bahía Blanca-Huinca Renancó line – was a valuable precedent, the ministerial working-party defined for this first concession a fan of broad-gauge lines converging on the grain-loading ports of Bahía Blanca, including the entire ex-RPBR from Villa Diego in Rosario. And it stated that this set of lines was the so-called Rosario-Bahía Blanca Corridor which Decree 666 had ordered to be privatised, a rather free interpretation even though this Corridor had not been clearly defined in the Decree. This network chosen by the Ministry was more than 5,000km long!

The network in question was formed of sections from three of the six regional Boards into which FA was divided. Almost all the still open parts of the old BBNWR were in the concession, but it also included parts of the Roca (ex-BAGSR) and Sarmiento (ex-BAWR) lines. From the Mitre line only the section of the ex-RPBR north of Timote was included, which at that time was almost abandoned. The objective of the Ministry was to create an extensive railway network flowing to Bahía Blanca with access to Rosario, which would be able to integrate itself into the grain and agro-industry business and operate independently of the traditional FA Boards:

- The design of the network had not included access to Buenos Aires, Bragado on the Sarmiento network being its most easterly point. With the benefit of hindsight, it would have seemed more logical to have included the whole of the latter network, which would have guaranteed access to the port of Buenos Aires. However, this would have led to huge complications during the preparation of the first tender, because it was not clear how the terms of the concession would deal with the problem of interactions between freight trains and suburban passenger services, which at that time were State-operated with no plans for privatisation. It must be remembered that this was the first CIE in Latin America, with no previous experience to draw upon.
- On the proposed network there were no important intercity passenger services, so their impact would be moderate, thus

simplifying the terms of the concession. It would have been much more complicated to plan a similar concession on the Mitre network, since passenger traffic to Rosario, Córdoba and Tucumán was the most important flow on FA, whereas cargo traffic might well have been regarded as marginal.

- In the Bahía Blanca area there were no serious conflicts over the railway lines passing through the city, nor did there exist any kind of complicated "ferro-urban" local agreements, which were generally hostile to the railway and might also, under certain circumstancies, have clashed with the concession for solely political reasons.
- In Bahía Blanca there were railway workshops (Spurr, Noroeste) and locomotive sheds (White, Maldonado) which when incorporated into the concession would give it full technical autonomy for the maintenance of its rolling stock fleet.
- The market seemed promising. The government had contracted with a foreign consortium to dredge the port and its access canals to a depth of 45 feet, which would make this port more competitive within a few years. Also, interest was being shown in establishing commercial private grain terminals at the port, as was already happening on the River Paraná.
- And finally, as has been noted above, the "R-PB Corridor" had already attracted the formal interest of several private investors.

Using a loan from the World Bank, the Ministry requested, from the international firm of consultants Booz, Allen & Hamilton, an analysis of the feasibility of the proposed concessions. This firm had carried out an assessment for the Ministry during the previous government and was familiar with the problems of the national railway network. Towards the end of 1989 the consultants concluded that the proposed Rosario-Bahía Blanca network would be viable provided it was exploited in accordance with North American operating practices. But the analysis also demonstrated that the feasibility indicators of this network were identified as being weak because of the specialised and seasonal nature of its traffic. This result could well have cooled the government's enthusiasm; but nevertheless the opposite happened, because the Ministry understood that, things being as they were, they could not be accused of "selling grandmother's jewels", given that "what was being offered" was precisely not the most valuable jewel.

This confluence of factors, some unpredictable, led to rapid progress of the first tender. It was launched on the 23rd of November 1989, after less than four months consideration by the railway working-party, with minimum documentation since the detailed conditions would only become available during the following months. It was some months before the first offers in response were received because opposition to the privatisation process had hardly manifested itself, and would grow during the first months of 1990.

From FA emerged an attempt to dilute the CIE concept by formally proposing that the concessionaire and FA compete over the same network, the survival of the latter being a given. Such a proposal was contrary to both the spirit and the letter of Decree 666, but it was considered seriously at the highest political level, and put aside probably because there were signals from the private sector that under those conditions there would be no interest in entering the railway business. What happened was that after a hard struggle, the initial Ministerial strategy was ratified in mid-1990.

As the tender process progressed, another obstacle was created by FA, which had signed a five-year contract with an important vegetable oil company, granting it very favourable operating and financial conditions on the network of the future concession. Without doubt this scenario would be harmful to the commercial interests of any future concessionaire, by depriving it of full control of a substantial part of its business, precisely during the initial period. Although the government obliged FA to rescind the contract shortly before the handover of the concession, the newly appointed concessionaire found itself, from day one, in conflict with a company which would naturally have been an important client, but had been suddenly deprived of favourable treatment.

FA also proposed that the Board of the Roca line should remain in operational control of the locomotive shed at Ingeniero White, leaving the concessionaire to operate the ex-BBNWR Maldonado shed (at that time used for stabling scrapped cargo wagons). Another FA proposal was that one track of the tranche of double track in the urban area of Bahía Blanca be allocated to the future Rosario-Bahía Blanca concession, and the other track left in the control of the Roca Board, its continued existence being discounted; and that the future concessionaire should carry out the modifications and other works that independent operation of the two lines would require. It was obvious that these expensive and unproductive modifications were all unnecessary, so this contrived initiative did not prosper either.

However, on the initiative of an influential legislator in the Province of Santa Fe who had long experience of rail-urban questions in Rosario, including the battle to close down the grain elevators at Rosario Norte station, a short tranche of the concession was removed, from Villa Diego to Rosario Port, to prevent this key link from becoming monopolised by the concessionaire. That this link would be under the control of FA was disregarded, as few doubted it would continue to exist.

All things considered, the decision to privatize having been taken, those taking it forward had to sort out all manner of ideological objections and proposals which were fallacious in spite of sounding reasonable to a lay person. That the Ministry working-party was able to make progress in this context was, apart from its own conviction, that it had been strengthened by the assistance of a co-opted group of railway specialists who agreed to embark on a project which, even in early 1990, was for many an experiment doomed to failure.

Offers, Awards and Transfer

Four groups purchased the tender documentation, but eventually there were only two offers, led by Techint (in association with Sociedad Comercial Del Plata) and RENFE, the Spanish Railways (together with the local firm Roman). The concession was awarded on 5th December 1990 to Techint, et al, but the actual takeover would have to wait for nearly a year because during this period it was necessary to resolve, for the first time, all the problems raised by the transfer of a railway concession, which included complex inventory questions, demarcation of boundaries with the rest of the non-concessioned network, the transfer of personnel, and the creation and application of new operational norms.

The Rules of Operation

Based on the spirit of Article 9 of Decree 666, though perhaps not strictly on the letter, the concession winner had included in its offer a proposal for new rules of operation, inspired by North American practice. This would replace the traditional system used in our country of giving "line-clear" to a train, derived from the British system, and which was anyway very antiquated. The Reglamento Interno Técnico Operativo (RITO, Internal Technical Operating Rules) had, in the 1970s, unified the rules of the old private and State railways. The system for giving line-clear was operated by station personnel communicating between themselves and with a remote "train control" centre. Line-clear was conceded following agreement between those responsible in the stations at either end of the track section – signalmen, station masters or assistant staff – with the coordination of the train control centre. The system required the presence of personnel on the ground to verify if line-clear could be asked for and given, and to verify the integrity of the trains. On the main lines there were stations located every 15km, 24-hour staffed every day of the year. The personnel obtained line-clear, operated signals and point levers in many stations. They also verified the integrity of the train by observing the tail disc or lamp and, for cargo trains, the presence of the guard's van.

The winner had commissioned an assessment from Paul Victor, an executive of a regional railway in the USA, who visited the network. He diagnosed that the installations were well maintained but were obsolete, and recommended the complete elimination of mechanical signals and simplification of the track layout at many stations. Victor proposed the adoption of rules similar to those employed on North American railways with medium traffic densities. The line-clear would be arranged between the locomotive crew and the control center by radio, without the need to involve station staff. The mechanical signals would be removed, and point position indicators would be installed. Setting of points in order to manoeuvre at a station, yard or branch would be done by the locomotive crew. The guard's van on the end of a cargo train would no longer be required because the integrity of the train would be guaranteed by requiring all cargo trains to be entirely fitted with compressed air brakes; an air pressure sensor would be placed on the last wagon of the train to monitor the air pressure in the train pipe, the sensor being connected via radio to the locomotive. Vacuum brakes would be eliminated, given that all the goods wagons purchased by FA since 1970 were provided with compressed air brakes. Guards, who until then had occupied the van at the end of the train, would no longer be necessary.

This proposal by the winner had advanced a theme which had been tabu in the railways of Argentina, where operating questions always had a touch of mystery, only accessible to a limited number of inscrutable specialists. For years before, different committees had considered questions like removing the guard's van without being able to reach any decision, because they lacked the will to take the bull by the horns and face up to a reform of the Ley General de Ferrocarriles (Regulation of Railways Act) and the Rules in its enabling Decree. The putative concessionaire had looked at the legal framework and reached an unexpected conclusion. The text of the Railways Act was completely general and did not impede the adoption of rules like those proposed. For example, the Act defined the figure of "Train Manager", but did not individualize it. The Rules, however, decreed that the Train Guard was that person; thus, in a cargo train, the Train Manager was someone who was located hundreds of metres behind the driver of the train, and even worse, unable to communicate except by using hand signals such as flags (during daylight) and lamps (at night). This proposal did not require what would be a very complicated reform of the Railways Act, but rather a modification of the Rules, which could be achieved by means of a government decree. In the case we are describing, the crew member until then acting as assistant to the driver of the locomotive would be appointed Train Manager. This man would cease to be merely the driver's assistant, becoming instead a key person responsible for seeing that orders received by radio from the control centre were obeyed, and for overseeing the correct setting of points for train manoeuvres.

During the complicated negotiations before the signing of the concession contract the text of the Rules was duly adjusted and when the concessionaire took charge, following the training of locomotive crews (and of the personnel at the few stations that would remain staffed), from one day to the next the railway ceased operating under the traditional rules of British origin using a whole set of apparatus dating back to the start of the century, and began operating under a form of North American rules depending on radio communication. Symbolic of the change, "line-free" was no longer called that and was transformed into "authorization for track use", a name change which could have been avoided, but the concessionaire insisted upon so that the new rules should not contain any terms from the old jargon with a different meaning, which could create difficulties of interpretation in the future.

Replacement of FA's RITO by a completely different set of regulations would have been unthinkable for the State-owned company. Trade Union inflexibility was always put forward as a reason for not facing up to a necessary reform of norms which had long been obsolete. In this case, however, the unions accepted the change in the rules of the game and came to negotiate with the concessionaire about new labour agreements, which also implied acceptance by the government of the novel operational regulations.

Workshops and Other Arrangements

From the start of the privatization of the "Corridor", the government remained ambiguous about its intentions with regard to the rest of the national network, and it could have been thought that FA would continue to survive. In any case, the position taken by FA to not include the workshops in the concession still prevailed, which created another considerable obstacle for the future concessionaire. However, this position was later modified, and during the negotiations for the concession contract Spurr Workshop was included, a compact but modern establishment, the latest opened by FA.

It was also necessary to resolve the situation of passenger trains on the Corridor, which continued to be run by FA without any decision by the government as to its long-term future. In the tender document it was specified that, even though the concessionaire would not operate these trains, they should be allowed to run without being charged a toll. FA continued to operate the trains using its own crews, and the concessionaire took over the station staff concerned with such services (ticket office staff, etc), while FA continued to pay their salaries. Later on operation of these passenger services was transferred to the Province of Buenos Aires.

Rolling Stock

The government offered aspiring concessionaires of the Rosario-Bahía Blanca Corridor a fleet of 1.600 wagons and some 30 locomotives. These quantities were really meager for a 5,000km line, a tiny proportion of the rolling stock available to FA. It was true that the wagons were almost all modern and suitable for the transport of bulk cargoes, but the locomotives were General Motors GR 12, 1.500 HP machines; that is, the higher power machines that FA had been incorporating since 1971 had been excluded. This stock was offered to rent, for which the concessionaire would have to pay an annual sum.

The Economic Conditions and Awarding Mechanism

The first tender faced the problem of how to award a novel kind of concession with very real political implications. The government chose to award the first concession to the offer which had gained most points, arising from a weighted average of criteria, of which only a few were economic. Although there were slight differences from tender to tender, the main factors which would be weighed up in the applicant's proposal were as follows:

- Proposed structure and experience of railway operation.
- Commitment to an investment plan which would be carried out during the first five years of the concession.
- Other investments.
- Maintenance plan.
- Amount to be paid to the State for the concession.
- Toll to be charged for accepting passenger traffic.
- Number of FA staff to be taken over.
- Percentage of national share.

With small changes between tenders, items 2, 3, 5, 6, and 7 in the above list amounted to two thirds of the weighted average in the awarding scheme. A candidate who aspired to achieve a high score needed to offer much investment, pay the State well for the concession, charge a reduced toll for accepting passenger traffic and take over a maximum possible number of FA staff. In other words, everything in the proposal which would inevitably make it less profitable. Implicit in this scheme was the supposition that these concessions would be highly profitable, so that they could compete by offering favourable conditions to the State, society and the workers.

The first concessionaire was baptised "Ferroexpreso Pampeano Sociedad Anónima" (FEPSA) and began its operations on 1st November 1991. The Iowa Interstate Railroad in the USA was to provide oversight for the railway operation aspects of FEPSA.

The installation of FEPSA was a significant landmark, given that it took place without any major disturbance to railway services. Once again it demonstrated what is common knowledge: well thought out technical decisions can be realized when decisive political power exists. The concessionaire showed that it could manage the business without serious operational or technical hitches. Yes, there was a commercial setback: a major vegetable oil company, the single most important client of FEPSA, would not agree new terms and conditions for the transport of its products.

As previously mentioned, this company had signed a rather generous five-year contract with FA, and resented the changed conditions. It announced that it would use trucks to transport its goods, and did so for a few years until eventually both parties were able to agree mutually satisfactory transport terms. But this incident, which might have caused the concession to fail if behind it had not been one of the strongest Argentine business groups, is evidence of the difficulties which would face those concessionaires which did not have their own traffic support base, given that the decline for decades of the railways had permitted the consolidation of a very large and efficient trucking industry.

Subsequent Cargo Concessions

In view of the success predicted in early 1991 for the first privatization, the government decided to continue with the privatization of all cargo services, by adopting a similar scheme. In some cases this involved modifying the spatial arrangement of the railway network, in order to correct mistakes committed during nationalization. For example, the San Martin tender included the Venado Tuerto – Villa Constitución and the Santa Isabel – Santa Teresa – Soldini lines, so that the future concession could have independent access to Rosario and the ports on the River Paraná. Less felicitous was the assignment to the concession of the section Mercedes – Bragado – Lincoln of the Sarmiento network, which was not generating significant cargoes of grain towards Buenos Aires, where the shipping of grain was anyway in decline. And it was an unwise decision to remove from the Roca network tender, after having received the offers, of the line between Bahía Blanca and Patagones-San Antonio Oeste, which ended up fragmented between the railway administrations of the Provinces of Buenos Aires and Río Negro.

Thus there followed the tenders for the Mitre, San Martín, Roca and Urquiza lines. There was competition for the first two, but only one offer emerged for each of the last two. This was because, as the scheme developed, all eyes were on the performance of the first concessionaire and the problems it was facing, which led to the private sector becoming more cautious.

The Case of the Belgrano Network

Finally, in 1992, the Belgrano network was tendered. Copies of the documentation were purchased, but no offers were received. A contributing factor was certainly a more realistic vision of the business, based on the initial experience, but above all the state of the network infrastructure was in this case more critical. There were several large bridges in vulnerable conditions, a fragile locomotive fleet owing to the bad spare-part policy of previous years, and a declining volume of traffic.

In the face of this failure, the government decided to reissue the tender and the ministerial team was enlarged in order to provide an outline of the scheme. But this work was never finished, as the government agreed to keep the network under State control for the time being, with a promise to award the concession to the Unión Ferroviaria (UF, the Union of Railwaymen, to which the majority of railway workers belonged, but not the drivers, the signalmen nor the senior staff). In 1993 the Belgrano network was "split" from FA and continued under State management until 1999 when, just before Menem stepped down from being President, it was formally conceded to the UF with a commitment that the State would provide the resources for significant annual investment.

This final process accomplished, the railway cargo network had been restructured as follows:

- Ferroexpreso Pampeano S.A. (FEPSA), appointed from 1st November 1991, extending over 4,952km, which included most of the Sarmiento network, sections of the Roca line in the Bahía Blanca area, and access to Rosario via the RPB line.
- Nuevo Central Argentino S.A. (NCA), appointed from 23rd December 1992, extending over 4.511km, which included most of the Mitre network (except the tranches passed to the BAP) and the Pergamino-Junin section.
- Ferrosur Roca S.A., appointed from 13th March 1993, extending over 3,342km, which included the Roca network (except for sections in FEPSA, the line to Mar del Plata and lines south of Bahía Blanca).

- Buenos Aires al Pacífico S.A., appointed from 26th August 1993, extending over 5,251km, which included the San Martin network (except for the Pergamino-Junin section), the Sarmiento network to Bragado and Lincoln, and sections of the Mitre network giving access to Rosario and Villa Constitución.
- Ferrocarriles Mesopotámicos S.A., appointed from 20th October 1993, extending over 2,737km, which included all the standard-gauge Urquiza network.
- Ferrocarril General Belgrano S. A. (a State company), in charge from 1st October 1993, extending over 6,335km, which included all the metre-gauge network except for the tranches either closed or ceded to the Provinces.

The overall network of concessions extended over about 27 thousand kilómetres, compared with the 34 thousand kilómetres nominally in operation towards the end of 1989. The difference consisted of the metropolitan network, of about 800km, together with a number of lines not included in the concessions and ceded to the Provinces.

The Suburban Passenger Service Concessions

While the cargo concessions were being drafted, an accord with the World Bank outlined an action plan for the future which, in the case of the metropolitan railways, would establish the creation of a specialised administration within FA – a re-creation of the Metropolitan Line Board of 1980 – and as a longer term objective, the creation of a State-owned company segregated from FA.

Towards the end of 1990 the economic state of the country was again deteriorating, inflation was increasing, and hyperinflation threatened. At this point dissident local leaders in the railway unions declared a strike which paralised the railways in the whole country. Unlike in previous conflicts, this time the strikers were faced by a government which stood firm, and was solidly backed by strong public opinion. This was the moment when President Menem coined his famous phrase "line on strike, line which closes". The government, far from giving way, ratified its privatisation of the cargo services, and in the case of the suburban railways decided to expedite the privatization stages. In March 1991, by Decree 502 suburban services were split from FA and a new public company was created, Ferrocarriles Metropolitanos S. A. (Femesa). Shortly afterwards, Decree 1143/91 approved the framework for privatization by concession of the Femesa network, jointly with the Subterraneo de Buenos Aires (Buenos Aires Underground) network, commonly known as the Subte.

The implementation of this privatisation was made the responsibility of the Unidad de Coordinación del Programa de Re-estructuración Ferroviaria (UCPRF, Unit for the Coordination of Railway Restucturing), originally created by FA to supervise the progress of the railway reform accords with the World Bank. In mid-1991 a working party began to formulate the tender process; towards the end of the year the general conditions were known, and during 1992 one by one the specific conditions for each of the seven business units or "service groups" were defined. Offers in response were also received one by one during that year, by end of which the offers for each concession were listed in order of suitability. 1993 was dedicated to negotiations with the listed candidates, and from 1st January 1994 the first concession was awarded, with the rest following one by one.

The tendering mechanism was significantly different to that used for the cargo network concessions. The concept of "Integral development Concession" was maintained, and each concessionaire was completely responsible for its suburban network, with the requirement that long-distance passenger and cargo trains must be allowed passage on payment of a toll. But in this case the rules of operation were not changed, because the signalling systems, even the more antiquated ones, were well matched to the levels of traffic, which always amounted to several tens of trains per day, as a minimum.

The selection process for awarding the concessions was also significantly different to that being used simultaneously for the ongoing freight concessions. It was accepted that a concession might receive a subsidy. Each bidder should quote the subsidy it required, from year to year. If the projected results of exploitation of the network permitted it, the responder could quote an annual tax payment, equivalent to a negative subsidy. The State recognised that it would not be possible to leave concessionaires free to invest on their own initiative and available means, given the magnitude of the sums required and the impossibility of ticket income financing them, in general. Therefore the State predetermined the level of investment which each concession should make, and the bidder should quote them as being charged to the State. The concessions would be for ten years, except in the case of the Urquiza-Subte concession (see below), which would be for twenty years. These periods were determined by the time it would take to complete the scheduled works, which was why the concession involving Subte had the longer period.

The bidders were subjected to a qualifying process in three stages. In the first, their business aptitude, financial ability and operating experience were graded. In the second, their Business Plan was evaluated, in which the responder should demonstrate the technical viability of their proposal. In these two stages, bidders who had not presented satisfactory documentation were disqualified. In the third stage only those who had passed the two previous stages were considered, and each case was evaluated by means of a single criterion: the total amount it would cost the State in subsidies and investments, as currently valued.

The tender process permitted bidders to bid for one or more suburban services, which resulted in the following six concessions:

- Metrovías S.A., from 1st January 1994, in charge of services on a 29.9km network which included the Urquiza Line and Buenos Aires Subte.
- Transportes Metropolitanos San Martin S.A., from 1st April 1994, in charge of services on a 56.3km network which included the Retiro-Pilar San Martin Line.
- Ferrovías S. A., from 1st April 1994, in charge of services on a 54.3km network which included the Belgrano Line from Retiro to Villa Rosa, known as the Belgrano North Line.
- Transportes Metropolitanos Belgrano Sur Line S.A., from 1st May 1994, in charge of services on a 66.3km network which

included the Belgrano Line between Buenos Aires Station and González Catán, and between Puente Alsina and Marinos del Crucero Belgrano.[7] known as the Belgrano South Line.
- Transportes Metropolitanos General Roca S.A., from 1st January 1995, in charge of services on a 260km network which included the Roca Line from Constitución to La Plata, Alejandro Korn, Cañuelas, plus the Villa Elisa-Temperley-Haedo line and the Ranelagh loop.
- Trenes de Buenos Aires S.A., from 29th May 1995, in charge of services on a 369.6km network which included the Sarmiento Line between Once, Mercedes and Lobos, and the Mitre Line between Retiro, Tigre, Capilla del Señor, Bartolomé Mitre and Zárate.

All these service transfers took place together on a holiday, during which there was no service, and normal service was resumed on the following day.

The Long Distance Passenger Trains

As part of the first freight concession, FEPSA had been required to accept that FA's intercity passenger trains would run over its network, and was charged with issuing tickets and care of passengers and trains. FA paid for salaries and a percentage of management and general expenses. This arrangement worked reasonably well because passenger services over the FEPSA network were both infrequent and relatively low speed and did not present special operational problems even over the busiest sections of the network.

The situation would change in the tenders which followed. The State determined that the bidders should quote a toll per train kilometre, which would be considered as one of the factors

[7] This station had been renamed in 1983 in memory of the crew members who died on the Argentine Navy cruiser Belgrano during the Malvinas/Falklands War in 1982.

used during the qualifying process. However, they were asked to provide tolls for two standards of passenger service: "commercial" and "social", "Commercial" service would mean that the passenger trains should operate at the speeds operated by FA at the time of receiving the concession. This would imply that certain stretches of track would need to be maintained for speeds of 100 or also 120km/hour. On the other hand, for "social" service the track maintenance would only need to be that required for freight trains. In the latter case, the effort required was assumed to be lower, and that consequently the toll quoted would also be lower. This approach was only adopted in 1992; it was arranged with the adjudicator of the Mitre network (the future NCA) and it was required for the Roca concession. It was stipulated that the State would have a period of time before deciding whether it would opt for commercial or social service. This solution was complicated and flawed, reflecting the difficulty of making long-term decisions about the passenger railway system at the political level.

During 1992, coordinated by the UCPRF – which was working on the privatisation of the suburban train services – there took place a study by a group of local and North American specialists, these last from the passenger train company AMTRAK. The study did nothing more than reiterate the results of all the objective analyses obtained over the last twenty years: many train services generated heavy losses, but a few covered their marginal costs, and another small number had moderate operational losses. All this gave rise to the expectation that it might be possible to achieve an equilibrium by improving capture of the demand for services with better marketing and better quality of service.

It is to be supposed that the study had followed from the decision to also privatize a basic network of long-distance passenger trains, which might be able operate with minimal State subsidy. However, something unexpected occurred: FA, via its administrator, expressed the need to immediately terminate the intercity train service, given that according to FA it was producing a loss which was about twice as large as that which the study had estimated. Eventually this matter rose to the level of the Finance Minister, who in this case was in agreement with FA and therefore decreed that all intercity trains would cease to run from March 1993. In the face of the protests generated in the whole country by this unconditional decision, the government searched for a political way out: given that the Provinces were demanding that these services should continue, they should take them over. FA would make locomotives and coaches available, and concessions would be given to those Provinces who wanted them, authorising them to run services and requiring them to pay the tolls specified in the concessions of the cargo and metropolitan networks through which they would run.

The government's offer was accepted by several Provinces: Córdoba, Tucumán, Chaco, Entre Ríos, La Pampa and Buenos Aires. But it was obvious that this political scheme was not a real solution. Was it logical that Tucumán should fund a service which would be used by many inhabitants of Santiago del Estero Province, with the latter not making the least contribution to the cost of the service? Such a scheme seemed most applicable in the case of the Province of Buenos Aires, where most passenger train services remained within its vast territory. So many Provinces adopted a cautious approach and let the offer pass.

Prior to this outcome, the government had tried to privatize the most promising service, Buenos Aires-Mar del Plata, where an average speed of 100km per hour would at that time have been competitive with road services. Various offers were received, but the commission evaluating them found that none were able to meet all the requirements of the tender, so the concession was not awarded. In the face of this failure, the government accepted an agreement to sign a contract with the Province of Buenos Aires for the Buenos Aires-Mar del Plata line. The whole of the intercity passenger services network within the Province was also included in the concession. The Province was permitted to subcontract the service; that is, to invite tenders for its private operation; but it did not do so. The Province was to act as an integral concessionaire for the line to Mar del Plata, and as a service concessionaire for the other lines.

In 1993 the Province created its own railway entity, Unidad Ejecutora del Programa Ferroviario Provincial (UEPFP, Provincial

Railway Programme Executive Unit), which took charge of a fairly large network of services inherited from FA and ran over the networks of four freight concessions. One of the first actions of the UEPFP was to reopen the branch from Guido to General Madariaga and to extend it to Pinamar, the first tranche of railway to be added to the national network since the extension of the Urquiza Line to General Lemos in 1981.

Liquidation of Ferrocarriles Argentinos (FA) and the Railway Heritage

Having successfully completed most of the concessions it had set itself to achieve, the government finally resolved to liquidate the State-owned railway companies; in that way transmitting the signal that there was not to be any reversal of the privatization process. Ferrocarriles Argentinos was liquidated, and later also Femesa, and the Ente Nacional de Administración de Bienes Ferroviarios (ENABIEF, National Entity for the Administration of Railway Assets) was created, dedicated to managing the immense railway heritage still held by the State. It consisted of an enormous number of buildings and other structures on abandoned lines and in vacated yards and stations which the State had deliberately not included in the concessions: many buildings which had formed parts of workshops, stores and locomotive depots, and a not insignificant amount of rolling stock in diverse states of repair, together with rails, materials and all kinds of spare parts.

On the other hand, several of the enormous workshops which were unnecessary for the activities of the concessions had been transferred to former workers cooperatives. Some of these cooperatives – Rosario and Perez, Laguna Paiva, Junin – continued to work on orders for the concessions, but never in sufficient quantity to sustain such activities in the longer term.

Later on, ENABIEF was dissolved and incorporated into the Organismo Nacional Administrador de los Bienes del Estado (ONABE, Organisation for National Administration of State Assets), responsible not only for railway assets but also for the heritage of other vanished companies and public organisations.

The destiny of the railway heritage ended up being one of the most questionable aspects of the railway reforms in the 90s. The State seemed to be unconcerned about its fate, and did not assign the resources which its preservation deserved.

For many years before privatization the property heritage of the railways was yet another unresolved matter. The State had inherited a huge amount of land embedded in almost all the major cities, sometimes magnified by the coexistence of several different railway companies, of which Rosario was the archetype, as it embraced the original installations of eight companies. This led, before nationalization, to the railways starting to work on the Plan Ferrourbanístico (Plan for Railways in Urban Locations), which envisaged unification of railway company installations, funded by the sale of the resulting spare land. In the decades which followed, Rosario, Mar del Plata, Córdoba, San Juan, Tucumán and other cities elaborated ambitious plans, which at best were only partially realised. These so-called ferro-urbanistic plans, were almost always too ambitious, and included unrealistic projects, with colossal yards for kinds of operations which no longer occurred in our railways. A case in point was in the Buenos Aires Central Market, where a railway yard was constructed capable of receiving a hundred or more goods wagons of vegetables, fruit and even fish, but where not even a single wagon of these items ever arrived.

Though FA collaborated with the provinces and municipalities in the planning of these projects, the central problem was that it did not have the funding to carry out the proposed works, since it first had to sell the spare buildings. In addition, many valuable plots of land were desired by municipalities in order to set up community parks, without having the budget to purchase them from the railway company. Because of this financial stranglehold, the few ferro-urbanistic works progressed very slowly and some were finally abandoned.

This problem changed when privatization began because, once the railway had concentrated on mass traffic flows and intercity passenger traffic had been abandoned, it became clear that the previous plans were almost all anachronistic. But the handling of this matter remained in the hands of an organization whose aim had nothing to do with planning for long-term railway requirements. An example of this was the Retiro Project in the City of Buenos Aires. With the aim of making land available for a property development of about 100 hectares along Avenida del Libertador and the Recoleta district, it was proposed to displace the three Retiro passenger termini and replace them with a single terminus which would be be constructed on the site of the Linea San Martín station. The magnificent edifice of the Linea Mitre Station would be converted into an enormous amusement mall, the Belgrano station would be demolished to allow extension of Eduardo Madero Avenue, and all cargo infrastructure in Retiro would be reduced to a few sidings because it was considered, against all informed opinion, that freight traffic to and from the port should operate, exclusively, via the small and disfunctional grid of tracks leading to the New Port. A competition for ideas in 1995 hardly improved on the scheme, but in the face of fierce opposition from railway, harbour and motor vehicle transport experts, this great project seems to have been abandoned, but without making known any alternative plan.

The Consequences of Railway Privatization

The crisis in the railway system had led the government of President Menem to embark on transfering it into private hands, initially rather timidly, almost as an experiment, with the Rosario-Bahía Blanca Corridor, but more generally and firmly from 1991. Once Decree 666/89 had been approved, after six years all the suburban system and the major part of the freight network had been privatized. This singular result was due to the political strength shown by the government during the whole period, which in any case led to the reelection of the President. Supported by a public opinion sensitized to the experience of hyperinflation, Menem imposed on his Party a policy which – for the railways, but not for them only – was the antithesis of that which had been applied immediately following the end of the war; in effect, during both periods, Argentina had aligned itself with the international trends of the time. Opposition to the reforms was lukewarm, and when radicalized factions tried to oppose by using the classic strategy of a strike, the reply was to deepen and accelerate the course of action chosen in 1989. The goodwill of political groups allied with the government and of the union leaders was won by means of some concessions: the decision to retain the Linea Belgrano in State hands with a promise to transfer it to administration by the UF; or the transfer of long distance passenger services to the Provinces, and to Buenos Aires in particular.

The economic and political changes which took place do not make it possible to clearly distinguish the effects of privatization, as they occurred, from the result of the application of contradictory policies following the crisis which befell the country at the end of the twentieth century. For this reason it is useful to examine the consequences with reference to three periods: that concluding in 1998 as hints of the crisis began, that terminating in 2003 as the worst of the crisis was over, and from then until mid-2007.

1991-1998: The Successful Reform

The initial consequences of privatization were considered to be very good, so much so that they aroused great international interest and experts from different places in the world arrived in Buenos Aires to closely examine what was happening. What did the success entail?

In the first place, an immediate and strong recovery of traffic; later, that this was achieved with a reduced complement of personnel such that the productivity index increased enormously; and lastly, that this attainment required far less government resource than during the period when the network had been a State-owned company. However, behind this optimistic panorama were unsolved problems which raised doubts about the long-term sustainability of the reform, but in the congratulatory atmosphere of economic success and political strength these were not attended to.

Recovery of demand began immediately for cargo and suburban services, of course relative to the extremely depressed levels of the period just before privatization, when FA felt it was doomed and had given up. But the recovery was real and rapidly rose above the levels in the second half of the previous decade. However, what happened in the suburban and freight markets was different, as we will soon see.

All the concessionaires were undeniably successful in achieving a rapid increase in the capacity of their transport services, by simply ensuring that sufficient motive power and rolling stock was available. Thanks to their superior agility in the purchasing of materials and spare parts, they were able to extend and maintain in service all their fleet. The cargo companies rested exclusively on their own financial efforts, given that they did not receive any cash from the State. On the other hand, the suburban companies benefitted from the State's undertaking to take on the cost of investment in renovations or major repairs and the purchase of second hand stock. During the early years the State punctually carried out those commitments.

Cargo

The cargo companies encountered very strong competition from road transport, and in some cases suffered from hard bargains driven by large potential clients. The railways had to fight for traffic, and even though their services increased rapidly, most companies were unable to achieve their optimistic traffic projections nor to reach expected charge levels. Cargo railway incomes were therefore appreciably lower than those projected in their tenders. Not all the companies suffered this problem in the same way: those in a better situation had been able to find a significant client for freight from among their group of shareholders. The income scarcity among the cargo concessions was a negative setback in the face of the initial optimism of the companies and the government. The firms ceased to pay the levies they had committed to, and kept a tight hold on the maintenance of the lines where it was not justified by the level of traffic. This situation became a weak point in the privatization process: although successful in restoring traffic levels, the concessionaires became easy targets for political attacks because of their abandoned lines and stations.

The cargo companies modernized their operational methods, but they did not comply with the investments which they had agreed to in their contracts; plans which, on the other hand, could well have merited a review from government to enable them to deal with the realities of the new market conditions. However, investments were made in branches and railway installations for access to new clients, and at certain junctions between lines which had always been disconnected, such as the crossings at Diego de Alvear and Coronel Suárez. The operational and commercial activities of the railways attracted significant investments from clients, as in the case of large grain elevators for the FEPSA network, the purchase by Minera Alumbrera of locomotives and wagons for the NCA network, or the cement discharging plant at Vicente Casares for Ferrosur.

If the cargo concession panorama was positive enough during this period, it was not so in the sectors which followed in the State or Provincial sphere. When the Belgrano Line tender failed, the government did not try again, but decided to recuperate this railway with strong State investment support. In fact, investment in the Belgrano between 1994 and 1998 amounted to almost the same as the total invested in all the private companies. But the result was not as expected, given that its traffic in 1998 became much lower than that in 1991, and the management of the new company which had been installed in 1994 was not able to reverse the decline.

Suburban Passengers

The demand captured by the suburban trains rose immediately following privatization, in response to the improved offer. But here there emerged a substantial difference between the two markets. For the suburban trains, as well as the better offer, the companies rapidly ensured a better service: trains became more frequent, and cleanliness of trains and stations was improved. Another not insignificant contributory factor was a public security programme funded by the State, which overturned the image of insecurity which the trains had acquired. In the face of this favourable mutation of service, demand responded very rapidly and demonstrated that, at least for the middle and low income portion of the population, the demand was not captive in any way, but was disposed to return rapidly to the train service as soon as the offer had become attractive. For certain, this strong recuperation was helped by the political decision of the government to maintain fares practically unchanged.

However, the set of concessions did not reach the maximum level of demand captured before the crisis in 1961, certainly under very different circumstances in the urban transport system: the demand in 1999 (480 million journeys) was 86% of that in 1957. Only the Roca Line concession managed to overtake its 1957 maximum, by capitalizing on the enormous investment that the State made by electrifying the Roca network, the number of journeys growing from 93 million in 1987 to 155 million in 1999. This result was obtained thanks also to the concession's good operational and commercial management and to the government's policy of reinforcing diesel-hauled services by taking advantage of the abundant availability of existing rolling stock together with new and refurbished locomotives; in that way gaining a notable improvement of locomotive-hauled services.

Among the other concessions, recovery of demand stood out in the two which had previously been doing badly: the North and South ex-Belgrano Line networks. This was also due to good management, which led to a substantial upturn in quality of service. In the Belgrano Sur this was due in particular to the re-use of idle long-distance passenger service coaches together with some locomotives supplied by the concessionaire. Other lines, which already had better levels of service, like the Mitre Line to Tigre and the Urquiza Line, consequently demonstrated more modest recoveries.

What seemed to be acting to limit an increase in suburban demand in almost all the concessions appeared to be the lack of rolling stock. Paradoxically, there was abundant inactive stock in the country, left over from the abandoned long distance services. Significant re-use of this stock would have meant putting a capital asset to work and creating a source of labour from its adaptation and maintenance. But having allocated 60 coaches to the Belgrano Sur Line, and other quantities to the Mitre and Urquiza Lines, the State chose to retain the remaining coaches for supposed Provincial projects, which never prospered. The least felicitous of these involved most of the metre-gauge carriages, which lay abandoned in closed yards and workshops, whereas their transfer to suburban concessions would have permitted a low-cost enhancement of the service offer. More or less the same limitation occurred in the broad-gauge networks. Another limitation which made itself felt was the number of level crossings, which by constraining train frequencies on the suburban lines degraded their services (and still does), particularly on the Sarmiento Line. This limitation was much more significant than that of the signalling system or the number of tracks.

Intercity Passengers

The national policy with regard to intercity passenger services was to have nothing to do with them, leaving the Provinces to make possible arrangements. Among the most significant initiatives was that of Buenos Aires, which had created the UEPFP, its Executive Unit for operating the Province's long-distance passenger services. The UEPFP seemed to want to set up a scheme opposite in concept to the railway concessions. The line from Alejandro Korn to Mar del Plata was transferred to the Province, and the Unit had a promising start with the inauguration of the service to Pinamar, but in the following years was in general unable to modernise the services nor to recover the demand. Taking advantage of the influence manifested by the Province, the UEPFP began a confrontational course of action with the cargo and metropolitan concessions, refusing to pay the required tolls owing to poor track maintenance and other alleged failures to comply. By 2000 the Unit owed some 40 million pesos (when one peso was still equivalent to one US dollar) to the cargo companies, in the face of inaction by the State, which neither insisted that the claimed poor track be maintained nor that the tolls be paid. The non-payment of the tolls gave the cargo companies a motive to defer maintenance on those lines which they were not using intensively, and was why the declining state of the tracks led to even further deterioration of the passenger services on some lines. On other lines service ceased because of flooding on the tracks.

The arrangements experienced in other Provinces was erratic. Tucumán supported the service to Retiro in Buenos Aires, but with long periods of discontinuity, Córdoba took over the concession for the "Tren a las Sierras" (a service through the northwestern tourist zone of the Province between the capital and Cruz del Eje), and on several occasions considered reopening traffic to Buenos Aires but never did, Rio Negro launched a rehabilitated service to Bariloche and imported some second-hand locomotives and carriages from Spain, Chaco did the same, but in this case it was for a local service based in Resistencia.

Not very many of these services experienced positive outcomes. They could not compete with omnibus services, given the low train speeds that were possible on the tracks maintained by the cargo companies. Their operations led to losses and though Provincial subsidies were provided, they were not sufficient for good rolling-stock maintenance, which raised many complaints from passengers because of delays and the poor state of the trains. Towards the end of 2001 everything pointed towards the disappearance of intercity passenger railway services in Argentina.

Role of the State

During this period the role of the State was ambiguous. On the one hand, the State had started and sustained a programme of reforms which would have been unthinkable a few years before, with many successes and some failures. However, it did not insist on engaging with the rejected concessions but instead used them as tokens for political negotiation with the Unions and the Justicialist Party in the Province of Buenos Aires. Once the privatization process had been completed, the moment for confirming the concession contracts arrived, and here the lack of adequate plans for subsequent stages became even more evident. A troublesome theme which emerged was to do with the entity in overall control. Since the dissolution of the National Railways Board, the public railway company had operated without any real external control, and the country had lost its previous experience of this delicate matter.

For irrational reasons, the State had carried forward the concession process by means of two independent technical groups, both subordinated to the Transport Minister, when really only one was necessary. In 1993 the cargo privatization group was moved into the recently created Comisión Nacional de Transporte Ferroviario (CNTF, National Railway Transport Commission) which took over control of the cargo and intercity passenger train concessions. On the other hand, the suburban privatization group, by ministerial resolution, took over control of the contracts of the respective concessions until an Autoridad de Transporte del Área Metropolitana (ATAM, Metropolitan Transport Area Authority) was created, which never happened. For a time there were two control entities, which led to frictions over certain matters where their competences did not seem to be clearly defined.

Finally, in 1996 the government decided to combine the control of all railway services with that of road transport, which had its own control entity, the Comisión Nacional del Transporte Automotor. The three control entities were unified into the Comisión Nacional de Regulación del Transporte (CNRT, National Commission for Transport Regulation). The name of this Commission was equivocal since more than one regulating entity – that is, an establisher of norms and conflict resolver – had been assigned control and supervision; regulation itself was actually in the hands of the Transport Minister. Also, the bringing together of road and rail transport under the control of the same entity did not signify an advance towards always desirable coordination, but rather involved an inefficient loss of specialization.

1999-2002: The Model Crumbles

From 1998, the Argentine economy began to suffer from growing problems: successive international financial crises (Mexico, Russia, Brazil), falls in the price of commodities exported by the country, depressed international commerce, overvaluation of local currency and growth of the external debt. To the economic crisis in the making was added the increasing political weakness of the government since the elections at the end of 1997 and during the following six-year electoral period, which deterred it from taking unpopular corrective measures. The change of government at the end of 1999 did not improve the situation: while the international scenario continued to worsen, the credibility of the new administration faded away in a few months and during all of 2001 found itself in a recession.The governing Alliance[8] was defeated in the elections held in October of that year and financial collapse in November together with an explosive social reaction did away with that government. The privatised railways suffered in the ways that follow below.

Cargo

The demand for cargo services had stalled 1998 and in 2001 had gone down by 15% with respect to the maximum level achieved in 1997 during the recovery phase. To the decrease of export sales and fall in construction activity was added the very seriously inundation of the low-lying plains in the west of the Province of Buenos Aires, which affected the Ferroexpreso Pampeano and BAP networks. In spite of the latter company having worked to raise the track level, for the first time in its history the line from Buenos Aires to Mendoza had been cut by the overflowing of La Picasa Lake, which obliged a deviation of its traffic over the NCA network, lengthening the end to end route by about 160km. All the companies suffered from the impact of the devaluation in early 2002, which immediately affected the purchase of spare parts abroad, upon which depended the maintenance of the locomotive fleet. The financial situation of several companies became fragile,

[8] This was a political alliance of the Unión Cívica Radical Party and a new Party called Frepaso (which does not exist today). This coalition won the presidential election, and for that reason the administration of President De la Rua became known as the Alliance Government.

while the failure to pay the required levies or make the obligatory investments created a context of great uncertainty with regard to the future of the concession contracts.

In spite of this, in 2001 company traffic had stopped falling and by the end of the year had slightly recovered. This was confirmed in 2002, helped by the great devaluation, which boosted the exporting sectors and reactivated construction activity. The five privatised networks ended 2002 with a traffic level just below those of the maxima either in 1983, under FA management, or in 1997, when privatization began. As their charges were not regulated, they could be adjusted to what the market would bear, particularly in the case of the transport of commodities, and this compensated for the rise in costs, so their financial situation began to improve.

As regards the Belgrano Railway, just before the change of government towards the end of 1999 the outgoing administration carried out its promise to the Union of Railwaymen, giving it a concession and agreeing to provide State funds for investment, which became impossible because of the crisis which followed. The Belgrano's income were falling because the company had less and less rolling stock in service. Its traffic, which in 1997 had been barely one third of that achieved in 1983, fell in 2002 to an insignificant sixth: less than one million tons on a several thousand kilometre network nominally in service.

Concerning the cargo concessions, the role of the State was absence and lack of interest. In contrast to those for passengers, these concessions required revision of their contracts, because failures to comply were building up both ways – no levy payments, no realisation of promised investments, no toll payments – and this created a growing uncertainty about the future of these concessions. But the State had no interest whatsoever in the revision of the cargo contracts. An important theme concerned the network in service, which owing to the lack of company finance was in fact being reduced to its productive components, leaving without service and maintenance those lines which lacked the capacity to attract cargoes. This reality had never been recognised during the State era and under the new conditions its indifference continued.

The privatised companies, left to themselves, necessarily had to cut absolutely unproductive costs, but this also placed them in a situation of presumed contractual failure. The State should have recognised the reality of the situation to impose on the companies, in any case, effective custody of their assets, while also permitting them to commercially exploit unused station spaces which would have contributed to alleviation of costs and preservation of the railway patrimony.

Suburban Passengers

The suburban railways also suffered from the impact of the crisis, which in their case was deferred but deeper. Until 1998 the concession contracts had been reasonably complied with by both parties. The railway's offering had been raised, quality of service had improved, and demand had responded positively on all the lines, limited only by rolling stock availability. But from 1999, the State began to falter in its financial commitments with the concessions, by delaying stage payments of works in progress. This situation accentuated during 2000, and the programme of investments continued to fall below that achieved in 1997, becoming virtually stalled in 2001.

From 1997 the Menem government had renegotiated the six suburban concession contracts, and finalised agreements with the four concessionary company groups: Trenes de Buenos Aires (TBA, the Mitre and Sarmiento lines), Metropolitano (the Roca, Belgrano Sur and San Martín lines), Ferrovías (the North Belgrano line), and Metrovías (the Urquiza and Subte lines). This implied investments of several thousand million dollars for modernisation of all the suburban system, particularly for the electrification of important lines where diesel locomotives were still being used. The agreements had maintained the original commitment with regard to subsidies and investments from the State, but it also wanted to create new resources: the companies were committed to converting any unpaid levies into investment funds, and a staged increase in fares was planned, so that they would be almost doubled in real terms. The funds so generated would be put towards the financing of a new investment programme. For this scheme to be viable, the period of the concessions was increased to thirty years.

The application in practice of these plans was not easy. Approval of the renegotiations was attacked by the political sectors then in opposition, self-designated organisations of users and other interest groups which manifested noisily at public discussion meetings. The Alianza government inherited this situation and decided to maintain the renegotiated contractual scheme, but for purely political reasons it chose to revise all the agreements and shorten their period to only 24 years. When in early 2001 the government decided to apply the delayed stage increase in fares recorded in the revised agreements, the opposition manifested itself again, and raised a legal challenge. The increase was finally put in place, but as time passed it began to be clear that the contracts thus renegotiated could not be adhered to.

In mid-2001 as the financial situation of the State worsened, subsidy payments began to be delayed together with, for the first time, a strong general decline in demand caused by the economic depression. In January 2002, following the devaluation of the peso to one third of its value, there started a series of price rises which affected all the population, while initially salaries remained the same. This deepened the effect on demand and during that year journeys on the suburban network fell by 25% compared to its maximum in 1999.

The new government reasoned that the social conditions did not permit raising fares, and that initially the companies should absorb the combined effects of rising costs, the fall in demand and the interruption of subsidy payments. The companies adjusted to costs by reducing services, train maintenance, surveillance and security, during a period when rolling stock and railway installations were being increasingly vandalized. Many of the advances brought about by privatization were rapidly lost during this period, but it should be said that not all the companies allowed normal services, cleanliness and a sense of safety to degrade. Metrovías and Ferrovías were the first to recover, also helped by the abrupt fall in service offerings of their rival, the Línea San

Martín. The performance of the different companies in the face of the crisis reflected the very different evolution of demand in each concession, under comparable social conditions. This continues to be the most reliable indicator of quality of service.

Investments became paralized and the renegotiation agreements remained dormant due to financial unviability. Despite this, the State believed it was not advisable to terminate the concessions when their original period came to term, which would have led it to recover five of the six concessions; it only cancelled the concession of the Línea San Martín to Metropolitano, the service of the former having worsened (and demand fallen) more than in any other concession.

With fares set at early 2001 levels, the State had to acknowledge the increase in costs faced by the companies, initially in the rising prices of consumables and spare parts, later of energy, and finally of staff salaries and diminishing subsidies, until in 2001 it initiated a cycle of growth. The State decreed a railway emergency, which meant a significant moratorium in the carrying out of company maintenance requirements, reducing them to only those essential for safety, leaving aside all other aspects, and making obvious the deterioration in the state of the fleet and installations in several sectors of the network.

The Role of the State

The role of the State in this stormy period was not at the high level required. It did not pay attention to the necessary formalisation of the situation the cargo concessions were in, but became involved in renegotiating the prematurely launched suburban contracts, ahead of what had been foreseen in the contracts themselves, and this was badly conceived because the government and the concessionaires then incurred an excess of optimism which led them to agree plans which later became unrealizable.

State and concessionaires fell into the same systemic error that was made during the FA period, of having unlimited confidence in great plans for electrification while omitting consideration of the excellent results obtained by the Ferrovías and Metropolitano concessions with diesel-hauled services. For example, simultaneous electrification of the lines to Pilar and La Plata were favoured, which would have generated an excessive number of coaches destined for the scrapyard, without contemplating that the rolling stock and locomotives released by the electrification of either one of those lines could be reused on the other line with fantastic results. At the same time, again left aside was re-utilisation on the suburban lines of the unused long-distance coaches, which slowly deteriorated in Provincial hands or while waiting for someone to decide to use them; stock which at moderate expense could have been adapted for suburban use, thus creating sources of work for declining local industry. High impact safety measures, such as raising platform levels for diesel services, were not even considered. Because of this, the proposed investment level was far above that available, as also was the fare rise which should fund it. From 2000 the government's decision was to go through said renegotiations, but without altering their substance, proposing irrelevant changes, such as reducing their period to 24 instead of thirty years.

During this transition period it was becoming clear that the power to make decisions was increasingly being transferred to the Transport Minister, which weakened the CNRT. The latter had been placed in administration in 2001; since then its Board had never been renewed, and the organisation lost influence over railway matters. As a positive move, for the first time a Sub-Secretariat of Railway Transport was created in 2001, but it was not endowed with a sound formal structure nor a cast of established and experienced staff.

The State also showed itself to be inactive in defence of railway spaces against intrusions and invasions, almost always organized and politically supported. Neither did it act in defense of the genuine interest which the community had in expanding railway transport; for example, in the case of the transport of methanol by the company Ferrosur, which was obstructed by a conjunction of political and trade union interests that led to the squandering of a railway investment already in place and left the traffic to road transport, without justification.

2003-2006: A Partial and Uncertain Recovery

The year 2003 was the start of the economic and politico-institutional normalization of the country, and there began an ephemeral cycle of growth. Railway activity shared this development with a recovery of traffic in both main railway markets.

Cargo

The cargo services were operated by six concessions, as previously noted. Five of these were in the hands of private companies: FEPSA, NCA, Ferrosur Roca, BAP San Martín and Ferrocarril Mesopotámico General Urquiza. The latter two were combined into a single administration, the Brazilian company called América Latina Logística (ALL, Latin America Logistics). These four privately-owned companies reached 2006 having transported 30% more than the last maximum of the State-owned company – for the broad and standard gauge networks – in 1983, and the growth trend continued. Several companies responded by acquiring motive power, in general second-hand locomotives which had been reconstructed and modernized. The concessioned companies continued without subsidies, relying on the income from transport charges, their investment and maintenance policy being that which was only adequate for the running of cargo trains. But in the end the State had decided that it would intervene actively in infrastructure investment, as it would do by supporting FEPSA in the reconstruction of some sections of flooded tracks, undertaking the work of reconstruction of the stone-ballasted embankment and tracks of the crossing over La Picasa lake, which could restore the direct connection between Buenos Aires and Mendoza for ALL. This willingness was appropriate, since the companies would not have been able to carry out, by themselves, works having a long useful life in order to correct the effects of recurring floods when not even 15 years remained before the termination of the concessions.

The good performance of the private cargo companies contrasted with the situation of the Belgrano, which under control of the Union of Railwaymen (UF) continued serving an insignificant demand until 2005. This extensive railway, which in 1983 had carried 22% of Argentine railway cargo traffic, saw this percentage fall to only 3% in 2005. The Belgrano situation was a great failure of the privatizing process because, when the first tender was frustrated, the government set up a unique form of privatization for the transfer to UF. Faced with this poor result, the government planned a new concession in 2004, but the tender failed. A private concessionaire withdrew at the last moment and two other companies were rejected for not following the rules of the competition. These rules implied enormous risks for future concessionaires because of poorly determined debts which would be transferred to them from the previous concession. Finally in 2006 a new private entity was constituted which took over the management of the railway under direct contract from the State, Called Sociedad Operadora de Emergencia (SOESA, Emergency Operating Company), it was formed from a Chinese investment group, the two companies which had applied for the failed tender, and three Unions: the UF, La Fraternidad and the Camioneros (Truck Drivers). The inclusion of the railway unions was a decision which, though without the support of previous demonstrably favourable results, could be justified in the political context; but not so in the case of the Camioneros, which represented interests essentially antagonistic to the railways, some way beyond any traditional references towards coordinating the systems of transport. In its initial years, SOESA should receive funds from the State to sustain its operations and to invest in the renovation of infrastructure and rolling stock, SOESA began its activities in mid-2006.

Cargo transport would benefit from some of the investments directed at passenger services, which are treated below, but as these develop they may cause problems which will need to be resolved. The government did not intervene in the cargo concessions, except on the matter of the infrastructure investments which itself had taken over, as mentioned above. Finally, during this period it was realised that the cargo concession contracts should be standardized by means of renegotiations. Guidelines for this included: that the companies transform the debts on their levies into investments, nett of any credits against the State (like the passenger train tolls); and that they should commit to investing a percentage of their income.

However, the cargo concessions were about to reach the halfway point in their terms of thirty years. This should have triggered a renegotiation of the extension of their terms in order to be able to promote investments which would lead to traffic growth. Not having done so could only lead to a new deterioration in the state of the railway system.

Suburban Passengers

Recovery of services and demand for traffic had continued in the suburban network, by 2006 reaching 90% of the maximum demand in 1999. But this overall result obscured significant differences between concessions, since Ferrovías and Metrovías had done much better than that maximum, whereas the situation of two concessions with poor operating performances had fallen well below those figures, at no more than to 25%. But perhaps even that figure did not completely reflect reality, since neglect had much increased in some concessions, the incentive to do better having disappeared following reductions in ticket prices and in the additional subsidies which the companies in question would receive. This neglect in turn deteriorated the social environment of the services and added to increasingly poor public safety in the suburban area. From this it followed that a sector of the public which had returned to the railway after privatization would once again abandon it.

The Línea San Martín concession is worth mentioning. It had been granted under conditions apparently very favourable to the State, but based on an exaggeratedly optimistic traffic estimate. By the end of 2004 service on this concession had shown the most deterioration, and its level of demand had almost halved since the maximum five years before. The government annulled the concession and entrusted its operations to a private company formed from the other three metropolitan concessions, the Unidad de Gestión Operativa (UGOFE, Unit for Operational Management). After two years this company had been successful and demand had risen to within ten percent of the previous maximum.

Fares had remained fixed until the end of 2006 and increases in wages and in the cost of fuel, spare parts and other items had been compensated for by the State, so that these operating subsidies had risen without interruption since 2002 and had amply overtaken their real values in 1996. In spite of this considerable additional subsidy, it was not possible for service quality to remain the same as that which had existed until 2001. On several of the lines, the apparent state of the trains had seriously declined, and service alterations were continuous and similar to those which had occurred during the previous period of State operation. But those companies which did not neglect quality of service experienced a rise in demand, which confirmed that the suburban system had the potential to capture traffic even if it was far from being fully realised.

Intercity Passengers

Long-distance or interurban passenger trains continued to be the sector with the poorest results, in the face of the failure of almost all the provincial iniatives which attempted to recover the services, except for the atypical case of a modest system of trains in the locality of Resistencia. Towards the middle of the first decade in the twenty-first century it seemed that intercity trains had entered an irreversible decline. But the State adopted a policy of recovery for this sector of the railway business, including actively intervening in its development without spurning the use of major technological advances. In Decree 1.261/04, the national State re-assumed the provision of long-distance inter-provincial services, and the action plan for these objectives received approval in Decree 1.683/05. As set out in its matters for consideration, these were directed mainly towards the transport of passengers on the suburban railways of Buenos Aires and on long-distance intercity routes. Decree 1683 did not explicitly mention freight services, but much of the investment in infrastructure intended for intercity passenger services would also benefit any freight operations using the same tracks.

As a first step towards this policy, the national State had taken over the re-establishment of the service between Buenos Aires and Córdoba. However, it did this not by creating a new public company, but rather by entrusting the matter to a company (Ferrocentral) created for the purpose by the NCA and Ferrovías concessionaires, the former being the operator of the tracks that the new service would use, and the second being an operator of suburban passenger trains. This service started in 2004, and offered a good level of quality, except for the time of the journey, which depended on the state of the tracks, until then maintained only as necessary for cargo trains. But it was a service which required a significant subsidy level. The government decided to make intensive use of a resource tried out during the previous decade: purchase in Spain and Portugal of second-hand rolling stock of the same (broad) gauge, which could be renovated by the local railway industry, thus usefully providing a source of work.

Going beyond Decree 1.683, there also had been launched a programme of high-speed and high-performance trains: the former foreseeing operation at the highest velocity provided commercially by railway technology, and the latter in accordance with the current European standards for lines not described as "high-speed", High-speed lines to Rosario and Mar del Plata had been put out to tender, and a high-performance line to Mendoza had been announced. However, these tenders were opened with no prior assessment of their feasibility and no preliminary engineering evaluation to justify them, leaving up to the bidders – from the large international groups which dominated in this field of technology – the choice of routes, gauges, and other essential characteristics. It repeats, perhaps in an aggravated way, the mistake made towards the end of the 1990s during the renegotiations of the metropolitan concessions, when the State had left strategic decisions in the hands of the concessionaires.

Conclusions

During the thirty years between 1977 and 2006 the reality of Argentine railways was transformed. The size of the system became drastically reduced. The great State-owned company vanished. Freight transport was taken over by private companies which on the whole provided a positive if variable service, particularly when compared with that of the Belgrano railway, which continued vegetating in a quasi-State limbo. Suburban trains offered a wide range of service quality which resulted in uneven recovery after 2001. Intercity passenger services seemed to disappear, until the national government again took them over, in spite of the lack of any demand which would justifying running them. Paradoxically, the government continually delayed investments in vital sectors of the network, while putting forward projects which would incur extremely costly investments in high-speed advanced technology where it was not necessary. Meanwhile, the enormous railway patrimony, especially its properties, continued deteriorating in the face of political indifference.

After nationalization, the railway did nothing but decay. This was due, to a great extent, to strong and inevitable competition from alternative modes of transport, modes which grew vigorously after the Second World War; this was no different to what happened in many other countries, and particularly in Latin America. However, in the case of Argentina there were local features which worsened the inevitable crisis, these being: an over-enlarged railway system; a seriously distorted network, with parallel routes, diverse gauges, and poorly integrated or interconnected component subsystems. All of this arose from a badly understood inheritance from the past, in which the supposedly endless riches of the country and its bright future of never-ending growth stimulated all kinds of foolish investments: a network which never arrived at some parts of the country; a geography which never produced abundant mass traffic over long distances, the main reason for being an active railway and justifies it as a necessary transport mode; and a poorly developed heavy industrial sector, which is the type of production which has most in common with the railway industry.

These realities, which technical studies clearly expressed time and again, were never taken on, together with their inevitable consequences, by most of the successive governments. There were long periods of immobility during which the underlying problems were not tackled as time passed. Governments limited themselves to the administration of a gigantic and difficult to manage organisation, and to plan proposals for works which lacked valid strategic objectives. This alternated with spasmodic processes of untimely adjustment or reform during which attempts were made to put into practice necessary measures which had been delayed for years.

The State company (FA) developed a gigantic internal bureaucracy which became another centre of power within the State, and at times imposed on the State a railway policy which tended to preserve the *status quo* in favour of contractors, trade unions, purveyors, and a few big clients, while putting disproportionate hopes on to costly technology modernisation programmes which were anyway never realised. In spite of its large cast of highly qualified technicians and professionals, the State company was unable to propose to the latest managers of the day an alternative railway policy which, while acknowledging the local conditions, would point towards the clear directions emerging in the international sphere. It was not possible, then, to provide a plan and a programme of action which could be sustained against political pressures; that is, the creation of what we would now call a Public Policy was impossible. The ephemeral leadership which came and went in the management of the public company was never decisive nor strong enough to face up to the interest groups, both internal and external, which interfered in the situation. Inevitable and painful measures, called "rationalizations" or "adjustments", could not be carried out "from within" in a planned, orderly and consensual manner between those involved, but instead they were imposed by the political authorities on the company and on the technical bureaucracy which managed it. But this could only be successful during exceptional and dramatic moments in the recent history of the country, when the rulers, legitimate or not, counted on the enormous powers given to them by society when it was faced with an abyss of violence and civil war on the one hand, or hyperinflation and economic ruin on the other.

In the last decade of the 20th Century a complex, flawed and controversial reform of the railway sector was carried out, which created a management model based on private companies. However, little by little, and more so after the turn of the century. State interference returned, and once again the railway began to depend more and more on the public accounts.

Electrification of part of the General Roca Railway suburban network was inaugurated in 1985. This was the most important railway development in the previous fifty years, which had been delayed for decades. An electric train at Temperley Station. *(Photo: Museo Nacional Ferroviario)*

Modernization of the privatized railways and of the cargo concession services which followed led to long double- or triple-headed freight trains. *(Photo: Guido Beck)*

Cargo train of the Nuevo Central Argentino (NCA) Railway, the company which transports the highest tonnage among the new set of freight concessions. *(Photo: Guido Beck)*

Modernized signalling and train control telemetry facilitated reduced costs and enhanced productivity, permitting the removal of guards, and guard's vans from the ends of trains. *(Photo: Jorge Nicolo)*

JORGE E. WADDELL

6 | The Railway System Becomes Worse, Smaller and More Costly 2007-2015

By 2006 rather more than two years had passed of the political cycle inaugurated by the presidencies of Néstor Kirchner and later of Cristina Fernández de Kirchner. This short period was dominated by the need to emerge from the economic emergency caused by the 2001 financial crisis. Government priorities were centred on renegotiating the external debt and dealing with societal demands. In this situation the railways were not a priority, and no significant policy changes took place. In the previous chapter some policy initiatives had been featured together with doubts regarding their efficacy. Now, ten years later and after the end of the Kirchner cycle of presidencies, an informed assessment of those policies can be undertaken.

During the presidency of Néstor Kirchner, characterised by recovery from the economic emergency and debt renegotiation, the country benefitted from the increase in funds due to a boom in production and the price of soya beans. But with regard to railway policy it was notable that things continued as before, except for slight nuancies. There were no drastic changes and any alterations took place gradually and were rather tentative. The railway system functioned on the basis of concessions to private companies granted during the 90s, with a few modifications introduced by the Alianza government and the transitional government of President Eduardo Duhalde. There was no intention of making essential changes but only to modify some of the details.

The two terms of office held by Cristina Fernández de Kirchner were rather different, characterised by economic ups and downs, times of rapid growth followed by crises, in the frame of a permanent confrontation between different economic and political protagonists. Railway policy now underwent drastic changes, although erratic and contradictory. The system entered the centre of the political scene, firstly because of serious service problems, secondly owing to certain accidents which caused a high number of victims, and lastly because the government itself used the railways as a central component of its political propaganda. But all of this did not prevent an enormous deterioration of the network.

Emergence of the Railways from the Economic and Financial Crisis 2003 to 2007

We can now assess the effect on the railways of the Kirchner presidences before moving on to the final years (2007-2015) we consider in this book, which begin at the 150th Anniversary of the first railway in Argentina. The analysis will be done in terms of the three major sectors of the railway service: cargo, suburban passenger and intercity passenger.

Cargo

Following the transfer of the San Martín and General Urquiza concessions into América Latina Logística (ALL) recorded in Chapter Five, the original six cargo service concessions had become five, of which four were in the hands of private companies: FEPSA, NCA, Ferrosur Roca and ALL. The fifth was the Ferrocarril Belgrano Cargas, which had been conceded to the Union of Railwaymen. The performance of this whole system, in terms of what had been foreseen ten years before, was positive if rather slow to improve. From the start the four private concessions had made a firm decision to recover the cargoes lost by Ferrocarriles Argentinos (FA). This was attenuated by several factors: the overvalued exchange rate damaged the export of agricultural products, which was the main cargo together with construction materials; rather low transport charges to offset competition from road vehicles; and finally the poor state of the railway infrastructure, which the concession companies could not afford to renovate, and the State did nothing to help with except in very few cases, such as the repair of ALL's San Martín trunk route across La Picasa lake. In spite of this, the cargo railway recovered the lost traffic, repaired old or purchased second-hand rolling stock, and transported an average level of 20 million tons per year. This, though small in comparison to the total goods transported in the country, was at least in absolute terms comparable with that of FA in 1983.

In 1998 the government had decided that it was necessary to renegotiate the cargo concessions, because of compliance failures by both parties and in order to make investment arrangements more flexible. The renegotiation was a slow process which took five years to finish, and in the end, ten years from the start, the government's Comisión Bicameral de Seguimiento de las Privatizaciones (Bicameral Privatization Commission) only approved three of the renegotiated concessions: FEPSA, Ferrosur Roca and NCA; ALL was never approved. The result of these renegotiations was to improve the situation of the companies, but not sufficiently to enable an increase in the scale of their businesses. Their main problem, which had not been discussed during the renegotiations, was the 30-year term of the concessions. Thirty years was not enough time to set up effective investments in the railway business, and they were already between 17 and 20 years into their terms, with no prospect of being awarded the possible 10-year extension originally offered. However, it is not correct to say that there was no investment in the privatized cargo network. Though there were no major infrastructure projects, the railways carried out works in order to improve system operations, including modifications to traffic intensive lines and better access to the ports. In addition, other non-railway companies invested significantly in grain elevators, industrial access spurs and private ports, all of which added value to the railway network.

By 2007 cargo network traffic had increased to 25 million tons, or 24.2 million tons not counting the Belgrano Cargas network. For comparison, this was approximately what FA was achieving before the disastrous general strike of 1961. The discordant note in this improvement was the narrow-gauge Belgrano network. It was larger than all the other cargo networks put together. This network was generally in poor condition, and only part of it was being operated. The earlier major investments during the 90s in infrastructure, motive power, cargo wagons and train control communications had increased performance by 50%, but when the Belgrano was handed over to the Union of Railwaymen in 1999 the network began to deteriorate again. The Néstor Kirchner government eventually cancelled the contract with the Union and in 2006 handed over Belgrano Cargas to SOESA (Sociedad Operativa de Emergencia S. A.) the absurdly named company described in Chapter Five, but the deterioration of rolling stock and tracks continued. The government neglected all the cargo networks, and ignored the growing occurrence of vandalism, intrusions onto the tracks and yards, obstruction of access to some of the ports, boycotts by truckers, and illegal actions such as impeding the loading of cargo and of stealing cargo from trains. Nevertheless, during these years the cargo lines managed to recover, except in the one case, but they did it with no support whatever.

Suburban Passenger

The six concessions to private companies established in the 90s, described in Chapter Five, had been able to grow considerably by much improving the quality, quantity and security of their services, leading to a maximum of almost 480 million passengers in 1999, the best performance achieved over the past fifty years of operation. The concessions had invested in rolling stock and track works, having had the benefit of gradually decreasing State subsidies. This success then led to demand exceeding the planned provisions, and caused the concessions to request renegotiation of their contracts, which was agreed to by the government. New contracts were set up, which included extending the duration of the concessions and requiring the companies to improve their networks by making large investments in electrification, raising platform height and complete renewal of rolling stock. These investments, amounting to thousands of millions of USDollars, would be funded by credits loans guaranteed by a gradual increase in ticket prices. All of these renegotiations took place as currency convertibility was coming to an end and the country was in a significant recession.

The 2001/2002 crisis, which caused the downfall of the Alianza government was disastrous for the suburban passenger system. Traffic demand had fallen, and the devaluation of the peso made it impossible for the companies to obtain the proposed international credits. In this situation the State should have acted to avoid major problems, but initially it moved in the wrong direction. Instead of cancelling the renegotiated contracts and reverting to the original set, the government and concessionaires agreed to return to the renegotiated contracts, but to delay the investments until the circumstances had improved. This of course never happened, and by Decree 2075 on 16th October, 2002, the government declared a "Railway Emergency" in the Buenos Aires Metropolitan area. This meant that all infrastructure works were suspended, whether started or not, including those that had been agreed in the renegotiated contracts. The only exceptions were emergency works necessary in order to guarantee services and maintain them for the lower traffic demands. These would be funded by the State, in recognition of the fact that its subsidy payments had been delayed. In addition, all the contractual arrangements for increasing ticket prices against performance criteria were also suspended.

The emergency declaration had been necessary, but should have been for a sensible length of time, until new contractual arrangements could be legally agreed between both sides. However, the emergency remained *sine die*, and its effects became disastrous. The Transport Ministry had enormous discretion in regard of service provision, ticket prices, subsidies, etc, but had an almost total lack of specialist economic or technical staff. Independent oversight by the CNRT had become ineffective, the concessions were less financially transparent, and they had initiated unplanned technical projects with dubious results. In summary, the Emergency Decree had established a new relationship with the concessioned companies: "Given the shortage of funds, the State will provide what it can when it can; in the face of this, the companies would have to provide indispensable services and maintenance". Thus the companies had great freedom of action without the State demanding much and as the government could not provide what was necessary to maintain continuity of service, it neither investigated nor controlled the companies. As the government's priority was to maintain the level and purchasing power of railway salaries, the Unions supported or at least offered no obstacle to this relationship. Thus the State, companies and Unions took part in an activity which denigrated both the service and its clients, and the Emergency was a perfect scheme for rapidly destroying all the achievements of the previous decade, which nobody realised nor cared about. The result was catastrophic. The government of Kirchner which took over in 2003 continued with the abnormality of the railway emergency. The enormous discretion available to the Executive fitted perfectly with its vocation of accumulating dominance over the other centres of power in the Republic, which included the total subordination of the concession companies, forcing them into being permanent suplicants for official favours. This was because the concession system had become entirely fictional. Non-existent contracts for railway services were replaced by arbitrary rules jointly agreed between the State and the concessionaires; that is, between the controllers and the controlled with no concern nor plan for technical or financial constraints.

By now the seven Metropolitan lines (originally six concessions) were operated by the following four concession companies: Trenes de Buenos Aires (TBA), Metropolitano, Ferrovías, and Metrovías, as set out in Chapter Five. Between 2003 and 2007 a gradual loss of traffic was noted because of the fall in quality of the services, especially the poor state of the rolling stock, bad timekeeping, the decline of safety and scarce cleanliness. All the lines had suffered in this way, but there were some differences. The two smaller companies, Ferrovías and Metrovías, had been able to better maintain their quality of service and lost fewer passengers; later on, their recovery was more rapid. On the other hand, TBA and Metropolitano lost many more passengers as their quality of service deteriorated. The three concessions in the Metropolitano Group, the San Martín, Belgrano Sur and Roca Lines were the most damaged. The company had been taken over by Taselli Group, a business which was dedicated to the purchase of failing companies in order to revive them or break them up, as they had done with the Altos Hornos Zapla steelworks and the Río Turbio coal mines. Probably this type of company might fulfil a useful function in an economy, but it was rare to hand over an indispensable public service. The policy of the Taselli Group was to maximise profits by reducing costs, which therefore minimized maintenance of the lines and stock. The services degraded immediately, which added to the suffering of the public caused by the 2001/2002 crisis, so they began to seek better ways to travel. Among the Metropolitano lines the worst affected was the San Martín, so much so that the government terminated its concession. Together with TBA, Ferrovías and Metrovías companies, it was managed by the newly formed UGOFE, introduced in the previous Chapter. This new company group would manage the lines on behalf of the State and would charge a percentage of the operating costs plus the expenditure on the works to be carried out, by way of compensation. This arrangement was highly beneficial for the companies in the group, but not for the public purse.

For the Roca Line the government had agreed with the Taselli Group that certain works should be carried out, especially extending electrification of the lines from Glew to Alejandro Korn, and from Temperley to Claypole. But for lack of technical expertise in the Transport Ministry, these works were poorly done: only one of the pair of tracks to Korn was electrified, so operating capacity was much reduced; and only one electric train at a time could run on the section from Temperley to Claypole for lack of sufficient electric power, which meant that diesel trains had to be intercalated. The Roca sought to gain favour by establishing middle distance services, including weekend trains to General Alvear. The TBA company, concessionaire of the Mitre and Sarmiento lines, also limited by the crisis restrictions, used its own workshops to reconstruct rolling stock. Installation of air-conditioning (A/C) in electric coaches was never properly conceived, with the result that a fleet of non-standard coaches with at least ten different A/C equipments entered service. A set of double-decker electric coaches was also constructed for use on the Sarmiento Line. As in the case of the Roca, TBA promised the Ministry it would run intercity services, and extended its Rosario service to the city of Santa Fe once a week. But these services had no success with the public, because of the long time they took to reach their destinations. Metrovías and Ferrovías achieved better performance in the face of the debacle, and were more organised in their proposals to the government for improvements. Ferrovías set out a modernisation scheme for the Belgrano North Line which included raising platform heights, automatic operation of coach doors and push-pull train operation, all of which were very sensible and necessary. Work began on some of the coaches, but an unexpected government plan paralyzed everything: the Tren de Alta Velocidad or "High Speed Train" (we will say more about this later), which would be using the track-bed of the Belgrano North Line. This halt to the modernisation of the Line was unfortunate for its passengers, but in spite of it both Ferrovías and the Metrovías Urquiza Line managed to control the vandalism of the period and the quality of their services, which was rewarded by them losing fewer passengers.

We have previously mentioned the lack of technical railway expertise in the government. This had come about because during the 90s the State had renounced any involvement in policy planning for the railways, and had left it to the concessioned companies. This now had a bad consequence for the latter's plans to incorporate new locomotives and rolling stock, because of the absence of any government oversight. Ferrovías had links with the Portuguese railways, became aware that they were modernising, and had obsolete rolling stock available for purchase at low prices. Some coaches and locomotives were shipped to Argentina, and this generated a certain optimism that the Metropolitan railways might be re-equipped by second-hand European stock, not just from Portugal but also Spain, where the broad gauge was the same as that in Argentina. In that way, between 2005 and 2009, 62 locomotives, 33 motor coaches, 93 trailer coaches and 15 electric coaches were imported. These surplus units were between 20 and 55 years old and, except for a very few, had been disposed of as only fit for scrapping. In addition, the units were far from being a homogeneous collection; for example, the 62 locomotives came in 9 different models. Some units entered service, but for lack of maintenance and spare parts were soon set aside. A few General Motors lcomotives proved to be effective, but all the rest were soon abandoned. Thus we can say that the original optimistic idea ended up as a grave mistake.

Intercity Passengers

Decree 1683 in 2005 declared that all intercity passenger trains, certainly already scarce, would be taken over by the national State, which would determine their implementation and operation, by itself or by third parties. This Decree was purely symbolic, and did not change the reality of the situation. Since the 90s when it was decided to withdraw all intercity services, only in two case was a certain continuity preserved: the Province of Buenos Aires had taken over various services within its territory, and the Province of Río Negro had run the Viedma-Bariloche service. Two other provinces, Córdoba and Tucumán, had attempted to run intercity services, but with very poor results so they did not last. Aside from these cases, only the Province of the Chaco successfully implemented some services within its territory.

Public opinion had always been sensitive to the theme of long-distance trains, which were especially missed in the interior. Governments had always tried, at least in their discourses, to respond to demands for their reinstatement. Within the framework of the new decree, a few experiments had been tried out. None were long-lasting, but did demonstrate a tepid official policy change: from a loss of interest in inter-city services to support for some trial schemes. Most successful had been the creation of the Ferrocentral company, formed from the suburban company Ferrovías and the NCA cargo company. This new enterprise had set up two services: the first being between Buenos Aires and Córdoba in 2004, and the second a year later between Buenos Aires and Tucumán. In both cases it had been possible to operate fairly frequent services with adequate rolling stock. However, the weak point of the services was the state of the tracks. Although these were improved, to ensure completion of the runs, in both cases the times taken for the journeys were far from those in the latest FA timetable. Two trains per week to each destination were established as an experimental stage, with the idea of gradually improving the frequency and speed of the services until a daily and reasonably fast train could be achieved. But, after the initial euphoria, the government lost interest in continuing to improve the services, which slowly declined. The worsening state of the tracks led to increasingly longer journeys, and although passenger numbers held up, this was because ticket prices were significantly reduced, making large subsidies inevitable.

Another emblematic case of these years was the service between Buenos Aires and Posadas, The Province of Corrientes, in contravention of Decree 1683, had conceded the operation of this twice-weekly service to a company called Trenes Especiales Argentinos (Argentine Special Trains). This company had neither technical nor financial solvency, not to mention any legal authorization or adequate rolling stock. The Urquiza Railway infrastructure was very poor, so the duration of the journey was interminable. Neither could they guarantee a minimum regularity of service. Trains halted or were cancelled, and when they did run the timetable was ignored. The position of the staff was precarious, and trains sometimes ran without the proper personnel. However, in the face of this the government did absolutely nothing. It never gave public support, but neither did it intervene to take over the running of the trains nor to order their withdrawal. The government, with its pro-railway discourse, did not want to suffer the political consequencies of shutting down a train service, and so by its inaction permitted this chaotic service to continue.

Thanks to it having received a great quantity of rolling stock in the 90s, the Province of Buenos Aires had managed to maintain FAs intercity services that ran within its domain. But after its successful early years there had begun a gentle decline which became more marked as time passed. Postponed maintenance and the state of the tracks had a negative effect on services, lengthening journey times and leaving the provincial company progressively shorter of coaches and locomotives. Services degraded and had started to be cancelled. As an example of this, the line from Buenos Aires to Mar del Plata, which was always the star of FAs services and had been in great demand during the summer, went from running ten trains per day in 1999 to run only four per day in 2007. Similar problems affected the line in the Province of Río Negro: two trains per week from Viedma to Bariloche had fallen to one per week because of scarce rolling stock, and trains could not be relied upon to run, leaving long periods without service.

Unfortunate Institutional Reforms 2007-2015

On 30th August 2007, 150 years had passed since the inauguration of the first railway in Argentina. This date was celebrated with festivities to mark an inflexion in railway policy. It had almost coincided with the transfer of the presidency to Cristina Fernández de Kirchner. As well as a difference in the style of the new President's form of governance, it was marked by some central changes in railway policy. The political euphoria of the election result and of a sustained growth in the economy led to the belief that this was a seminal moment. Regarding the railways, a process began characterised by the conception of Pharaonic projects and the creation of new laws, all of which implied that drastic changes would follow.

The government announced its Tren de Alta Velocidad (High Speed Train) project. This involved the construction of a new line between Buenos Aires, Rosario and Córdoba. There had been no consultation about this project, but it was presented as definitive and no objections or observations were allowed. As well as the high cost of constructing it, probably unrealistically so for the Argentine economy, its low potential demand for traffic made it hard to justify. But also various technical questions had not been taken into account. First, existing high-speed technology uses standard-gauge track, which is not compatible with Argentina's broad gauge system. Consequently, construction of the track, the most costly part of the project, could not make use of local infrastructure. Second, the chosen route was not adequate. Access to Buenos Aires would be along the Belgrano North suburban line, necessitating enormous adaptation works along that line which would constrain its future development. Lastly, the section between Del Viso and Villa Rosa (Pilar) and Rosario would follow the Belgrano Cargas line, which would impede its access to the Port of Buenos Aires. Just the announcement of the project had the effect of cutting off the planned modernisation of the Belgrano Norte line which, as we have said, still remains paralyzed. Without any form of analysis of the impact of the project on the existing railway network, the contract with the awarded consortium was duly signed. In 2009 the international financial crisis put the group of banks which had offered funding into a very difficult financial situation, and it was for that reason the high-speed project was never started.

The second Pharaonic project which had negative consequences was the tunnelling of the inner suburban section of the Sarmiento Railway. The initial idea was to construct a tunnel between Caballito and Villa Luro, as this would solve the problem of the large number of level crossings on this section. Soon after this plan was announced, the Mayors of the districts through which the rest of the Sarmiento suburban line ran questioned why they were not included in the work. So the government modified the initial plan by proposing to construct a tunnel for the whole length of the electrified section of the line up to Moreno. This work, apart from its enormous cost in competition with other priorities, also raised certain technical difficulties with regard to future developments. There were two basic objections: in the first place the idea of constructing a tunnel, instead of the trench cutting which had been proposed since 1903, would impede the running of non-electric trains. Thus suburban trains serving Luján, Mercedes or Lobos, together with intercity trains would no longer directly be able to reach the terminus of the Sarmiento line at Once. In the second place the proposed tunnel would provide only two tracks, eliminating the existing four-track sections and the possibility of fast and semi-fast trains serving outer destinations being able to overtake slower traffic. The lengthy tunnel proposed ran the risk of converting a railway service into a metro disconnected from the rest of the network. As in the case of the High Speed Train, international finance problems made it difficult to start the project, although periodic announcements continued to be made in favour of the work.

With regard to the institutional reforms, these emerged in two laws, Law 26352 in 2008, called Reorganization of Argentine Railways, and Law 27132 in 2015, called New Argentine Railways. Both these legal instruments fundamentally changed the institutional organization of the railway system in Argentina.

On 15th March 2007 at the Plaza Constitución terminus of the Roca line, there was a violent reaction by passengers to the cancellation of trains during the rush hour, which ended with coaches being set on fire and a fierce battle between activists and the security forces. The government reacted immediately with the announcement of a new law for the reorganisation of the railways. In the hurry to respond and to show that the authorities were taking charge of the railway's problems, a bill sent to the Congress was copied almost literally from Spanish legislation on the same theme. The bill was sanctioned as Law 26352 on 28th February 2008 after almost no legislative discussion. This Law set aside the principle of an "integrated public company" which had always been used in the organisation of the railway system, and had been reaffirmed in the concessions awarded in the 90s. Instead, this Law had adopted the European system of "separation of the infrastructure from its operation", an idea which had originated in Sweden in the 80s. This implied that a State company owning and administrating the infrastructure, which absorbed the main costs of the railway, did not impact on the firms operating the servicies on the railway, because they would only pay a levy for using the tracks. This separation policy aspired to generate profitable railway companies while leaving the major infrastructure costs to be picked up by the State. Then this would be comparable with how the public roads were funded. Of course this is no more than an accounting disposition, since the real costs remain the same and have to be paid one way or another, but it was believed that public opinion regarded separation of costs to be more presentable than the State entirely subsidising an integrated organisation.

The Swedish model has extended over the whole of Europe, but to date it cannot be said that it has clearly improved the circumstances of the railways.

In order to begin applying this Law based on the Swedish model, two new State companies were created, the Administración de Infraestructura Ferroviaria Sociedad del Estado (ADIFSE, Railway Infrastructure Company) and the Sociedad Operadora Ferroviaria Sociedad del Estado (SOFSE, Railway Operation State Company). Both began to function in 2009, having been handed, for the administration of what needed to be done, to the Unions: ADIFSE to the Brotherhood of Engine Drivers and SOFSE to the Union of Railwaymen. The problem with this new arrangement, apart from certain complications to do with operating the train services, was that the companies were not in control of the running of the trains. In reality the application of laws in Argentina, until this point, had been purely in theory, given that most cargo and suburban passenger services had continued being operated under concession contracts based on the integrated system model. In fact this Law had specified that it should be applied once the existing concessions had come to an end or were terminated. However, the Law was applied neither in the Belgrano Cargas Railway (State-operated) nor in the suburban service lines having terminated concessions, all of which continued functioning as integrated companies. In practice, therefore, the ADIFSE became only the manager of infrastructure project works and the SOFSE began to function as an intermediary which supervised the servicies provided by the companies. The creation of these two entities certainly implied a dispersal of responsibility for real problems and a progressive rise in bureaucracy.

The second unfortunate reform was the almost unanimous approval on 15th February 2015 of Law 27132, known as the New Argentine Railways Law. This Law had been inspired by the latest reforms carried out in France. On the one hand, it created a holding which brought together ADIFSE, SOFSE and the Railway Personnel Administration. This last entity, successor of the Belgrano S.A, in the 90s, had been used to centralise all the personnel of the rescinded suburban concessions. On the other hand, it established the rule that the whole Argentine railway network would be "open access", which meant that no company would operate exclusively in any sector of the network, and that it would encourage competition between existing railway companies, whether cargo or passenger, as well as encouraging any new company that wanted to enter the railway business.

The two reforms were unfortunate and damaging for railway services. The separation of the infrastructure, to the extent which it was applied as established in Law 26352, implied that the railway companies would not have control over the running of their own rolling stock. As this is essential for achieving profitability, being dependent on an alien entity would result in the companies not investing in their rolling stock, and thus unable to participate fully in the transport market. The second reform, that of Law 27132, was based on a mistaken supposition. This was the assumption that there was a railway monopoly problem, which required open access and the encouragement of competition. The fact was that cargo services had not been a monopoly because of the permanent competition from road transport, which effectively set the price the railways could charge. On the other hand, a monopoly implies excessively high tariffs, whereas the reality in Argentina was to the contrary. The tariffs were very low which meant that there was no justification for encouraging intra-modal competition. If this were to be applied as established by the Law, encouraging competition in a context of low tariffs would have provided yet another incentive to not invest in rolling stock, which would have weakened the railway even more against its rival, the truck. In any case, Law 27132 had been approved not long before, and how it would be implemented was unknown.

Cargo

In 2007 the group of six concession companies transported almost 25 million tons of cargo, which constituted a record over the previous 50 years. This was achieved, as had been anticipated, without making large infrastructure investments, but by putting to work existing assets together with small spends on reconditioning rolling stock and the acquisition of a few second-hand locomotives on the international market. This was helped, we should point out, by capitalizing on contributions by other, non-railway, companies which provided storage facilities, port installations and multimodal stations. But in 2008 an unexpected conflict broke out between the government and the farming sector, which paralized its commercial activities for several months. The impact on the railway companies, which mainly transport agricultural produce, led to a traffic loss of more than 4 million tons in 2009. Although in the following two years high international commodity prices led to a recovery in the amount of cargo transported, it did not reach the maximum level of 2007 and was not maintained over time. From 2011 onwards a steady decline was observed until 2015, when it had fallen to 18.5 million tons, a figure comparable with the average FA figures in the 70s and 80s.

As well as the conflict with the farmers, in recent years the cargo companies have suffered the consequencies of a lack of concrete policies for the sector. Increases in costs, especially labour costs, were caused by government-supported agreements between the passenger railway companies and the Unions. In the case of the passenger railways, these above the cost of living wage improvements were covered by increases in government subsidies; but in the case of the cargo lines, which were not subsidized, the extra cost could not be covered by increasing the tariffs charged. Also, the proliferation of anti-rail attitudes not faced up to by the government continued: cutting of tracks, boycotts of companies which shipped by rail, and municipal governments which supported trucking companies against the railways. And lastly, after twenty years of operation without adequate renovation of the infrastructure, problems arose which led to reduced line speeds without being able to prevent an increasing number of derailments. From the start of their concessions the cargo companies had not been in a position to take carry out track renovations. The cargo system has had an approximate gross turnover of between 15 and 16 thousand USDollars per kilometre of track per year, which shows that the business is very small and its profits are not sufficient for investment on tracks. Together with this inability they were faced with an absent government which, even though it had been evident since the beginning, did not take on the problem, letting deterioration continue and gravely compromising the future of the railways.

In facing up to the reduction in goods carried during the last four years, the companies reacted in different ways. Of the six cargo companies, three continued under the original renegotiated concessions. The other three were taken over by the State. The three surviving private companies achieved a much better performance than the State-owned ones. Ferrosur Roca, Ferroexpreso Pampeano and Nuevo Central Argentino were able to maintain traffic levels close to those previously recorded. In 2015 these three companies carried 86% of the total cargo; whereas the other three carried the remaining 14% in spite of operating over a nominal network almost twice the size, because they had not fared well in the past. On the one hand the Belgrano Railway, with the largest but least used network, which as we noted above was operated by SOESA from 2006, had not been able to grow its insignificant traffic. With the SOESA it managed to transport a million tons, which even though it is twice the amount Belgrano Cargas had transported when operated by the Union of Railwaymen, is a long way from the figures it achieved in the 90s as the State company Belgrano S.A, and is much less than the 4 million tons carried during the final years of FA. In order to reverse the situation of the Belgrano the government decided to implement a plan to renovate its tracks by means of a major project with international funding. These works would concentrate on the Belgrano's route delivering soya beans to the port of Rosario. However, the implementation of this work did not significantly change the performance of the Belgrano. In 2013 the government terminated the contract with SOESA and took over direct operation of the Belgrano. To implement this it created the State company Belgrano Cargas and Logística (Belgrano Cargo and Logistics). In spite of this, the performance of the Belgrano has not shown any significant improvements.

The other two companies, the former Urquiza and San Martín Railways concessioned to ALL but now State-owned, suffered from a particular circumstance. For many years, the Brazilian company ALL had a policy of reducing its costs to a minimum in order to maximize profits. This policy mainly affected the schedules for maintenance, which led to the deterioration of its rolling stock and tracks. Nevertheless it achieved a useful level of traffic on the San Martín line amounting to rather more than 4 million tons. The situation was worse on the Urquiza line, because of major infrastructure problems, shortage of rolling stock and its traffic being strongly affected by commercial relations with Brazil. For these reasons the traffic level of 1.5 million tons in 2006 and 2007 could not be maintained and began a decline. By 2012, ALL indicated its intension to withdraw from Argentina and sell its concession. Ferroexpreso Pampeano expressed an interest in taking over ALL's network in Argentina and entered negotiations which reached an advanced stage. The government had initially encouraged the negotiations, but in 2013 changed its opinion and decided to terminate the ALL concession and take upon itself the operation of the network. It immediately incorporated the San Martín and Urquiza lines into Belgrano Cargas and Logística. But after three years under State control the lines have suffered badly, The San Martín lost 70% of its cargo traffic and the Urquiza 80%. In fact the Urquiza has become almost paralysed as its trunk line into the Metropolitan area has been abandoned. State management has not been able to overcome the inherited condition of the line. Additionally, inconsistency of official policy meant that 100% of the investment on tracks for cargo lines were supplied to the three State-managed lines which only transport 13% of the goods, while the lines which carry the other 87% is left to use its own resources for infrastructure renovation without State intervention.

Regarding the previously mentioned institutional reforms, separation of infrastructure and open network access, these have not been applied to the cargo concessions, whether privately or State owned. In no case has an operating scheme as specified in Law 26354 and the new open network regulation been enforced. However, their existence has had an effect: in the face of this new situation the cargo companies have suspended even minor infrastructure investments while awaiting the new regime.

Suburban Passengers

Following the 2001 crisis, the system of suburban services peaked in 2008, reaching 448 million passengers carried, much better than the record in 1999. This level of traffic was not sustained, however, and from 2009 onward there was a constant and steady fall in demand. This tendency arose from the notorious degradation in cleanliness, security and regularity of the services. Checking of tickets was also relaxed, so that fare evasion increased and this in itself contributed to the decline in takings. The economic equation for the companies, as the cost of operations rose while having to maintain stable ticket prices affected by inflation, deteriorated more and more. Increases in staff numbers, reduction in working hours, incorporation of staff from outsourced activities and equipping them for their railway employment, all served to increase the subsidy required for the suburban passenger services from 45 million USDollars in 1999 to 500 million in 2015. To this was added the fact that during this emergency the railway companies did not have any stimulus to be more efficient and to amplify their services. Their only objective was to survive by trying to maintain the simplest possible operation and shifting all major costs onto their subsidies.

In 2008 the Belgrano Sur and Roca line concessions, still in the hands of the Taselli Group, were rescinded, following a marked deterioration of their services. The government handed over the management of their services to UGOFE, which had operated the San Martín line since 2004. In order to improve the services. UGOFE proposed the carrying out of some track work and rolling stock restoration for the two lines, which was paid for by the State, and in this way the decline in demand on the two lines was reversed. But UGOFE operated the services as the agent of the National State, and administered the carrying out of agreed works in return for charging a management fee and a percentage of its cost. All of this meant that UGOFE, constituted by the three surviving concessions, put more effort into construction activities, mainly refurbishment of stations and relaying certain sections of track, rather than into genuine service improvements. All things considered, apart from the recovery of demand on the Roca and Belgrano Sur, after a while the other concessions suffered a continuous decline in their services, markedly so in the two TBA lines, Mitre and Sarmiento.

By 2012 the situation could be summarised as that of a system which was losing passengers, with a quality of service which had seriously deteriorated and was more and more onerous to maintain with the high operating subsidy it received. On 22nd February of that year a tragedy occurred in the Buenos Aires Once Terminus of the Sarmiento line. A very crowded morning rush hour train collided with the buffer stops. This disaster cost the lives of 51 people and had important consequences for Metropolitan services. To start with the TBA company was placed into administration, subsequently lost its concession, and management of its services was passed to the Unidad de Gestión Operativa Mitre Sarmiento (UGOMS, Unit for the Operational Management of the Mitre and Sarmiento Lines), which was formed from the Ferrovías and Metrovías companies. Emergency measures were instituted for the running of the few available trains in suitable condition, and line speeds were reduced. The bad state of the trains, the limited services offered, and the fear that another tragedy could occur led to the public shunning trains on these two lines. The Mitre lost 75% of its passengers and the Sarmiento nearly 90%. But services on the other suburban lines also suffered consequent losses.

The Once accident also led to drastic changes in railway policy. The Transport Ministry was transferred from the Ministerio de Planificatión Federal (Ministry for Federal Planning) to the Interior Ministry, which from then on was called the Interior and Transport Ministry. The agitation of public opinion led the government, which had been badly hit by the accident, to try out a new policy for the Metropolitan train services. Thus the new Minister activiated the agreements which had been previously made with the Chinese government, among which figured the acquisition of railway equipment. Contracts were rapidly formalised and a great quantity of equipment arrived in the country. This consisted of the purchase of 24 locomotives and 180 passenger coaches for the San Martín line; 610 electric train coaches for the Roca, Mitre and Sarmiento lines; 27 diesel trains for the Belgrano Sur; as well as 220 passenger coaches and 22 locomotives for long-distance trains. This constituted the most significant investment in the railways since the electrification of the Roca in the 80s. But the political need to provide results rapidly meant that the incorporation of the equipment was improvised, with insufficient technical consideration. For example, for the electrified lines, the power available from the substations needed to be upgraded, as it was found that the new electric trains were unable to run together at the full capacity of the line and at the speeds they were capable of. For these reasons hundreds of the coaches had still not entered service by March 2016.

All these innovations and associated works were concentrated on the lines operated by the Management Units subordinated to SOFSE (the State operator). The two remaining concessions, Urquiza and Belgrano Norte, did not benefit from the State's investment. This led to a paradoxical situation, since the two companies which had always had better quality of service and were the best organised and most favoured by the public, were relegated to making do with obsolescent rolling stock. Both Metrovías and Ferrovías have proposed to the government that their lines be modernised, but so far have not received an official response.

Significant institutional changes occurred during 2014 and 2015. The Ferrovías and Metrovías companies had together formed two administration companies. UGOFE and UGOMS, and proposed to the government that they become independent. The Metrovías created a company called Corredores Ferroviarios (Railway Corridors) for the administration of the San Martín and the Mitre, while Ferrovías created Argentren to do the same for the Roca and the Belgrano Sur. The Sarmiento passed into direct administration by State operator SOFSE. This scheme lasted for only a short time, however, as in 2015 the State rescinded the management contracts with these companies and, via SOFSE, took over direct operation of all the suburban services with the exception of the Urquiza and the Belgrano Norte, which remained under the original concessionaires since the decade of the 90s.

We can say that management of the suburban system in the hands of the State had its ups and downs. On the one hand, the installation of the new rolling stock represented a significant improvement. However, demand responded timidly, probably because on the contrary, even with the new trains, journey times and regularity of services did not get better. In spite of this, from 2013 demand increased by almost 50% to reach 329 million passengers by 2015, an improvement over figures in previous years but still much lower than the levels in 1999 and 2000, during the operation of the original concessions.

A series of emblematic projects for the suburban railways have been announced more than once over the years. The electrification of the line to La Plata was announced seven times in the past five years, and only became a reality from Plaza Constitución as far as Quilmes with an infrequent emergency service, owing to a lack of power because the power substation needed at Berazategui had still not been provided. Tunnelling for the Sarmiento was also announced many times with no sign of a start, and it continues to hang like a sword of Damocles over the future of the line. The idea of connecting the Belgrano Sur into Plaza Constitución station has been another of these Pharaonic projects announced with no consideration of what effect it would have on the operation of the Roca line. Lastly, a Regional Express Network like the RER in Paris has been announced, which would include a tunnel under the Avenida Nueve de Julio to permit trains from the Roca and Belgrano Sur in the south of Buenos Aires to run through to stations on the Mitre, San Martin and Belgrano Norte lines in the north, and *vice versa*. In addition, a plan to extend Sarmiento line trains past Plaza Once station into downtown Buenos Aires has been suggested, via a disused cargo tunnel to the Port. All of these projects were formulated without any technical or operational assessment studies, and the little which has been implemented, as in the case of the La Plata electrification, has been carried out in a very improvised manner. Railway policy has centered on announcements in the media of grand and costly projects, instead of taking forward the implementation of timely and specific works of limited cost on the actual lines, which would improve the operation of the service used every day by millions of people.

Intercity Passengers

As we mentioned previously, long-distance trains had been reduced to services in the Provinces of Buenos Aires and Río Negro, together with services from Buenos Aires to Córdoba, Tucumán and Posadas. Of these, the most significant services provided were those run by the Buenos Aires provincial company, UEPFP. Their most successful service was that between Buenos Aires and Mar del Plata, which generated 55% of intercity ticket sales in the country. But the UEPFP, which had a policy of increasing its labour force, suffered from a decline of its subsidy from the provincial treasury. This led to a fall in the standard of track and rolling-stock maintenance, which began a decline in the quality of its services. Reduced availability of locomotives and coaches led to the initial ten trains per day to Mar del Plata falling to four in 2007, one in 2014 and none in 2015. Most other services in the Province had already been discontinued, except along the corridors to Bahía Blanca on the Roca and to Junin on the San Martín. The quality of the trains had been degraded to a level not seen before. The Río Negro provincial company found itself in a similarly poor situation. The lack of resources, its operational costs, and the absence of maintenance reduced its services to one per week. This line runs parallel to a road which is in the process of being paved, so its future is foreseeable.

The trains to Córdoba and Tucumán, operated as we have said by the company Ferrocentral, did not survive their initial success and although the company did its best to maintain the quality of the services, degradation of the infrastructure caused journey times to increase, making them less and less competitive. In addition, it was never possible for the company to enhance the initial offering of two trains per week to each destination. This gradual decline led in 2015 to the government rescinding their contract and taking over the operation by means of SOFSE. The frequency and travel times of the services has not changed, and their only improvement has been the incorporation of new rolling stock purchased from China. The infrequent trains to Posadas operated, as we have said before, by a company with neither technical suitability nor financial solvency which operated under illegal conditions, simply ceased to function, although replaced for a short time by a TBA service.

But as we have noted, yearning for the restoration of long-distance trains is a part of Argentine nostalgia. This influences public opinion, and during during election periods is used by the political parties. In recent years this has led to the precarious restoration of intercity services, mostly lacking either economic or social justification anywhere in the country. Thus in the Province of Córdoba the Tren de la Sierra was restored together with an urban service in Córdoba City itself which lasted for only a few weeks. A few trains were run on the Sarmiento line to Realicó, General Pico and Santa Rosa, all very slow and infrequent. In 2008 the government also established a binational service entitled "Tren de los Pueblos Libres" (Free Peoples Train) with the intention, which made no sense, of linking Buenos Aires and Montevideo in a two-day journey. Its route was never fully determined, and when the state of the tracks in Uruguay showed that the project was infeasible, it ceased to run.

Countless projects for regional trains also appeared, and some came to pass. In Salta a service between the City of Salta and Güemes was established. In Entre Ríos a number of regional services within the Province were planned which though they began to circulate never acquired regularity, especially so in the case of the principal service, that between Paraná and Concepción del Uruguay, always intermittent and unpredictable. Also in Entre Ríos a suburban service was implemented in Paraná using a set of precarious vehicles called Technotrén, which was irregular and uncertain in operation. Santa Fe is intending to install a similar suburban service using these vehicles, while Santiago del Estero has implemented a service with the same vehicles between Santiago and La Banda. All these regional services lack economic rationality and are of dubious social utility. Technically they are not really sustainable, and were established without feasibility studies and no analysis of public demand. The only variable taken into account is their electoral political advantage.

In many cases the Provinces have been unable for financial reasons to maintain this regional policy. This was the case in Entre Ríos, but they were able to transfer the operation of the provincial railways into the hands of the National State. Chaco Province was able to do the same. In this case a local railway in Resistencia and two intercity railways had been operated by a provincial company. Sefecha. Ironically, at the same time this was happening, the national government was putting pressure on the City of Buenos Aires to take over the underground railway network, for being a local operation which should not fall to the State to sustain. However, this argument did not seem to apply in the Chaco and Entre Ríos cases, and to the running of regional services in other parts of the country.

However, the most ambitious government projects were those relating to the reinstatement of intercity trains between large cities. In a 2008 proposal was made to reestablish a service between Buenos Aires and Mendoza with a significant investment in rolling stock and infrastructure, but the 2009 crisis meant it was put aside. Recently, fomented by the new Minister of the Interior and Transport two projects were launched for intercity express trains: Buenos Aires – Mar del Plata and Buenos Aires – Rosario. For these 220 coaches and 22 locomotives from China were purchased. In reality this equipment had been ordered previously for the Mendoza reinstatement project, and had included sleeping coaches, which did not make sense on routes of length 300km and 400km respectively, though of course it did for the at least three times longer Mendoza route. The establishment of these express services, without any serious assessment of the demand for them, implied making a start on the complete renewal of the track to Rosario and a large part of the track to Mar del Plata. However, in 2015 the track works on both the lines were suspended. In spite of this, for electoral reasons both services started to run; to an improvised station on the outskirts of Rosario which took over 6 hours, and to Mar del Plata taking about the same time but then soon suspended because repairs to a bridge on the line had not been completed. The Rosario service, with an inappropriately long journey time and a badly located terminus, attracted hardly any passengers. All of this leads us to maintain that, in the matter of intercity train services, there has existed irrationality and improvisation, just as it has always occurred in most Argentine railway policy in the years since nationalization.

Epilogue | Rise and Decline of the Railway in Argentina

Railways as a means of transport, having revolutionized transport systems all over the world, began in the early twentieth century to lose ground against the growth of road transport. And later on it also lost some traffic to the rise of aviation. In consequence, the railway crisis was not exclusive to any one country. Everywhere, the possibility of retaining independent, comprehensive service railway companies disappeared, in a double sense. On the one hand, using only the income from charges for the services provided was becoming insufficient to maintain their infrastructure, to meet their operational costs, and to obtain investment capital for technology upgrades and adaptation to changes in the transport market. On the other hand, being expected to provide a public service in response to all that was demanded of it, without being able to refuse certain services, was becoming less profitable. Also, for the same reasons, the possibility of providing railway services as the business of a private company had disappeared, at least in its traditional form.

Facing this new reality, practically all railway systems began to reduce their coverage, by closing lines and branches which failed to justify their continuing existence for economic or social reasons. Many services which had belonged on the railway moved over to road transport. The survival of railway services which were judged essential started to require the support of State contributions, such as in the case of passenger services in large urban conurbations. The construction of new railway infrastructure works, the necessity for which should result from careful prior study, began to depend more and more on the fiscal coffers. Participation of the railway in the transport system began to diminish, as much for cargo as for passengers, except in the particular case just mentioned above.

However, in this general panorama Argentina occupies a special place. There the railway crisis was even deeper than in the majority of other countries. At the time of the Second World War it had one of the most significant railway systems in the world, both in terms of its size and the range of activities it provided, fundamental to the economic life of the country. Today only the remains are left. This book has gone some way towards describing this growth and decline, and tries to offer an explanation.

In this sense, the six periods into which the text has been divided can be reduced to two. The first three describe the rise, growth and peak of the system; and the remaining three its fall. And, perhaps, if we want to be more precise, we might say that the beginning of the fall should be placed in the middle of the third period, in the decade of the 1930s, when in Argentina economic recession, rise of the motor vehicle, and devaluation of the national peso combined to severely damage rail transport in the country. Given that until then the railway had been completely dominant, and that the motor vehicle had started from a very low level, for a time the problems did not reflect clear evidence of loss in the transport market. The war, however, enabled the railway to recover some of its market loss. Thus, maybe it is more correct to say that the decade of the 1930s, rather than being the start of a downward slope, was only a flattening out of the importance of railway transport. Therefore, the fall really did begin in the fourth period.

Also, the 1930s led to a change in the attitude of Argentine society and government. Until then the railway had been considered the essential transport mode, backbone of economic performance and of the possibility for growth. For that reason, it had received incentives which, since the Mitre Law in 1907, had stayed centred on a special tax regimen. Suddenly, due to a combination of factors, this until then essential transport mode began to be considered obsolete, and in the years that followed, guilty of a growing fiscal deficit. The railway companies were left to take their chances, without major resources, just when they needed to reconfigure themselves against the new reality of motor vehicle competition.

Until 1930 the model of railway system exploitation had operated without any major questions being raised. The most important railways were private companies funded by British capital which had consolidated extensive exclusion zones, with their activities regulated by a series of laws and controlled by the State via the General Railways Board. These companies were autonomous businesses, because of how they were created, the source of their capital, the composition of their Boards of Directors and because of their size. They were the result of direct investment by means of a procedure which had involved concessionary promoters, construction companies and investment banks which channeled investors' capital in the form of shares into new companies not linked to any others. That capital, which had multiplied in time with the growth of the networks, belonged to thousands of shareholders, most of which were small or medium size investors none of which would be able to dominate at an annual meeting. The Board, which itself selected new directors, had initially consisted of persons of sufficient prestige to attract investors. In time, the first directors were replaced by professional railwaymen. Many of these had been trained in the company itself, and had won places as directors by virtue of the experience and ability which they had demonstrated, indispensible qualities for the effective management of an organization which had become enormously complicated. Constant growth had converted them into the largest companies in the country, in terms of their capital investment, their income and operational expenditure, and because of the numerous personnel employed.

The railway companies thus established were profitable. The average return was not high, but was sufficient to service their bonds and reasonable dividends on their shares, in such a way that the great companies were always able to obtain new capital by issuing more bonds. Relations with successive governments were not without problems, the most common one being to do with the setting of fares and charges, as much because the companies felt it necessary to raise them because of increasing costs; or as shippers affected by a fall in the price for their goods, pressed for them to be lowered. But the authorities, who understood that profitability, which was limited by legislation, needed to be maintained so that the system could continue to function, allowed for this situation when they intervened in disputes.

The companies were extremely specialized, and did not aspire to do business outside their railway activities. They were not subordinate to the interests of other companies. When they understood that it was convenient to make an incursion into some related activity they did so, even though they might affect the activity of companies which also had British capital (i.e., there was no cartel). This had happened when the large railway companies acquired ships to transport the coal which they used as fuel at a lower price, or when they undertook the task of replacing that coal, which had become expensive and hard to obtain, with nationally produced oil. Or also when they resolved to manufacture rolling stock locally, in their own workshops, to replace imported coaches, goods wagons and locomotives. In the same way, they were not tied to the interests of any other sector. For this reason, when seeking to increment their traffic, they were not deterred from taking actions which led to the division into lots of lands adjacent to their lines which resulted in an increase in the number of agricultural colonists, even though this would mean making enemies of the large landowners. All their actions were oriented towards increasing their income from railway traffic and reducing the cost of providing their services, because this enhanced their income and profitability.

The year 1930 changed this reality. The companies suddenly lost their profitability, just at the moment when they needed more capital in order to continue electrification of the suburban networks and to start replacing steam traction with diesel locomotives. The government became disinterested in the railways, and left them free to find their own way, though it continued to finance the State company in less developed regions. The hostile environment which began to develop and prolongation of the crisis situation convinced the managers of the companies that the age of the railway business had come to an end. Sale of the assets to the State appeared to be the only possible way out.

Finally, between 1947 and 1948, the State purchased the companies, which were able to recover part of the capital invested. But the Argentine government did not comprehend the problem which they were facing. Nationalization was thought of as a solution, as a worthy end in itself, and it was extolled in empty phrases so devoid of significance that the railway purchase was seen as "buying back sovereignty". In reality, with this purchase the State was taking over a task whose principal requirements can be described as follows: (a) it should organise a new business structure to efficiently manage and defend the railways in the way that the private companies had; (b) it should adapt the railways to the new reality and determine which traffics should be preserved and which left to road transport; (c) it should procure capital to invest in an infrastructure which had been intensively used during the war years and needed to be renovated and to be provided with up-to-date technology, particularly with regard to locomotive traction.

The Argentine government did not give significant attention to this problem. As had been seen during the post-war bilateral negotiations with Great Britain, during which purchase of the railways was one theme, it appeared that the State had no great interest in the future of rail transport, and this attitude did not change after nationalization. It did not seriously consider the requirements listed in the previous paragraph. It delayed the organization of the State company, it was never concerned about which railway traffics to preserve and it invested little in a disorganized manner. Quality of service declined, the operational deficit steadily increased and the negative attitude which had arisen for ideological reasons in the 1930s grew stronger. The role of the railway in the transport system fell much further than was justified by the rise in road traffic.

After much delay, some improvisation and little enthusiasm, the Argentine government initiated a process of change in the two last decades of the twentieth century. It was not clear if this acknowledged that the railway was still important, or because the authorities wanted be rid of the responsibility which had fallen on their shoulders after nationalization. Some acquired experience was taken into account in implementing the change. For example, the importance of and necessity for the railway should be considered under three distinct scenarios: the suburban passenger service in the City of Buenos Aires, the transport of cargo, and the long-distance passenger service. For the first of these it was clear the railway was irreplaceable. Also, an idea taken for granted was that a cargo railway, effectively operated, would be a self-funding business. Lastly, experience with the intercity (long-distance) passenger scenario demonstrated that each service proposal would need to be properly assessed on a case-by-case basis, in order to resolve whether investment in a particular route would be justified in the face of motorcar, omnibus or even aeroplane competition.

In the end, the government decided to liquidate the State railway company, and to offer all the services as concessions to private companies. As a general rule, companies holding cargo concessions would pay a levy to the State for the use of the assets they received; and the suburban passenger concessions would receive a State subsidy. None of these concessions specified precisely how investments would be financed for the network, which had become extremely neglected and needed to be modernised and returned to effective operation. In the case of the long distance passenger concessions, the government became completely disinterested and ended up abandoning them. As time passed, half of the chosen concessionaires proved to be incapable of seriously undertaking the task of running a railway business. In addition, the State failed to draw up new regulations for the concessionary railway system, and to create adequate control arrangements, the latter having disappeared since nationalization in 1948.

This drastic change seemed to produce good results. The tons of cargo transported increased. In the metropolitan area of Buenos Aires more people returned to travelling by train. But this improvement proved to be ephemeral. The country was facing one of its recurrent economic and social crises, and more and more frequently the weak regulation of the concessions, and the unwillingness of successive governments to continue with them, again caused a deterioration of services and the loss of a major part of the traffic which had been recuperated. The emergency measures then adopted fell down because of the unclear rules under which the concession system functioned.

State indifference, and doubts as to the direction which exploitation of the railways should take, were shaken by the tremendous but predictable accident at Once Station in the City of Buenos Aires, where more than 100 people were victims, 51 fatally. The shock of this event resulted in two responses. On the one hand, it led to expenditure on rolling stock, in order to curb the decline which time, lack of investment and scarce maintenance had caused. The suburban railways of Buenos Aires in 2010 were essentially those left by the British companies in 1948, run down as we have described. In practice the only significant investment which had occurred since then was the partial electrification of the Southern railway in early 1980. On the other hand, the second response was that the management of the railways was being thought about seriously once again.

More than half of the sixth period in our history of the railway in Argentina has passed since it began in 2007. The best that can be said about this period is that it has generated an uncertain situation. Everything remains undeveloped: the concession system, the resurgence of nationalization, the specification of a new model for railway exploitation. Three cargo railway concessions have survived, operating under precarious contracts without the possibility of realizing investments which would assure continuity of service. Two suburban railway concessions have also survived, in the same situation and a permanent state of emergency. The State management Operating Units continue their tendency to increase the numbers they employ with no regard for productivity and efficiency. The new legal model has not been implemented. And, of course, the railway continues to lose relevance in the transport system of the country, while continuing to weigh heavily on the already enlarged costs of financing the State.

Maps and Tables

Map 1. Railways in service, 1886

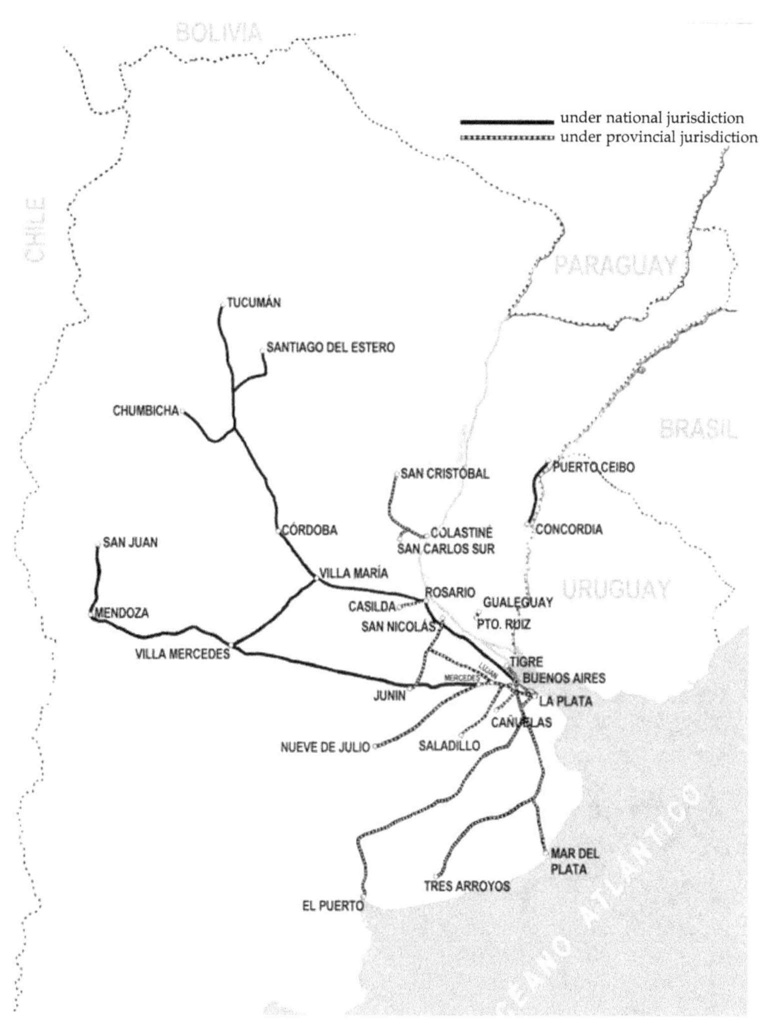

Map 2. Railways in service, 1916

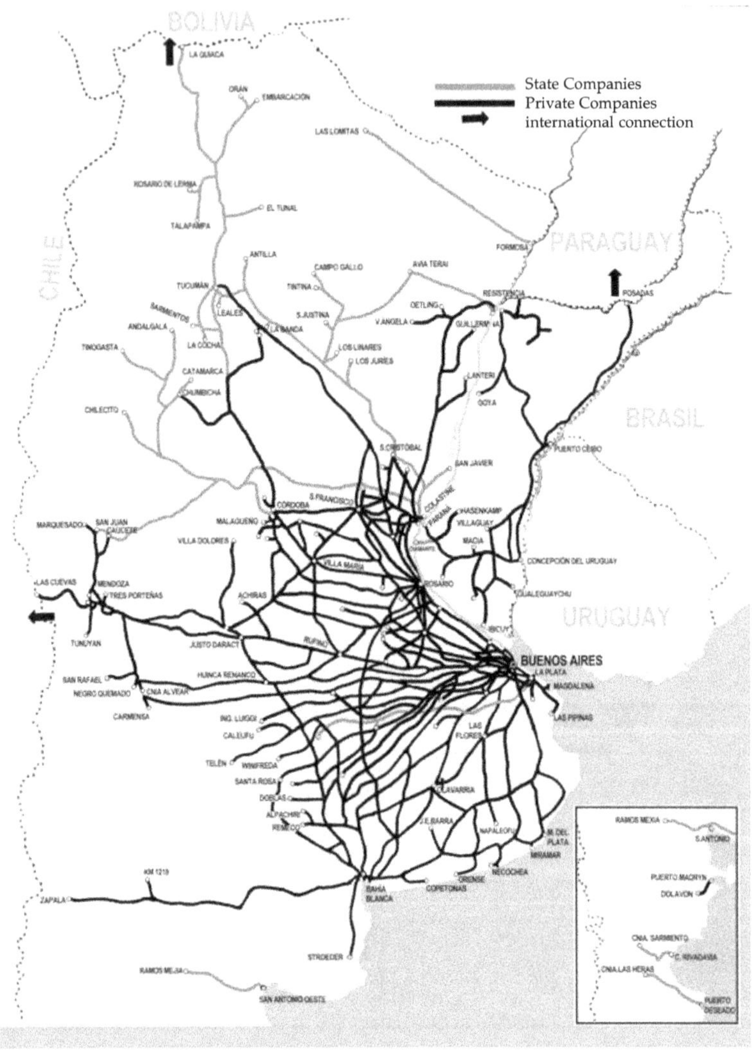

Map 3. Railways in service, 1946

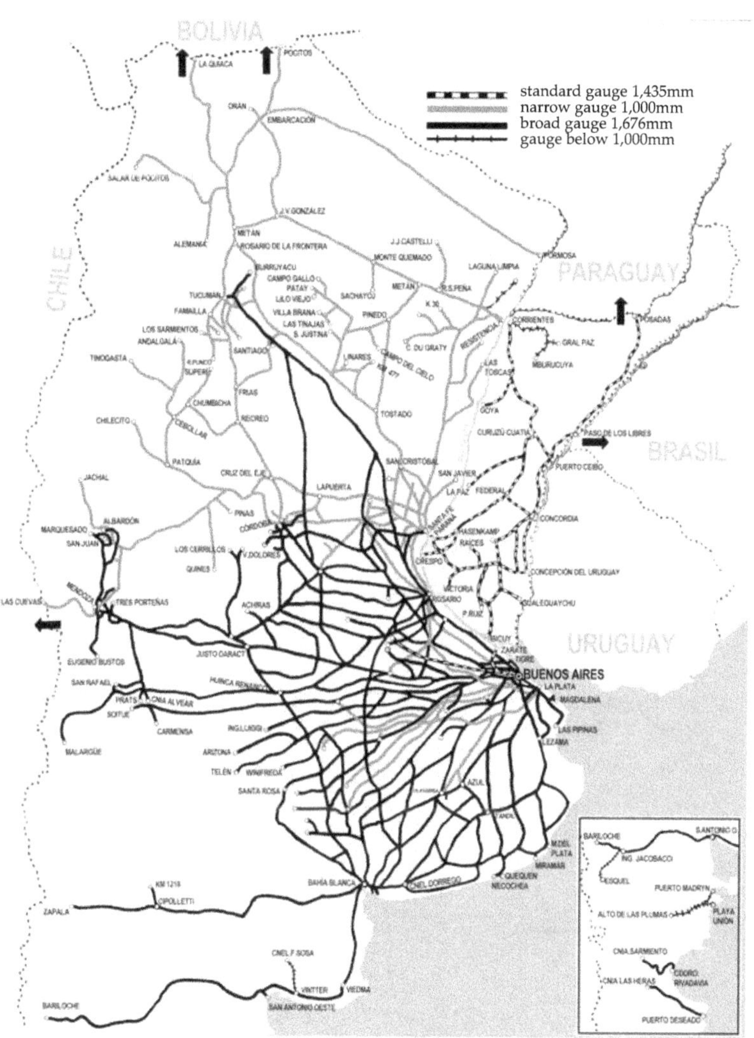

Map 4. Railways in service, 1976

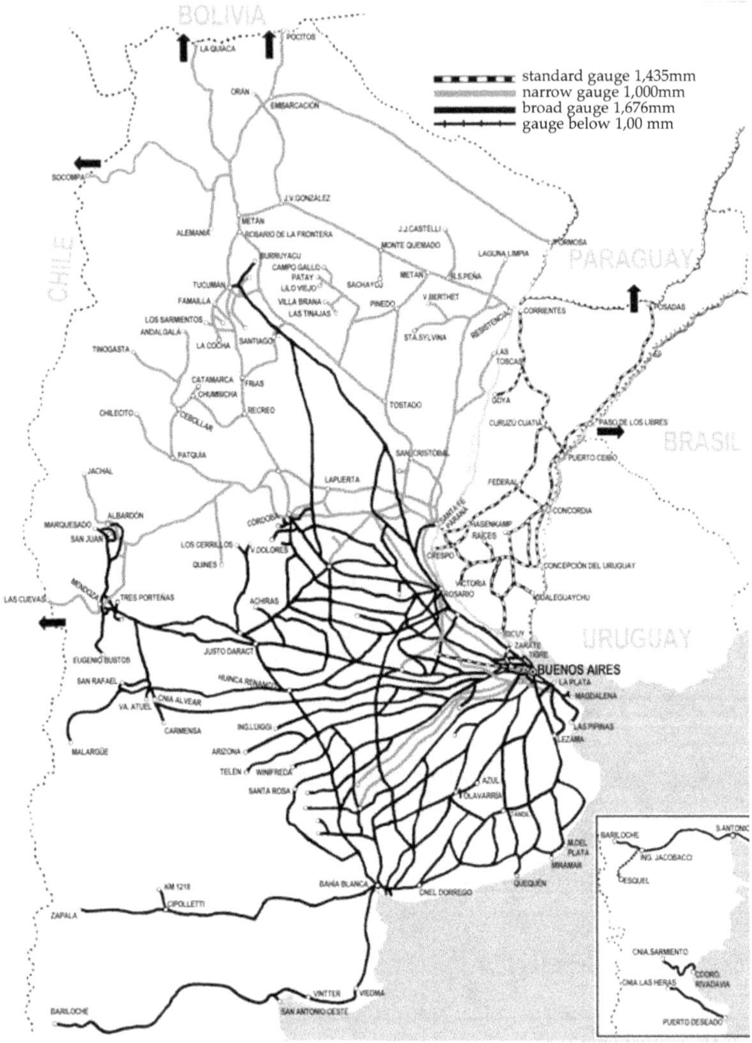

Map 5. Railways in service, 2006

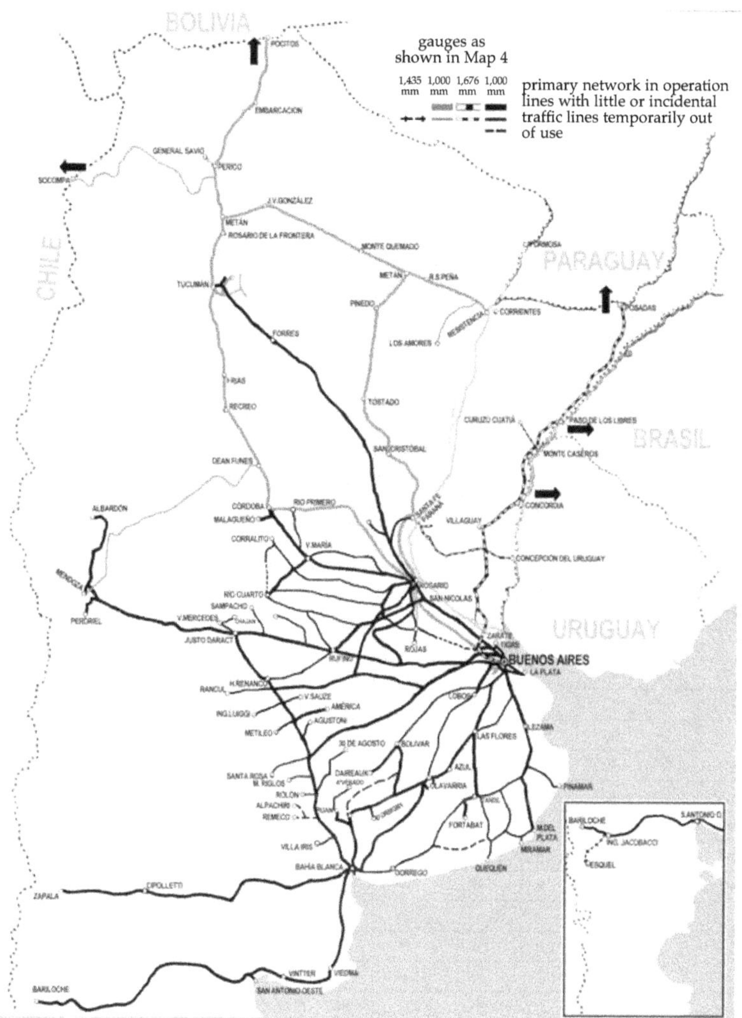

Table 1. Length of provincial and national company networks, 1857-1886 (km)

	Province of Buenos Aires					National					Province of Santa Fe	
Year	BAWR	BANR	BAGSR	BAEPR	BARR	CAR	AR	EAR	NCR	BAPR	WSFR	SFPR
1857	10	-	-	-	-	-	-	-	-	-	-	-
1858	18	-	-	-	-	-	-	-	-	-	-	-
1859	23	-	-	-	-	-	-	-	-	-	-	-
1860	39	-	-	-	-	-	-	-	-	-	-	-
1861	39	-	-	-	-	-	-	-	-	-	-	-
1862	39	8	-	-	-	-	-	-	-	-	-	-
1863	39	22	-	-	-	-	-	-	-	-	-	-
1864	69	25	-	-	-	-	-	-	-	-	-	-
1865	101	29	114	5	-	-	-	-	-	-	-	-
1866	160	29	114	6	-	196	-	-	-	-	-	-
1867	160	29	114	6	-	254	-	-	-	-	-	-
1868	160	29	114	6	-	254	-	-	-	-	-	-
1869	160	29	114	6	-	286	-	-	-	-	-	-
1870	177	29	114	6	-	396	-	-	-	-	-	-
1871	240	29	170	7	-	396	-	-	-	-	-	-
1872	240	29	235	20	-	396	-	-	-	-	-	-
1873	246	30	235	55	-	396	132	-	-	-	-	-
1874	329	30	324	55	-	396	132	55	-	-	-	-
1875	329	30	324	58	-	396	254	155	400	-	-	-
1876	329	30	433	58	77	396	254	155	400	-	-	-
1877	380	30	433	58	77	396	254	155	547	-	-	-
1878	380	30	433	58	77	396	254	155	547	-	-	-
1879	380	30	433	58	77	396	254	155	547	-	-	-
1880	426	30	563	58	77	396	254	155	547	-	-	-
1881	426	30	563	58	77	396	254	155	547	-	-	-
1882	542	30	563	58	77	396	254	155	547	-	-	-
1883	594	30	765	58	77	396	470	161	547	-	56	-
1884	754	30	1,026	58	77	396	523	161	547	-	56	-
1885	804	30	1,159	58	145	396	712	161	781	97	56	93
1886	831	30	1,249	58	417	396	767	161	1,110	578	56	163

Table 2. Company Performance, 1857-1886 (%) (nett profit/capital)

	Province of Buenos Aires					National					Province of Santa Fe	
Year	BAWR	BANR	BAGSR	BAEPR	BARR	CAR	AR	EAR	NCR	BAPR	WSFR	SFPR
1857	2.4	-	-	-	-	-	-	-	-	-	-	-
1858	4.8	-	-	-	-	-	-	-	-	-	-	-
1859	-	-	-	-	-	-	-	-	-	-	-	-
1860	-	-	-	-	-	-	-	-	-	-	-	-
1861	-	-	-	-	-	-	-	-	-	-	-	-
1862	2.4	-	-	-	-	-	-	-	-	-	-	-
1863	4.9	-	-	-	-	-	-	-	-	-	-	-
1864	7.3	0.5	-	-	-	-	-	-	-	-	-	-
1865	5	1.2	1.3	-	-	-	-	-	-	-	-	-
1866	9.1	2	2.6	3.4	-	0	-	-	-	-	-	-
1867	7.1	5.2	4.7	6.5	-	1.3	-	-	-	-	-	-
1868	5.2	6.1	6.3	5	-	2.8	-	-	-	-	-	-
1869	7.7	6.1	7.5	4	-	2.5	-	-	-	-	-	-
1870	7.9	8.2	7.9	2.7	-	3.4	-	-	-	-	-	-
1871	6.9	15.2	6.8	2	-	4.8	-	-	-	-	-	-
1872	6.7	10.2	7.8	1.2	-	4.8	-	-	-	-	-	-
1873	8.8	8.6	6.1	loss	-	4.2	-	-	-	-	-	-
1874	8.9	9.6	5.6	0.5	-	7.9	-	0.1	-	-	-	-
1875	7.3	8.5	7.9	loss	-	6.6	0.2	0.1	-	-	-	-
1876	8.6	6.4	6.4	1.7	0.6	3.1	0.2	loss	-	-	-	-
1877	9	4.2	6.3	1.5	1.3	3.2	0.3	loss	-	-	-	-
1878	7.3	2.8	7.9	1.3	1.6	3.5	0.4	loss	1.6	-	-	-
1879	8.2	4	9.6	1.8	1.7	4.1	0.5	0.1	2.4	-	-	-
1880	7.9	5.4	9.6	2.1	1.9	6.9	1.2	0.9	4.3	-	-	-
1881	8.6	5.3	9.7	3.2	2.5	7.6	0.9	0.5	3.5	-	-	-
1882	6.5	4.1	9.3	3.3	3.4	10.8	2.1	1	3.8	-	-	-
1883	7.6	4.9	6.8	5.2	3.6	14.7	1.7	0.9	5.1	-	loss	-
1884	10.5	6.4	6.5	8	2.5	16.8	2.5	2	8.8	-	loss	-
1885	4.2	7.1	5.6	7.6	2.3	13	2.1	1.5	3	loss	loss	1.9
1886	4.8	6.2	7.2	7.8	5.6	12.4	1.3	1.6	2	loss	loss	3.7

Table 3. Length of the Argentine railway network (km), 1886-1916

Year	broad-gauge	standard-gauge	narrow-gauge	Total	Growth (%)
1886	4,832	171	1,273	5,826	
1891	7,269	1,022	3,457	11,748	100
1896	8,719	1,118	4,625	14,462	23
1906	12,890	1,882	5,788	20,560	30
1913	20,177	2,507	9,809	32,493	60
1916	20,748	2,680	10,394	33,822	4

Table 4. Lengths of company networks (km), 1886-1916

Notes: The companies are in the merged economic groups which existed in 1916, without taking into account that they may have been previously independent or in another group. The BAGSR/WR group included the BAGS, BAW and Midland Railways. The CAR group included until 1908 the BARR and CAR, and until 1898 the BAEPR which in that year joined the BAGSR. It had also taken over the BAN, SFCGS and WSF Railways. The BAPR group included the BAP, AGW, VMR, BBNW and Transandine Railways. The ERR/ANER group included those two railways and the EAR until 1905. Provincial control of the ERR for the first four years has not been taken into account. This group also covers the First Entre Ríos Railway from 1896, which was previously controlled by AGFE (Administración General de Ferrocarriles). The BACR is set under British Capital because of its debentures issued in 1906, all placed in London. The Northern Section of the CCR was controlled by the AGFE until 1888. The CCR group included itself, its extension to Buenos Aires, the CRR and the RST. The SFPR lies under French Capital from the beginning of this period, ignoring provincial control during the first two years. All the railways owned by the Nation are classified as under NRB control even though the NRB was only created in 1909. Included there are the AR until 1909, as well as the NCR and the ANCR. Also included is the railway from Córdoba to the Northwest even though it was only bought by the State in 1910. From 1911 the railways in Formosa, Chaco and Patagonia were also included. The PBAR column included the BAWR until 1890 and the PBAR from 1910.

Table 4. Lengths of company networks (km). 1886-1916

	British Capital						French Capital			State	
Year	BAGS/ WR	CAR	BAPR	ERR/ ANER	BACR	CCR	SFPR	RBPR	BAPGRC	AGFE	PBAR
1887	2,281	1,135	1,091	449	-	-	289	-	-	1,374	1,022
1888	2,344	1,288	1,198	449	104	-	587	-	-	1,374	1,078
1889	2,741	1,338	1,198	449	145	1,245	698	-	-	556	1,210
1890	2,585	2,371	1,198	513	145	1,245	812	-	-	556	1,022
1891	2,464	3,249	1,723	1,012	145	1,534	1,110	-	-	1,231	-
1892	2,811	3,321	1,752	1,012	165	1,534	1,302	-	-	1,798	-
1893	2,913	3,381	1,752	1,012	165	1,534	1,306	-	-	1,801	-
1894	2,957	3,422	1,752	1,105	181	1,534	1,306	-	-	1,801	-
1895	2,962	3,463	1,788	1,105	181	1,536	1,308	-	-	1,801	-
1896	3,181	3,473	1,845	1,118	225	1,580	1,308	-	-	1,886	-
1897	3,332	3,516	1,924	1,118	225	1,580	1,308	-	-	1,907	-
1898	3,557	3,646	1,926	1,254	225	1,580	1,308	-	-	1,907	-
1899	4,607	3,463	1,947	1,273	225	1,580	1,311	-	-	2,110	-
1900	4,632	3,463	2,065	1,273	225	1,580	1,311	-	-	2,160	-
1901	4,706	3,463	2,157	1,466	225	1,580	1,311	-	-	2,167	-
1902	4,706	3,648	2,316	1,581	225	1,580	1,311	-	-	2,167	-
1903	5,297	3,804	2,584	1,581	225	1,580	1,311	-	-	2,167	-
1904	5,545	3,804	2,584	1,581	225	1,580	1,502	-	-	2,538	-
1905	5,610	3,804	2,723	1,581	225	1,580	1,502	-	-	2,699	-
1906	5,819	3,827	2,937	1,657	225	1,580	1,523	-	-	2,923	-
1907	6,238	3,876	3,563	1,711	225	1,580	1,752	-	-	3,112	-
1908	6,510	3,876	3,963	1,797	225	1,665	1,752	-	507	3,379	-
1909	6,614	4,098	4,678	1,852	269	1,667	1,752	-	618	3,047	-
1910	7,846	4,281	5,128	1,940	269	1,956	1,752	797	964	3,491	305
1911	8,625	4,639	5,194	2,032	269	1,980	1,752	797	1,166	4,961	305
1912	9,142	4,874	5,439	2,165	276	1,988	1,880	797	1,268	5,057	305
1913	9,352	5,071	5,640	2,165	340	1,991	1,920	797	1,268	5,265	553
1914	9,579	5,367	5,695	2,384	359	2,002	1,940	797	1,268	5,806	553
1915	9,604	5,367	5,695	2,384	373	2,023	1,947	799	1,268	6,001	553
1916	9,609	5,367	5,695	2,450	378	2,023	1,964	799	1,268	6,088	553

Table 5. Lengths of the networks of company groups (km), 1917-1946

	British Capital						French Capital			State	
Year	BAGS/ WR	CAR	BAPR	ERR/ ANER	BACR	CCR	SFPR	RBPR	BAPGRC	AGFE	PBAR
1917	9,629	5,348	5,668	2,300	378	2,023	1,947	799	—	1,374	1,022
1918	9,629	5,348	5,668	2,300	378	2,023	1,947	799	—	1,374	1,078
1919	9,629	5,348	5,668	2,300	378	2,023	1,947	799	—	556	1,210
1920	9,629	5,348	5,668	2,300	379	2,023	1,947	799	—	556	1,022
1921	9,806	5,348	5,516	2,302	379	2,023	1,964	799	—	1,231	—
1922	9,896	5,348	5,516	2,302	379	2,023	1,964	826	—	1,798	—
1923	9,901	5,348	5,585	2,302	379	2,024	1,964	826	—	1,801	—
1924	9,901	5,348	5,601	2,302	379	2,024	1,916	826	—	1,801	—
1925	11,128	5,348	4,447	2,302	379	2,019	1,916	829	—	1,801	—
1926	11,157	5,346	4,515	2,299	379	2,028	1,916	826	—	1,886	—
1927	11,218	5,346	4,515	2,299	379	2,033	1,989	826	—	1,907	—
1928	11,222	5,346	4,625	2,299	379	2,044	2,006	826	—	1,907	—
1929	11,580	5,368	4,695	2,219	379	2,044	2,077	826	—	2,110	—
1930	11,678	5,567	4,695	2,224	379	2,044	2,085	826	—	2,160	—
1931	11,786	5,567	4,704	2,253	379	2,044	2,085	826	—	2,167	—
1932	11,786	5,873	4,704	2,253	379	2,044	2,085	826	—	2,167	—
1933	11,786	5,994	4,704	2,253	379	2,044	2,085	826	—	2,167	—
1934	11,786	5,994	4,525	2,253	379	2,044	2,085	826	—	2,538	—
1935	11,786	5,994	4,525	2,253	379	2,044	2,085	826	—	2,699	—
1936	11,786	5,994	4,525	2,253	379	2,044	2,085	826	—	2,923	—
1937	11,786	5,994	4,525	2,253	379	2,044	2,085	826	—	3,112	—
1938	11,787	5,994	4,525	2,253	379	-	2,085	826	507	3,379	—
1939	11,787	5,994	4,525	2,253	379	-	2,085	826	618	3,047	—
1940	11,787	5,994	4,525	2,253	379	-	2,085	826	964	3,491	305
1941	11,787	5,994	4,525	2,253	379	-	2,085	826	1,166	4,961	305
1942	11,787	5,994	4,525	2,253	378	-	2,085	826	1,268	5,057	305
1943	11,765	5,985	4,456	2,242	378	-	2,166	828	1,268	5,265	553
1944	11,764	5,954	4,463	2,252	378	-	2,194	827	1,268	5,806	553
1945	11,764	5,954	4,160	2,252	378	-	2,194	827	1,268	6,001	553
1946	11,764	5,954	4,463	2,252	378	-	2,194	827	1,268	6,088	553

Notes: The BAGS/WR group includes the Buenos Aires Midland and the BBNWR from 1925. The BAPR group includes the the BBNWR until 1924 and the FCT until 1933. The CCR includes the RST. The AGFE/NRB also includes the NCR, the ER, and the San Antonio to Nahuel Huapí, Comodoro Rivadavia, Puerto Deseado, and Formosa-Embarcación lines. From 1922 it also includes the Chubut Central and from 1938 the CCR and the Transandine.

Table 6. The Argentine Railways Network (FA), 1947-1976

Year	Length (km)	Passengers carried (millions)	Cargo Carried (mill. tons)	Personnel	Operating Ratio
1947	42,578	313.7	34.2	158,092	1.13
1948	42,578	350.6	34.2	173,206	1.09
1949	42,578	470.1	31.6	184,418	1.31
1950	42,865	490.9	32.8	188,568	1.27
1951	42,855	524.2	32.9	184,734	1.38
1952	42,968	531.2	29.6	200,065	1.17
1953	43,952	541.0	30.5	198,871	1.17
1954	43,922	572.2	31.0	204,336	1.29
1955	43,930	578.6	28.7	209,854	1.33
1956	43,933	605.1	27.7	214,698	1.43
1957	43,938	618.5	26.8	218,513	2.02
1958	43,932	622.5	25.3	219,917	1.85
1959	43,931	604.0	26.7	220,591	1.56
1960	43,923	579.8	26.1	200,590	1.74
1961	no data	444.9	21.9	152,153	2.02
1962	no data	449.2	17.2	157,705	2.02
1963	42,419	485.4	16.3	162,051	2.13
1964	no data	479.9	20.6	166,478	2.13
1965	no data	479.3	23.1	no data	2.18
1966	41.941	no data	no data	no data	no data
1967	no data	499.1	20.8	163,196	no data
1968	no data	491.5	19.6	153,772	1.44
1969	no data	492.5	20.7	149,003	1.35
1970	39,905	439.8	22.1	145,460	1.46
1971	39,822	434.6	21.5	143,472	1.88
1972	39,816	405.7	18.3	140,580	1.66
1973	39,805	391.1	19.1	141,760	1.81
1974	39,782	422.8	19.1	141,228	1.88
1975	39,787	446.8	16.2	153,308	2.70
1976	39,779	444.9	17.8	154,949	2.01

Source: derived from official FA and Ministry of Public Works information.

Table 7. Cargo Traffic carried by Argentine Railways (FA), 1970-1993 (millions of tons)

Year	Sarmiento	Mitre	San Martín	Roca	Urquiza	Belgrano	Total
1970	1.7	4	5.5	4.8	1.4	4.7	22.1
1971	1.2	3.8	5.5	4.7	1.5	4.9	21.5
1972	1	3.4	4.2	4.1	1.3	5	19
1973	1.5	4.1	3.9	4.2	1.2	5.1	20
1974	1.6	4.7	3.6	4.3	1.2	4.7	20.2
1975	1.4	3.9	3.1	3.6	1.1	4	17.1
1976	1.6	3.9	3.8	3.7	1.3	3.5	17.8
1977	1.8	4.3	4.5	4.1	1.2	4.3	20.2
1978	1.4	3.4	4.5	3	1.2	3.5	17.2
1979	2.1	3.5	4.7	3.6	1.3	4	19.1
1980	1	3.2	4.2	3.2	0.8	3.9	16.3
1981	1.5	3	4.4	2.9	0.9	3.6	16.3
1982	2	3.6	5.2	3	1	4.3	19.1
1983	2.7	3.9	6.2	3.7	1.1	4.8	22.5
1984	2.1	3.5	5.5	2.6	1.4	4.4	19.5
1985	2	3.2	4.2	2.9	0.7	4.2	17.2
1986	1	3	3.6	2.6	1	3.9	15
1987	0.7	2.7	2.9	2.4	1.2	3.7	13.6
1988	0.6	3.2	3.2	2.5	1.4	4	14.9
1989	0.9	2.5	3.4	2.6	1.2	3.6	14.2
1990	1.1	3.3	2.4	3.2	1	3.2	14.2
1991	0.5	2.5	1.6	2	0.8	2.3	9.7
1992	0.1	1.5	1.2	1.3	1	1.5	6.6
1993	no data	no data	no data	no data	no data	no data	no data

Source: 1970 to 1990: FA, "Statistical Summary of the railways in operation"; 1991 & 1992: FA, Department of Statistics, "Síntesis Estadística 1988/1992" (internal document).

Table 8. Suburban Passenger Traffic carried by FA and Femesa, 1970-1995 (millions of passengers)

Year	Mitre	Sarmiento	Roca	San Martín	Urquiza	Belgrano Norte	Belgrano Sur	Total
1970	87.3	113.7	84.9	48.8	22.8	55.6		413.1
1971	89.6	116.2	81.4	48.2	21.9	51.8		409.1
1972	84.1	108.6	78.2	44.4	20.2	43.4		378.9
1973	79.1	108	75.4	42	18.7	39.8		362.9
1974	83.4	116.4	82.6	46.1	20.5	44.2		393.1
1975	88.9	124.4	84.9	45.6	23.7	44.5		412
1976	88.3	123.3	84.2	47.7	22.4	45.3		411.1
1977	81.1	119.5	76.8	49.3	22.7	40.8		390.3
1978	74.4	114.1	71.8	47.2	21.9	37.9		367.2
1979	70.7	114.3	69.2	48.5	23.4	40.3		366.4
1980	72.2	117.6	73.6	51	24.4	44.2		383.1
1981	66.4	108.4	54.4	42.6	24.4	38.5		334.8
1982	59.6	92.7	46.2	37.3	24.6	22.8	11.4	294.6
1983	57.9	92.4	33.8	35.2	24.4	24.6	12.1	280.4
1984	55.5	96.7	24.6	36.3	27.3	25.2	13.6	279.1
1985	55.5	94.6	33	39.3	25.9	24.9	15	288.1
1986	55.7	97.8	85.7	41.6	24.6	24.6	15.6	345.7
1987	53	95.2	93.3	39.3	24.5	22.5	12.1	339.9
1988	44.1	80.9	79.1	34	22.9	17.6	7.7	286.3
1989	44.6	73.9	74.3	33	19.9	15.7	7.2	268.7
1990	46.8	75.6	80	33.6	16.4	15.1	5.7	273.2
1991	30.5	62.4	57.3	25.2	15.5	14.5	3.6	209
1992	35	59.2	55.5	22.8	17.8	14.2	4.9	209.4
1993	34.4	60.5	64.9	21.7	16.8	11.8	2	198.3
1994	38.3	61.3	75.8	5.4	-	2.4	0.7	180.7
1995	17	22.8	-	-	-	-	-	39.8

Source: 1970 to 1990, FA (Ferrocarriles Argentinos) "Síntesis estadística de los ferrocarriles en explotación"; 1991 to 1993: Femesa (Ferrocarriles Metropolitanos S. A., Metropolitan Railways), "Control de gestión, diciembre 1993".

Table 9. Cargo Traffic carried by the Concessions, 1991-2006 (millions of tons)

Year	FEPSA	NCA	BAP/ALL	FSR	FM/ALL	FGB/...	TOTAL
1991	0.1	-	-	-	-	-	0.1
1992	2	0	-	-	-	-	2
1993	2.3	2.8	0.6	1.1	0.1	1.2	8.2
1994	2.5	3.5	2.4	2.5	1.2	1.1	13.2
1995	2.9	3.5	2.9	3.3	1.2	1.4	15.2
1996	2.9	4.1	3.2	4.2	1.1	1.6	17
1997	3.2	4.9	3.6	4.5	1	1.7	18.9
1998	3.3	5.5	3.3	4.1	0.9	1.7	18.8
1999	2.5	5.5	3.1	4.1	1	1.3	17.5
2000	2.4	5.5	2.9	3.1	1	1.4	16.3
2001	2.4	6.2	2.9	3.7	0.7	1.1	17
2002	2.4	7.3	3	3.3	0.7	0.8	17.5
2003	2.8	8.1	3.2	4.3	1.2	0.9	20.5
2004	3	8.3	3.4	4.8	1.4	0.8	21.7
2005	3.6	9	3.5	5.1	1.4	0.8	23.4
2006	3.4	8.7	4.2	5.5	1.5	0.6	23.9

Source: Comisión Nacional de Regulación del Transporte(CNRT), information from the CNRT website; Year 1993, Línea Belgrano, "Five years of operation 1993/1998", Ferrocarril General Belgrano S. A.

Table 10. Suburban Passenger Traffic carried by the Concessions, 1994-2006 (millions of passengers)

Year	Mitre TBA	Sarmiento TBA	Roca Metro-politano	San Martín (*)	Urquiza Metro-vías	Belgrano North Ferrovías	Belgrano South Metro-politano	Total
1994	-	-	-	23.9	22.4	12.6	3.4	62.4
1995	36.5	38.5	116.5	38	23.2	25.4	8.3	286.3
1996	69.8	99.3	136	43.5	24.7	28.8	11.3	413.5
1997	80.6	111.5	147	46.6	25	32.3	13.1	456.1
1998	84.1	113.2	152.1	50.4	25.6	35.9	16.2	477.5
1999	83.5	111.7	155.3	50.7	25.8	36.3	16.1	479.4
2000	81.7	111.5	155	49.6	25.1	36.6	16.3	475.9
2001	74.5	100.3	139.1	45.2	22.6	34.1	14.4	430.2
2002	65.7	88.2	108.2	34.3	21.9	29.3	9.3	356.8
2003	68.7	97.2	109.8	29.9	26.7	34.8	10.4	377.5
2004	69.7	105.1	111.2	31.6	28.3	38.7	11.6	396.2
2005	71.4	109.3	117.2	34.9	27.7	40.6	12	413.1
2006	75.5	114.6	118.3	41.2	27.5	44.1	12.1	433.2

(*) Línea San Martín: until 2004, Metropolitano "Management Control Report"; from 2055 to 2006, Unidad de Gestión Operativa (UGOFE, Unit for Operational Management).
Source: Comisión Nacional de Regulación del Transporte (CNRT, National Commission for Transport Regulation) .

Table 11. Intercity Passenger Traffic carried by Ferrocarriles Argentinos (FA) 1970-1995 (millions)

Year	Total	Year	Total
1970	26.69	1983	9.61
1971	25.58	1984	11.53
1972	26.82	1985	11.88
1973	28.26	1986	12.88
1974	29.78	1987	12.53
1975	34.76	1988	10.06
1976	33.83	1989	11.73
1977	19.41	1990	11.16
1978	12.94	1991	6.79
1979	10.78	1992	5.26
1980	10.62	1993	no data
1981	8.17	1994	no data
1982	7.72	1995	no data

Source: 1970 to 1990, FA (Ferrocarriles Argentinos), "Statistical Summary of the railways in operation"; 1991 to 1993: FM (Ferrocarriles Metropolitanos S. A.), "Management Control/Report", December 1993

Table 12. Intercity Passengers carried by the Concessions, 1994-2005 (millions of passengers)

Year	Total	Year	Total
1994	s/d	2000	2.46
1995	2.4	2001	2.02
1996	2.57	2002	1.86
1997	2.65	2003	2.45
1998	2.66	2004	2.69
1999	2.57	2005	2.65

Note: Línea San Martín, until 2004; Metropolitano,2005 & 2006, UGOFE.
Source:CNRT (National Commission for Transport Regulation)

Table 13. Argentine Railways (FA): Performance Indicators

Year	Lines in operation (km)	Employees	Diesel locomotive equivalents	Operating Ratio
1970	39,905	145,460	1,073	1.46
1971	39,822	143,472	1,061	1.88
1972	39,816	140,580	1,050	1.66
1973	39,805	141,760	1,033	1.81
1974	39,782	141,228	922	1.88
1975	39,787	153,308	861	2.7
1976	39,779	154,949	848	2.01
1977	36,930	126,039	857	1.78
1978	34,327	111,339	855	1.69
1979	34,284	106,393	892	1.94
1980	34,192	96,935	840	2.14
1981	34,106	95,804	864	2.11
1982	34,029	96,095	808	2.13
1983	34,061	103,102	818	1.84
1984	34,057	107,837	774	2.06
1985	34,159	102,941	760	2.28
1986	34,140	99,897	694	2.43
1987	34,150	97,218	659	2.88
1988	34,115	98,134	670	2.19
1989	34,059	93,445	634	1.69
1990	no data	82,270	no data	no data
1991	no data	53,331	no data	no data
1992	no data	36,557	no data	no data
1993	no data	no data	no data	no data

Source: 1970 to 1990: FA, "Síntesis estadística de los ferrocarriles en explotación", 1991 y 1992: FA, Department of Statistics, "Síntesis estadística 1988/1992", Internal document.

Table 14. Cargo carried (millions of tons), 2006-2015

Año	FEPSA	Ferrosur	NCA	ALL-SM	ALL-GU	Belg Cargas	Total
2006	3.4	5.5	8.7	4.2	1.5	0.5	23.9
2007	4.1	5.5	8.6	4.4	1.5	0.7	24.9
2008	3.8	5.5	8.3	3.7	1.2	0.9	23.7
2009	2.9	5.1	7.2	3.5	0.8	1.1	20.7
2010	3.8	5.2	8.3	4.1	0.9	1.1	23.5
2011	4.0	5.6	8.6	4.3	0.6	1.1	24.2
2012	4.1	5.2	7.7	3.7	0.5	0.8	22.0
2013	3.6	5.7	7.3	2.9	0.4	0.8	20.8
2014	3.5	5.2	7.4	1.9	0.2	1.0	19.3
2015	3.5	5.1	7.4	1.5	0.1	0.8	18.5

GU: General Urquiza Railway

Table 15. Suburban Passengers carried (millions), 2006-2015

Year	Mitre	Sarmiento	Urquiza	Roca	San Martín	Belgrano Norte	Belgrano Sur	Total
2006	75.5	114.5	27.5	118.3	41.2	44.1	12.1	433.2
2007	75.8	116.0	24.9	101.1	46.6	45.6	10.5	420.6
2008	73.2	118.1	24.2	125.7	49.6	45.8	11.3	448.0
2009	64.5	108.2	22.6	131.8	48.2	43.7	11.9	430.9
2010	61.0	99.5	22.5	130.8	49.8	42.7	12.7	419.1
2011	51.4	88.6	18.5	91.5	48.5	32.1	13.3	343.9
2012	35.6	39.1	19.0	97.1	48.9	30.5	12.2	282.4
2013	15.9	11.4	15.4	104.8	44.6	33.4	10.4	236.0
2014	18.3	39.6	12.6	115.0	39.2	29.9	11	265.7
2015	41.3	55.2	18.5	128.8	47.1	26.7	11.8	329.5

Table 16. Intercity Passengers (millions), 2006-2015

2006	2.8
2007	2.3
2008	2.1
2009	1.8
2010	2.1
2011	2.1
2012	1.9
2013	1.9
2014	2.3
2015	no data

Bibliography

Archival Sources

Museo Nacional Ferroviario (National Railway Museum) (Buenos Aires): Archivo de la Dirección General de Ferrocarriles (National Railway Board Archive); Private Railway Companies Annual Reports and Statements; State Companies (AGFE, EFEA, FA) Annual Reports and Statements.

Guildhall Library (London): Stock Exchange Yearbook Archive (*Prospecti* and Private Railway Companies Annual Reports and Statements).

The National Archives (former Public Record Office) (Kew, Greater London): Board of Trade, Dissolved Companies Files (BT31).

University College Library (London): Latin American Business Archive (Buenos Ayres and Pacific Railway Company and River and Mercantile Trust files).

Secondary Sources: Books, Articles and Working papers

Badaloni, Laura, 2022, *Ferroviarios del Central Argentino. La conformación de un colectivo de trabajadores (1902-1933)*, Buenos Aires: Editorial Imago Mundi.

Bunge, Alejandro 1918, *Ferrocarriles argentinos. Contribución al estudio del patrimonio nacional*, Buenos Aires: Imprenta Mercatali.

Coronell, Juan Carlos, 1990, *Los ferrocarriles en la Argentina (1948-1962). Aspecto político-social*, not published.

Corti, Celestino, 1926, *Investigaciones sobre algunos problemas ferroviarios*, Buenos Aires: Imprenta de la Universidad de Buenos Aires.

Cuccorese, Horacio Juan, 1969, *Historia de los ferrocarriles en la Argentina*, Buenos Aires: Editorial Macchi.

Damus, Sylvester, 2008, *Who Was Who in Argentine Railways. 1860-1960*, Ottawa, DIA Agency.

———, 2008, *Argentine Railways. Seven Papers on their Economics and History*, Ottawa: DIA Agency.

Ensinck, Oscar Luis, 1980, *Historia de los ferrocarriles en la Provincia de Santa Fe*, Rosario: Universidad Católica Argentina.

Escudé, Carlos y María T. Carballo de Cilley, 1979, "Perón, Miranda y la compra de los ferrocarriles británicos", en *Todo es Historia*, nº 142.

Fernández Priotti, Carlos Alberto, 2006, *El Ferrocarril Oeste Santafecino. Carlos Casado y la Colonización de la Pampa*, Rosario.

———, 2017, *Historia del Ferrocarril Central Argentino (1854-1901)*, Rosario.

Fleming, William J., 1991, "Profits and Visions: British Capital and Railway Construction in Argentina. 1854-1886", en Clarence B. Davis and Kenneth E. Wilburn (Jr.), *Railway Imperialism*, New York: Greenwood Press.

García Heras, Raúl, 1983, *Los ferrocarriles británicos en la Argentina. 1928-1943*, not published.

———, 1985, "World War II and the Frustrated Nationalization of the Argentine British-owned Railways, 1939-1943", in *Journal of Latin American Studies*, vol. 17, issue 1.

———, 1988, "Los ferrocarriles británicos y la política de coordinación de transportes en la Argentina durante la década del 30", en Mario Rapoport (comp.), *Economía e historia. Contribuciones a la historia económica argentina*, Buenos Aires: Grupo Editorial Norma.

———, 1990, "Las compañías ferroviarias británicas y el control de cambios en la Argentina durante la Gran Depresión", en *Desarrollo Económico*, vol. 29, nº 116.

———, 1994, *Transportes, negocios y política. La Compañía Anglo Argentina de Tranvías. 1876-1981*, Buenos Aires: Editorial Sudamericana.

Goodwin, Paul B., 1974, *Los ferrocarriles británicos y la UCR (1916-1930)*, Buenos Aires: Editorial La Bastilla.

Gordillo, Mónica R., 1988, *El movimiento obrero ferroviario desde el interior del país, 1916-1922*, Buenos Aires: Centro Editor de América Latina.

Huergo, Pedro J., 2011, *Une aventure ferroviaire franco-belge en Amérique du Sud: La Compagnie Générale de Chemins de Fer dans la Province de Buenos-Ayres (1905-1946)*, Bruxelles: Presses Universitaires de Bruxelles.

Lacoste, Pablo, 2000, *El Ferrocarril Trasandino (1872-1984)*, Santiago de Chile: Editorial Universitaria.

Lewis, Colin M., 1968, "Percival Farquhar and the Argentine Railways. 1912-1914", in *Transport History*, vol. I, nº 3.

———, 1977, "British Railways Companies and the Argentine Government", in D. C. M. Platt (ed.), *Business Imperialism. 1940-1914. An Inquiry Based on British Experience in Latin America*, Oxford: Oxford University Press.

———, 1983, *British Railways in Argentina. 1857-1914. A Case Study of Foreign Investment*, London: The Athlone Press.

———, 1991, "Railways and Industrialization: Argentina and Brazil. 1870-1929", in Christopher Abel and Colin M. Lewis (Eds.), *Latin America: Economic Imperialism and the State*, London: The Athlone Press.

———, 2007, "Crisis, tecnología y eficiencia. Los ferrocarriles de capital británico durante los años de transición. 1912-1933", en Mario Justo López and Jorge Eduardo Waddell (comps.), *Nueva historia del ferrocarril en la Argentina: 150 años de política ferroviaria*, Buenos Aires: Editorial Lumière.

———, 2008, "'Anglo-Criollo' rather than British: Early Investments in Argentine Railways and Utilities", in Jorge Schvarzer, Andrés Regalsky and Teresita Gómez (comps.), *Estudios sobre la historia de los ferrocarriles argentinos (1857-1940)*, Buenos Aires: Universidad de Buenos Aires.

López, Mario Justo, 1991, *Historia de los ferrocarriles de la Provincia de Buenos Aires. 1857-1886*, Buenos Aires: Editorial Lumière.

———, 1994, *Historia de los ferrocarriles nacionales. 1866-1886*, Buenos Aires: Editorial Lumière.

———, 2000, *Ferrocarriles, deuda y crisis. Historia de los ferrocarriles en la Argentina de 1887 a 1896*, Buenos Aires: Editorial de Belgrano.

———, 2008, "El problema ferroviario argentino y la nacionalización de las compañías de capital británico en 1948", en

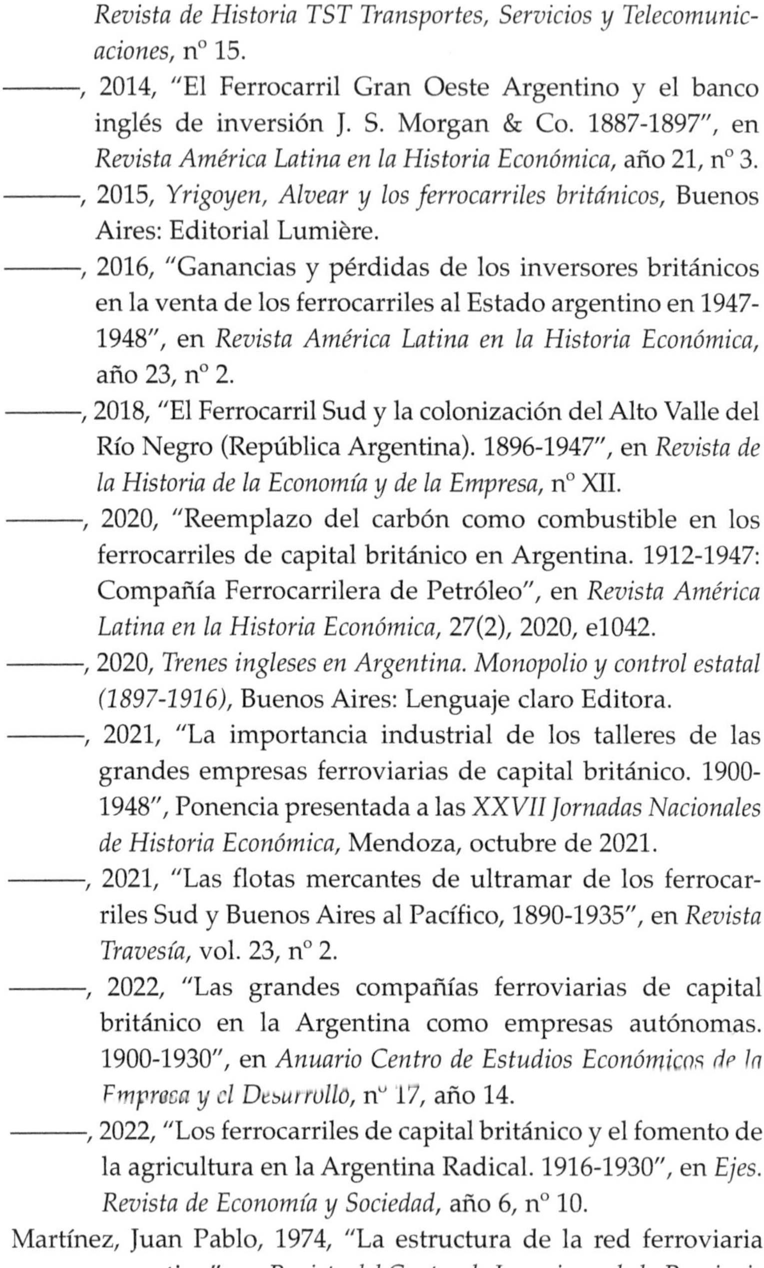

Revista de Historia TST Transportes, Servicios y Telecomunicaciones, nº 15.

———, 2014, "El Ferrocarril Gran Oeste Argentino y el banco inglés de inversión J. S. Morgan & Co. 1887-1897", en *Revista América Latina en la Historia Económica*, año 21, nº 3.

———, 2015, *Yrigoyen, Alvear y los ferrocarriles británicos*, Buenos Aires: Editorial Lumière.

———, 2016, "Ganancias y pérdidas de los inversores británicos en la venta de los ferrocarriles al Estado argentino en 1947-1948", en *Revista América Latina en la Historia Económica*, año 23, nº 2.

———, 2018, "El Ferrocarril Sud y la colonización del Alto Valle del Río Negro (República Argentina). 1896-1947", en *Revista de la Historia de la Economía y de la Empresa*, nº XII.

———, 2020, "Reemplazo del carbón como combustible en los ferrocarriles de capital británico en Argentina. 1912-1947: Compañía Ferrocarrilera de Petróleo", en *Revista América Latina en la Historia Económica*, 27(2), 2020, e1042.

———, 2020, *Trenes ingleses en Argentina. Monopolio y control estatal (1897-1916)*, Buenos Aires: Lenguaje claro Editora.

———, 2021, "La importancia industrial de los talleres de las grandes empresas ferroviarias de capital británico. 1900-1948", Ponencia presentada a las *XXVII Jornadas Nacionales de Historia Económica*, Mendoza, octubre de 2021.

———, 2021, "Las flotas mercantes de ultramar de los ferrocarriles Sud y Buenos Aires al Pacífico, 1890-1935", en *Revista Travesía*, vol. 23, nº 2.

———, 2022, "Las grandes compañías ferroviarias de capital británico en la Argentina como empresas autónomas. 1900-1930", en *Anuario Centro de Estudios Económicos de la Empresa y el Desarrollo*, nº 17, año 14.

———, 2022, "Los ferrocarriles de capital británico y el fomento de la agricultura en la Argentina Radical. 1916-1930", en *Ejes. Revista de Economía y Sociedad*, año 6, nº 10.

Martínez, Juan Pablo, 1974, "La estructura de la red ferroviaria argentina", en *Revista del Centro de Ingenieros de la Provincia de Buenos Aires*.

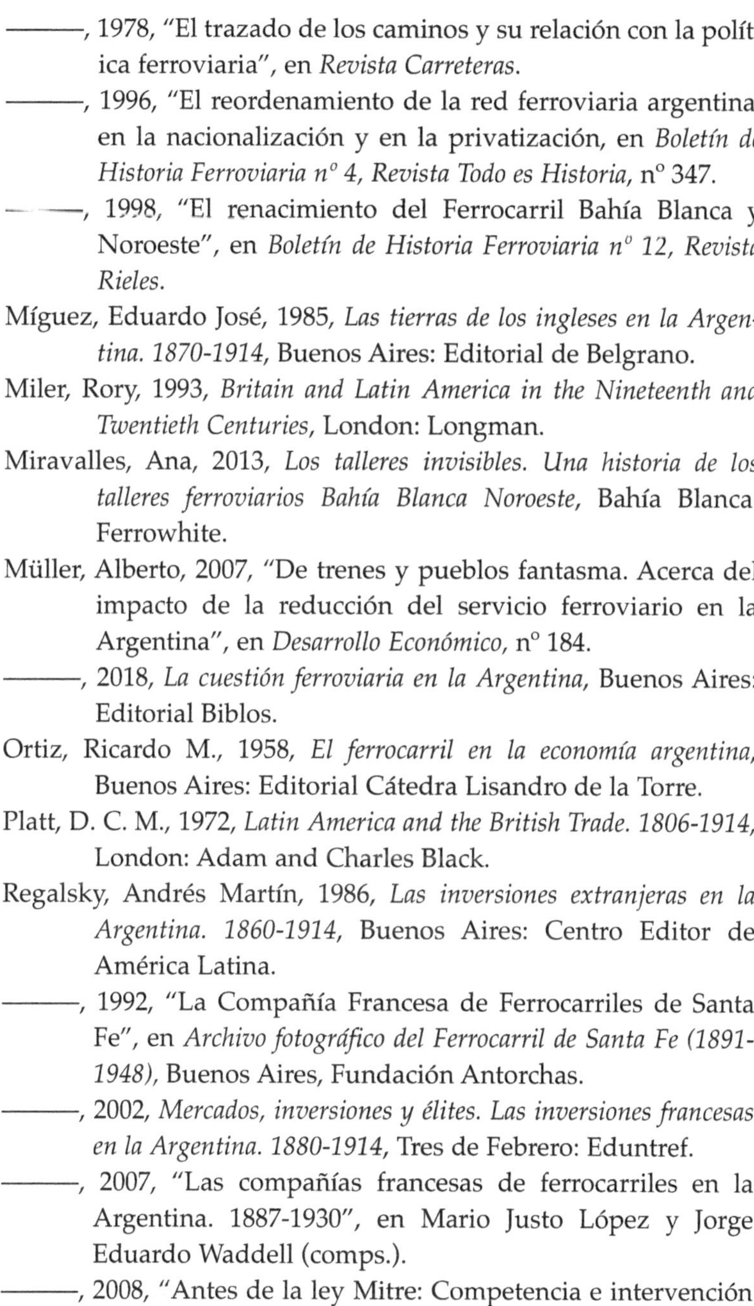

———, 1978, "El trazado de los caminos y su relación con la política ferroviaria", en *Revista Carreteras.*

———, 1996, "El reordenamiento de la red ferroviaria argentina, en la nacionalización y en la privatización, en *Boletín de Historia Ferroviaria n° 4, Revista Todo es Historia,* n° 347.

———, 1998, "El renacimiento del Ferrocarril Bahía Blanca y Noroeste", en *Boletín de Historia Ferroviaria n° 12, Revista Rieles.*

Míguez, Eduardo José, 1985, *Las tierras de los ingleses en la Argentina. 1870-1914,* Buenos Aires: Editorial de Belgrano.

Miler, Rory, 1993, *Britain and Latin America in the Nineteenth and Twentieth Centuries,* London: Longman.

Miravalles, Ana, 2013, *Los talleres invisibles. Una historia de los talleres ferroviarios Bahía Blanca Noroeste,* Bahía Blanca: Ferrowhite.

Müller, Alberto, 2007, "De trenes y pueblos fantasma. Acerca del impacto de la reducción del servicio ferroviario en la Argentina", en *Desarrollo Económico,* n° 184.

———, 2018, *La cuestión ferroviaria en la Argentina,* Buenos Aires: Editorial Biblos.

Ortiz, Ricardo M., 1958, *El ferrocarril en la economía argentina,* Buenos Aires: Editorial Cátedra Lisandro de la Torre.

Platt, D. C. M., 1972, *Latin America and the British Trade. 1806-1914,* London: Adam and Charles Black.

Regalsky, Andrés Martín, 1986, *Las inversiones extranjeras en la Argentina. 1860-1914,* Buenos Aires: Centro Editor de América Latina.

———, 1992, "La Compañía Francesa de Ferrocarriles de Santa Fe", en *Archivo fotográfico del Ferrocarril de Santa Fe (1891-1948),* Buenos Aires, Fundación Antorchas.

———, 2002, *Mercados, inversiones y élites. Las inversiones francesas en la Argentina. 1880-1914,* Tres de Febrero: Eduntref.

———, 2007, "Las compañías francesas de ferrocarriles en la Argentina. 1887-1930", en Mario Justo López y Jorge Eduardo Waddell (comps.).

———, 2008, "Antes de la ley Mitre: Competencia e intervención estatal en la región pampeana en los comienzos del siglo

XX", en Jorge Schvarzer, Andrés Regalsky y Teresita Gómez (comps.).

Rippy, J. Fred, 1959, *British Investments in Latin America. 1822-1949. A Case Study in the Operations of Private Enterprise in Retarded Regions*, Minneapolis: University of Minnesota Press.

Roccatagliata, Juan Alberto, 1987, *Los ferrocarriles en la Argentina. Un enfoque geográfico*, Buenos Aires: Eudeba.

———, 1998, *Los ferrocarriles ante el siglo XXI*, Buenos Aires: Editorial de Belgrano.

Rögind, William, 1937, *Historia del Ferrocarril Sud*, Buenos Aires: Establecimiento Gráfico Argentino.

Salerno, Elena, 2003, "Los comienzos del Estado empresario. La Administración General de los Ferrocarriles del Estado. 1910-1928", *Documento de Trabajo nº 6*, Centro de Estudios Económicos de la Empresa y el Desarrollo.

———, 2007, "La evolución y los problemas de los ferrocarriles del Estado durante la primera mitad del siglo XX", en Mario Justo López y Jorge Eduardo Waddell (comps.).

———, 2008, "La inversión pública en los Ferrocarriles del Estado (1930-1940)", en *Revista de Historia TST Transportes, Servicios y Telecomunicaciones*, nº 15.

———, 2020, "Los Ferrocarriles del Estado durante la década de 1930: una aproximación a la gestión del Administrador General Pablo Nogués", en *Coordenadas. Revista de Historia Local y Regional*, año 7, nº2.

———, 2020, "El final de la primera empresa estatal nacional: La Administración General de los Ferrocarriles del Estado. 1943-1948", en *Pasado Abierto*, nº 12.

Schvarzer, Jorge y Teresita Gómez, 2006, *La primera gran empresa de los argentinos. El Ferrocarril Oeste (1857-1862)*, Buenos Aires: Fondo de Cultura Económica.

Schickendantz, Emilio y Emilio Rebuelto, 1994, *Los ferrocarriles en la Argentina. 1857-1910*, Buenos Aires: Fundación Museo Ferroviario.

Skinner, Kenneth, 1984, *Railway in the Desert. The Story of the Building of the Chubut Railway and the Life of its Constructor Engineer E. J. Williams*, Wolverhampton: Beechen Green Books.

Skupch, Pedro R., 1971, "Las consecuencias de la competencia de transportes sobre la hegemonía británica en la Argentina (1919-1939)", en *Revista Económica de La Plata,* n° 1.

Stones, H. R., 1993, *British Railways in Argentina. 1860.1948,* London: P. E. Waters.

———, 1999, *International Railways over the Andes,* London: P. E. Waters and Fundación Museo Ferroviario.

Vera de Flachs, María C., 1982, *El ferrocarril Andino y el desarrollo del sur de Córdoba,* Buenos Aires: Fecic.

Waddell, Jorge Eduardo, 2005, "La idea de redimensionamiento de la red ferroviaria argentina entre 1930 y 1962", ponencia presentada a las *X Jornadas Interescuelas Departamentos de Historia,* Rosario.

———, 2006, "Discusión en torno a los planes ferroviarios de la década del sesenta", Ponencia presentada a las *XX Jornadas Nacionales de Historia Económica,* Mar del Plata.

———, 2008, "Los ferrocarriles británicos en la segunda mitad de la década de 1930 y la explotación de sus líneas", en Jorge Schvarzer, Andrés Regalsky y Teresita Gómez (comps.).

———, 2009, "La red ferroviaria argentina en la actualidad", en *Revista GEA,* n° 127.

———, 2013, "Los límites culturales del desarrollo ferroviario en la Argentina", Ponencia presentada al *V Congreso Internacional de Historia Ferroviaria,* Asociación Internacional de Historia Ferroviaria, Santiago de Chile.

Wright, Winthrop R., 1980, *Los ferrocarriles ingleses en la Argentina. Su influencia en el nacionalismo económico. 1854-1948,* Buenos Aires: Emecé.

Zalduendo, Eduardo A., 1975, *Libras y rieles. Las inversiones británicas para el desarrollo de los ferrocarriles en la Argentina, Brasil, Canadá e India durante el siglo XIX,* Buenos Aires: Editorial El Coloquio.

———, 1980, "Aspectos económicos del sistema de transportes de la Argentina (1880-1914)", en Gustavo Ferrari y Ezequiel Gallo (comps.), *La Argentina del Ochenta al Centenario,* Buenos Aires: Editorial Sudamericana.

Index

About the Authors

Mario Justo López is a lawyer and PhD in the specialty of History of Law by Universidad of Buenos Aires. He has specialized in the study of Argentine railway history, on which he has published numerous articles and books. He is a member of the International Association of Railway History, based in Paris, and president of the Fundación Museo Ferroviario.

Jorge E. Waddell is a lawyer from the University of Buenos Aires (UBA). He works as a Regular Adjunct Professor of State Theory and researcher at the Faculty of Law (UBA). Specialized in Political and Economic History, he has dedicated himself to the study of Argentine railway policy, a subject on which he has published articles in Argentina and foreign media.

Juan Pablo Martínez is an engineer (UBA) with a postgraduate degree in Railway Engineering. In 1967 he joined Ferrocarriles Argentinos, occupying from there in diverse positions in public functions. He participated in the implementation of the railway lines privatization processes and in 1996 he was director of the Coordination Unit of the Railway Restructuring Program.

www.ingramcontent.com/pod-product-compliance
Lightning Source LLC
LaVergne TN
LVHW050528160826
845677LV00011B/1978

* 9 7 8 9 8 7 3 7 6 4 4 6 2 *